STONEWALL JACKSON'S LITTLE SORREL

An Unlikely Hero of the Civil War

SHARON B. SMITH

Guilford, Connecticut

An imprint of Rowman & Littlefield

Distributed by NATIONAL BOOK NETWORK

British Library Cataloguing in Publication Information available

Library of Congress Cataloging-in-Publication Data available

Names: Smith, Sharon B., author.
Title: Stonewall Jackson's Little Sorrel : an unlikely hero of the Civil War / Sharon B. Smith.
Description: Guilford, Connecticut : Rowman & Littlefield, 2016. | Includes bibliographical references and index.
Identifiers: LCCN 2016024509 (print) | LCCN 2016025121 (ebook) | ISBN 9781493019243 (cloth : alk. paper) | ISBN 9781493028467 (Electronic)
Subjects: LCSH: Little Sorrel (Horse), –1886. | Jackson, Stonewall, 1824–1863—Friends and associates. | United States—History—Civil War, 1861–1865—Campaigns. | War horses—United States—Biography.
Classification: LCC E467.1.J15 S7525 2016 (print) | LCC E467.1.J15 (ebook) | DDC 636.10092/9 [B]—dc23
LC record available at https://lccn.loc.gov/2016024509.

∞™ The paper used in this publication meets the minimum requirements of American National Standard for Information Sciences—Permanence of Paper for Printed Library Materials, ANSI/NISO Z39.48-1992.

CONTENTS

Foreword

"Is this the place with the horse?" is a frequent question asked by visitors entering the Virginia Military Institute Museum for the first time. "Yes!," has been the proud reply since 1948, the year Little Sorrel arrived from the Confederate Soldiers' Home in Richmond, Virginia.

I have always thought it appropriate that the war horse of Stonewall Jackson spent his last days being cared for by veterans, many of whom had been with him in their youth. Little Sorrel earned the honor of "veteran" status, carrying his master over some of the most famous battlefields of the Civil War. The physically unimpressive horse was a witness—a participant— throughout the Shenandoah Valley campaign. He carried Jackson into the chaotic barrage of Confederate musket fire on the dark evening of May 2, 1863, which resulted in the mortal wounding of the General.

Fredrick Weber, the leading American taxidermist, arrived at the Confederate Soldiers' Home in March 1886 prepared to start the mounting process as soon as the end came for the thirty-six-year-old Little Sorrel. Taking measurements from life, Weber prepared a steel armature which was then wrapped in sisal and plaster. The last step was to place the hide over the form. Webster's work was so well done that there has only been a need for conservation twice in the intervening 130 years.

Little Sorrel is among a very select list of historically significant horses mounted and exhibited in museums worldwide. Napoleon's Le Vizir can be seen at the Musee d'Armee de l'Hotel des Invalides in Paris. Phar Lap, the great Australian race horse, is in the Museum Victoria in

Melbourne. Comanche, the lone survivor of the Battle of the Little Big Horn resides at the University of Kansas. Cowboy actor Roy Roger's Trigger was mounted at the time of his death in 1965.

During the Civil War more than 3,000,000 horses and mules were pressed into service. One-half of that number perished during the four years of struggle. Only two survivors—one Union, one Confederate—still stand in silent tribute to the tremendous sacrifice of equines in the Civil War. The first to be mounted was Union General Philip Sheridan's Renzi, who died in 1878. Today Renzi, renamed Winchester after the general's famous 1864 ride to that town, is exhibited in the Smithsonian Institution's American History Museum in Washington DC. The other mount, representing the South, is Little Sorrel.

Little Sorrel was frequently the subject of comment by war-time observers. Like his famous rider, the reddish-brown horse was "deceptively plain." He was not anyone's ideal of the war charger so often depicted by artists; yet he possessed stamina and character that amazed and amused admirers. He could live on "a ton of hay or live on cobs," recalled Henry Kyd Douglas of Jackson's staff.

Sharon Smith's work sheds light on why Little Sorrel was a good fit for Jackson. She offers a convincing argument suggesting that the general might have been a better horseman possessing a better understanding of the requirements of a good officer's mount than previously thought. In a broader way, Smith helps readers appreciate the role of the horse in mid-century America.

It was the courageous image of a commander on horseback that compelled soldiers into battle or rallied a faltering line. Rider and mount became an inseparable image: Lee on Traveller; Sheridan astride Rienzi; Mead's Old Baldy; Grant's beautiful chestnut Cincinnati. Necessity dictated that officers had more than one mount. Frequently the officer's horse was a casualty. (Little Sorrel was wounded at least twice.) Confederate cavalry commander Nathan B. Forrest had the most mounts shot from under him: thirty-nine. The flamboyant George Custer is reported to have had eleven horses killed in battle.

George W. Grayson, a leader of the Creek Nation and Captain of the 2nd Creek Mounted Volunteers, CSA, stated that "One becomes greatly attached to any horse that he has had the exclusive use of for any considerable time, but especially fond and friendly becomes this attachment when he feels that his horse has on occasion been the means of helping him through, probably saved his life in many thrilling junctures and hair raising escapades."

Such a relationship no doubt existed between Stonewall and Little Sorrel. If there had not been a Civil War, Thomas Jackson would have continued his quiet life as a college professor at VMI. Little Sorrel most likely would have had an equally uneventful existence on a farm somewhere in Ohio. Fate created a relationship between the unlikely general and the unlikely war horse.

This is the story of that relationship.

Author's Note

Confederate General Thomas J. "Stonewall" Jackson's favorite and best warhorse was an animal of many names, and sometimes no name at all. When Jackson acquired the horse, on May 10, 1861, the little gelding came without a name attached. There is some faint evidence that his original name was American Traveler, but that is unproven, perhaps improvable, and probably untrue.

Jackson's widow and staff members said after the war that the general called his horse Fancy, although they gave different reasons for that choice of name. Mary Anna Jackson, known as Anna, said that her husband intended the little horse for her and that the name was suitable for a lady's mount. Others claimed that the name was a joke since the horse was anything but fancy. There are problems with both explanations.

Jackson kept the horse, even though he had ample opportunity to turn him over to Anna, especially during the first year of the war. As for the other possibility, Stonewall Jackson was not inclined to joke and the concept of irony was a mystery to him. The most likely explanation is that Jackson had previously owned a horse named Fancy, one that in all probability came with the name. So he kept it and repeated it with his new horse.

Civil War–era writers didn't call the horse by name. Newspaper reporters, letter writers, and memoirists who didn't revise their work later referred to him as Jackson's little sorrel, or Jackson's old sorrel, or just Jackson's sorrel. After the war, the "old" became the most common adjective. At war's end, he was fifteen and that *was* approaching old age for a horse in an era when equine life expectancy was no more than twenty.

The description became the name. At the time of his death in 1886, most newspapers reported the passing of Stonewall Jackson's warhorse Old Sorrel. Some noted that the general called the horse Fancy, and most remarked on his small size. As the great flood of Confederate memoirs arrived during the last fifteen years of the nineteenth century, the name "Little Sorrel," already used occasionally, became the name of choice for veterans who actually remembered him.

The variety of names has led to confusion. Some writers have referred to Stonewall's two favorite horses, Fancy and Little Sorrel. They were the same horse. Jackson did own a second sorrel horse, one who also had a variety of descriptive names: Big Sorrel, Gaunt Sorrel, Young Sorrel, and perhaps others. This horse was not a favorite, usually lent out and finally given away to an aide.

There is no evidence that Stonewall Jackson himself called his favorite horse Little Sorrel, although he may have used the phrase "the little sorrel" to differentiate him from the other sorrel horse he owned. But the name Little Sorrel has conquered all others, and that's the name modern historians, writers, and artists use. It's the name used here.

INTRODUCTION

Laid to Rest at Last

Juanita Allen, president of the Virginia division of the United Daughters of the Confederacy, was a woman on a mission during the winter of 1996–1997. She had a Confederate hero to honor, although some of her friends questioned the method she chose to bestow the tribute, if not its recipient.

"Southerners are a very devoted people and we believe in honoring heroes of all types," she explained to the *Washington Times*, responding to critics. To be fair, very few of those critics came from the South, and those who did weren't especially critical. Mrs. Allen, looking around for projects for her organization, had already settled upon a few related to Thomas J. "Stonewall" Jackson, second only to Robert E. Lee in the esteem of Virginians to whom the Civil War was still important. There were plans under way to erect a new marker near the spot where Jackson was shot down by friendly fire at Chancellorsville.

Also in Mrs. Allen's sights was a new grave marker for Jackson's widow, Anna, the first president of a United Daughters of the Confederacy chapter. A visit to the museum at the Virginia Military Institute (VMI) in Lexington,

Virginia, where Jackson was a professor when war came, produced a plan to restore the general's first uniform, which had become a little threadbare over the past century. But the visit produced something else as well.

In a place of honor in the military museum, next to the bullet-torn raincoat Stonewall Jackson wore at the time of his mortal wounding in 1863, not far from the famous shiny helmet of World War II hero General George S. Patton, near a massive exhibit of nineteenth-century firearms, stood the mount of a small red horse. The horse was as famous as he was unimpressive.

It was Little Sorrel, Stonewall Jackson's favorite—although unlikely—warhorse. He was renowned throughout the South during the war and had become even more famous, North and South, during the long years of his retirement. At first, his fame was as a reflection of his legendary master, an eccentric and implausible military genius. Eventually the horse's very survival became legendary too.

When Little Sorrel died in 1886, at the improbably advanced age of thirty-six, he was mounted by one of the world's foremost taxidermists. Frederic S. Webster maintained an elaborate studio on Pennsylvania Avenue in Washington, D.C., and was known as an artist among mere technicians, a taxidermist who made his subjects compelling and real. He specialized in manipulating them into lifelike positions, often placing them in dioramas using the increasingly sophisticated art of photography.

Webster had recently left Ward's Natural Science Establishment in Rochester, New York, making himself available for private commissions. He had learned his trade at Ward's, best known in the taxidermy world as the place that P. T. Barnum had sent his famous Jumbo to be mounted after the elephant's untimely death. Although Webster didn't work on Jumbo, he had recently become known worldwide for a taxidermy grouping that he called "The Flamingo at Home." Webster's flamingoes were the talk of the scientific world since the display so accurately showed a group of birds in a typical habitat, a rare technique in Victorian taxidermy.

Celebrated taxidermist Frederic Webster.

Webster was a brilliant—and expensive—choice to mount the beloved Little Sorrel. Unlike most other taxidermists of the era, Webster disdained wire frames with sawdust filling. He first created a plaster-of-Paris sculpture in an appropriate head-up position as if the little horse had just heard the sound of bugles and cannon. He then artistically stretched the red hide over the statue. The horse's skeleton wasn't needed, so Webster took it as partial payment for his work.

Frederic Webster carried Little Sorrel's skeleton along with him ten years later when he took a job as curator and chief taxidermist of the Carnegie Museum of Natural History in Pittsburgh and articulated it into a lifelike position, tensed and ready to charge. Little Sorrel's skeleton was then placed on display. There it stood for fifty years, gathering dust and losing the occasional tooth and section of bone.

In the 1930s, several Southern museums began inquiring about the skeleton. Little Sorrel might have been an object of mild curiosity in Pittsburgh, but he remained a hero south of the Mason-Dixon Line. Webster, as much a survivor as the little red horse, expressed no serious opposition to its repatriation, although he grumbled a little at the idea that it might be done without formal consultation with him.

Meanwhile, Webster's mount of Little Sorrel had remained in Virginia, first at the Lee Camp of the Confederate Veterans Home in Richmond, a residence for elderly Confederate soldiers. By the late 1940s, when the last veteran was gone and the need for the residence had passed, Little Sorrel's mount was moved to the VMI Museum. By then, Webster himself was gone, although just barely, having died in 1945 at the age of ninety-five. VMI was a suitable destination for the bones as well, so the skeleton was taken apart and shipped to Lexington, where it remained in storage for nearly half a century.

Then Juanita Allen showed up, looking for a project for the Daughters of the Confederacy. It was well over a century since the horse's demise and more than one hundred thirty years since the death of his

Mount of Little Sorrel at the VMI Museum in Lexington, Virginia.

master, but both horse and general were important enough to rouse the patriotism of a Confederate Daughter. When she learned that only part of Stonewall Jackson's horse was on display and that the bones lay nearly forgotten, Mrs. Allen knew she had her project.

"We petted his nose and told him he was going to be laid to rest," said Mrs. Allen to the *Roanoke Times*. The mount itself was going nowhere. It remains the museum's most popular exhibit. Mrs. Allen was referring to the skeleton.

"I felt so sorry for him that he'd never been laid to rest," she told the reporter. "Everything should be buried. It's just the Christian thing to do."

Webster would have approved. He had, he said, begun work on Little Sorrel just after Stonewall's horse "went over the green fields of some animal heaven to rest in peace and honor."

Little Sorrel's master might have been a little more troubled by anything resembling a funeral for a horse, even his loyal Little Sorrel. Jackson was a famously religious man, a Presbyterian, and a great believer in the Bible. He would have known well and believed thoroughly the words of Genesis that give to man supremacy over livestock. Jackson's denomination, as most others did and still do, taught that animals do not possess immortal souls and certainly don't require a religious service to see them off to heaven, even one made up of green fields.

But some believe as cowboy philosopher Will Rogers did. "If there are no dogs in heaven," Rogers often said, "then when I die I want to go where they went."

The Daughters and the VMI Museum staff were careful not to describe the event they planned as a funeral, but it certainly looked to be one to the nearly four hundred people who showed up on a hot and sunny day in July 1997. The attendance came as a surprise. The event was to honor a horse, after all, and one who had died 111 years earlier. But it was not just any horse. He was Stonewall Jackson's favorite, to be sure. But the honoree was famous in his own right.

Little Sorrel was a survivor. He had carried Jackson in all but one of the great general's battles and apparently suffered only one minor injury. He had then lived on longer than almost any other horse who had participated in the Civil War, longer even than thousands of human veterans. People wanted to see him buried, just as people had poured into Lexington to see his master buried a couple of miles away 134 years earlier.

At 3:00 PM on July 20, 1997, a procession of dignitaries emerged from the Jackson Memorial Hall on the VMI campus, the building that houses the museum where Little Sorrel's mount remains the most popular exhibit. At the head of the procession was a young cadet carrying a specially made eighteen-inch-high walnut box into which the cremated skeletal remains of Little Sorrel had been placed. Accompanying them were a fife and drum corps, a cavalry unit that included a dozen horses, VMI officials, a bagpiper, costumed reenactors, descendants of Confederate veterans, and, although it was not a funeral, a Presbyterian minister.

After suitable prayers and speeches, four men dressed in Confederate uniforms lowered the walnut box into a prepared plot on the VMI parade ground directly in front of a life-size statue of Stonewall Jackson himself. As the remains entered the earth, reenactors fired three volleys over the horse's grave. Added to the dirt placed on top were handfuls of soil from each of the battlefields where Little Sorrel carried Stonewall Jackson, usually to victory.

George Moor, a Jackson reenactor and head of the cavalry unit that accompanied the walnut box, dismounted to say a prayer over the still-open grave. He carefully placed two horseshoes inside and was asked the meaning of his token.

"So he may be shod wherever he goes," Moor told the crowd.

James Robertson, author of the definitive biography of Stonewall Jackson, ended the ceremony with a wish for Little Sorrel. "May you continue to have good grazing in the boundless pastures of heaven," he said to the remains of the unlikely hero.

Little Sorrel's gravestone in Lexington, Virginia.
KEITH GIBSON, VMI MUSEUM, LEXINGTON, VA.

No, it wasn't a funeral, because you don't have funerals for horses. But it probably was the last original burial of a Civil War veteran, and an appropriate tribute to a horse who had become a unique symbol of a vanished country.

CHAPTER 1

Warriors under Saddle

During the first week of May 1861, the major in command of Virginia volunteers at Harpers Ferry had horses on his mind. Thomas J. Jackson, a West Pointer, Mexican War combat veteran, and longtime instructor at the Virginia Military Institute in Lexington, Virginia, knew all about the value of horses in wartime. He also knew that he was exceedingly short of them.

Virginia was a relative latecomer to rebellion. The state's secession convention was able to produce enough votes only after South Carolina's troops fired on Fort Sumter in Charleston Harbor on April 13, leading President Abraham Lincoln to call for volunteers to put down the rebellion. Although most Virginians weren't secessionists, they wanted no part of fighting fellow southerners and joined the other states of the new Confederacy on April 17. The complexion of the rebellion changed immediately.

Virginia was the biggest, the richest, and the closest to Washington of any state in the new Confederacy. It was also, of all the southern states, home to the largest number of West Point–educated current and former officers of the U.S. Army. Like Jackson, most of them would follow their state into rebellion.

Nearly all the West Pointers were offered significant assignments from Virginia's new governor, John Letcher, who would control his state's military manpower until the Confederacy organized its own army. Major Jackson received one of the most important posts when he was sent to command the thousands of volunteers and militia members pouring into Harpers Ferry, site of one of the two major Federal arsenals in the country. The amateur soldiers took control of the town and the arsenal the day after the secession vote, but the military minds in Richmond, including a recently resigned U.S. Army colonel named Robert E. Lee, knew the Federal army would soon want the town back.

On April 27, Jackson received his orders to Harpers Ferry, arriving there two days later. He had left the U.S. Army a decade earlier, taking a job as a professor at VMI, where he taught natural philosophy, the nineteenth-century version of physics. But he also taught artillery tactics, and so he knew immediately upon arrival that horses, lots of them, would be needed in Harpers Ferry if the town were to be saved for the Confederacy.

Harpers Ferry wasn't a particularly congenial spot for an army of rebellion. It was snugly situated across the Potomac River from the still-loyal Maryland, a slave-holding state destined to stay with the Union thanks to an early order from President Lincoln calling for Maryland to be occupied by Federal troops and several of its civil liberties to be suspended.

On the other side of Harpers Ferry lay the mountainous western part of Virginia, where a majority of citizens resisted secession. Many had no use for the institution of slavery that helped instigate the breakup of the Union in the first place. Others may not have minded slavery but owned no slaves themselves and resented the political power of wealthy eastern Virginians who did hold slaves.

Thomas "Stonewall" Jackson in 1863.

But Harpers Ferry was geographically significant in another way, situated as it was at a key stop on both the Baltimore and Ohio Railroad and the Chesapeake and Ohio Canal. Both systems linked east and west for the Union and might do the same for the Confederacy. The town, important beyond its size, also stood as a gateway to the Shenandoah Valley of Virginia, the rich and fertile land between the Allegheny and Blue Ridge Mountains. The valley was a vital corridor to anybody traveling north and south in the western half of Virginia. It was also a breadbasket of great importance to anyone trying to feed an army.

Major Jackson's orders were to guard this crucial spot, a town that stood at the foot of three elevations, two of them towering over the town. He had seen the topography and sensed its military implications eighteen months earlier, when he, two undersized cannons, and twenty-one VMI cadets trained in artillery were sent to Harpers Ferry to protect against an uprising of slaves or abolitionists (both equally feared) as raider John Brown awaited execution in nearby Charles Town.

Brown's initial attack on the Federal arsenal in October 1859 had failed since few slaves joined in. There had been no evidence that further trouble was coming, but Virginia was taking no chances. Jackson and the cadets stayed a few days, witnessed Brown's execution, and returned to Lexington.

The artillery professor learned a couple of things from his stay. First, Harpers Ferry would be exceptionally difficult to defend without placing troops and artillery on the heights overlooking the town. Second, undersized cannons, small enough to be hauled by cadets, wouldn't do the job if real shooting started.

So Jackson wrote to Richmond for cannons, ammunition, caissons, wagons, and anything else he could get, and he began to look around for horses to haul all that equipment. He also looked around for somebody to help him procure those horses, and his attention fell on a man he knew well, at least by reputation.

Harpers Ferry during the Civil War.
NATIONAL ARCHIVES

John Alexander Harman of Staunton was a member of the family that operated Harman Brothers Stage, a coach line that carried mail and passengers between valley towns poorly served by rail. Jackson himself had traveled on a four-horse Harman coach between Lexington and Staunton on the first leg of his journey to Richmond on April 21, his usual practice when he left Lexington during the decade he spent there.

Harman was a man who all his life had been eager to get on with challenges and new experiences, no matter what the potential danger. He had arrived in Harpers Ferry a week and a half ahead of Jackson, the day after the passage of Virginia's secession ordinance. He wasn't sure he wanted to remain. Harman was a busy man and expected to become busier with the outbreak of war. But he was head of a volunteer militia unit in Staunton and felt obligated to make the trip.

In addition to the stagecoach business, Harman procured and butchered meat for a wholesale grocery business, edited a local newspaper, and ran a substantial farm two miles east of Staunton. In his early twenties, before business interests burdened him, Harman had gone off to Texas in search of adventure. His experiences there became the stuff of legend in Staunton, Lexington, and the other Shenandoah Valley towns.

A first wave of Americans, mostly southerners, had arrived in Texas in the mid-1830s to answer settlers' call for help in executing a revolution against Mexican control of the land north of the Rio Grande. Among those who responded was Ben McCulloch of Tennessee, whose fortuitous case of measles prevented him from being present at the Alamo when it fell to Mexican troops in March 1836.

Unlike the defenders of the Texas shrine, McCulloch survived to prosper during the years of Texas independence. In 1845, Texas was annexed by the United States and admitted to the Union with a boundary chosen by President James K. Polk, over the bitter objections of Mexico. War broke out the following year and McCulloch raised a company of volunteer rangers to defend Texas from Mexico.

A young John Harman made his way to Texas, joined up with McCulloch, and rode along as McCulloch's Rangers performed as regular cavalry, dismounted cavalry, guerrilla cavalry, scouts, and spies. The rangers also procured horses for the U.S. commanding general Zachary Taylor and protected Taylor's long and vulnerable supply lines.

After the war, Harman returned to Virginia and a more conventional life. Thomas Jackson may or may not have known about Harman's Texas adventures, but in Harpers Ferry he learned quickly that the businessman from Staunton was just the man to find him some horses.

Jackson asked Harman to ride out into the Virginia countryside east of Harpers Ferry to acquire horses suitable to pull artillery pieces, supply wagons, and ambulances. He would ask for donations, which neither man expected, or offer to buy the animals, which they equally doubted would work. They could give only IOUs drawn on the Commonwealth of Virginia in payment, a proposal that would be unpopular under any circumstances, but even more so in Loudon County.

It wasn't just proximity that made Loudon a likely target of forced Confederate horse procurement. The county was famous throughout Virginia for the quality of its livestock. Its pastures were superb, thanks to the careful management and crop rotation practiced by its small farmers, mostly Quakers and Germans whose ancestors had traveled south from Pennsylvania a century earlier.

The new Confederacy had another reason to look first to the Quaker and German farmers for horses. No farmer would like to be given an IOU for a good horse, and Jackson, a man of great common sense, was reluctant to offend men he hoped would join or send their sons to his rapidly organizing companies and regiments. But enlistment of the Germans was unlikely and that of Quakers essentially impossible.

Deep within Quaker doctrine was the belief that slavery was an absolute evil. Virginia Quakers who lived in Loudon County tended to be quiet about their beliefs, unlike their cousins over the Mason-Dixon Line in Pennsylvania. But the fact that they could run such admirable small farms without slave labor often rankled some of the larger plantation owners of Loudon and other northern Virginia counties.

For several decades there had also been rumors about Quaker farmhouses in Loudon County sheltering runaway slaves, but that would have been so dangerous to slave and protector alike that there were probably few actual occurrences. However, the farmers would certainly have looked the other way as runaways dashed north to freedom.

All in all, John Harman was inclined to look first on the Quaker and German farms of Loudon. He quickly hit equine pay dirt, seizing dozens of horses and leaving pieces of paper behind. He also left simmering resentment. A month after Harman completed his search, the Quaker and German districts of Loudon County would vote overwhelmingly no in the referendum that finalized Virginia's secession, while most of the rest of the county and state voted to leave the Union.

Quakers and the few other Unionists in Loudon suffered so much from loss of livestock and crops to the Virginia and then the Confederate armies that some were driven to violate another profound Quaker doctrine: that of nonviolence. In the spring of 1862 Quaker farmers and businessmen organized the Loudon Rangers, a partisan cavalry unit later absorbed into the U.S. Army. Although Union regiments did come out of Virginia's forty-one western counties, they represented West Virginia, which separated from the Confederacy and became the state of West Virginia in 1862. Only the Loudon Rangers came out of Virginia itself to fight for the Union.

The Rangers fought for most of the war with prices on their heads, knowing that capture meant hanging as traitors to Virginia. As Quakers, they were not particularly effective soldiers, but they persevered to the end of the war, perhaps remembering all those fine horses lost to Harman and Jackson.

Harman's success in rounding up good horses prompted Jackson to ask him for additional help. Although he had ridden out of Lexington on his own horse, Jackson had sent that animal home to continue his journey by stage and train, first to Richmond and then to Harpers Ferry. It's not clear why Jackson didn't keep the horse with him or have him sent along later, since he knew that officers were expected to provide their own mounts. Regardless of the reason, Jackson asked Harman to be on the lookout for a suitable horse, one that might stand the stress of battle, should it come.

The search began just as the relationship between the two sides of the Baltimore and Ohio Railroad was beginning to change. For the first two weeks of Southern control of Harpers Ferry, each side permitted trains to pass, even if they appeared to be carrying supplies that might be used for military purposes. That changed after the first week in May.

On May 9, a westbound train headed to Harpers Ferry was captured by Federal troops in Maryland. Aboard were inventor Charles Dickinson and his new steam-operated artillery piece intended for the Confederacy. The peculiar gun was confiscated, Dickinson arrested and sent to Annapolis, and a round of train seizures and counterseizures was under way.

The day after the steam gun seizure, on Friday, May 10, 1861, a five-car livestock train headed to Baltimore from southern Ohio was stopped at the Harpers Ferry station. Four of the cars were filled with beef cattle, a hundred of them, and they were enthusiastically confiscated for use by the troops, who had been stretching the limited food supplies of the town.

The fifth car contained ten horses, good enough horses that John Harman was called in to take a look. The exact makeup of the horse consignment is lost, and it is now unknown if Harman found some draft animals to add to his supply. But an army needs horses that can be ridden as well as driven. Harman, having learned recently that Major Jackson was in need of a mount or two, checked the consignment carefully, found a few prospects, and sent for his commander.

Jackson liked a handsome horse as well as the next man, and he had owned a few in his time. He had bragged in Mexico about a particularly beautiful and expensive horse acquired for a hefty price, but that animal had been used only during peaceful months of occupation and had never seen action. The carload of Ohio horses may have included one or two handsome ones, but the two that caught his eye were more ordinary.

One was a big sorrel horse, a little angular but clearly strong enough to carry a man of almost six feet. The second, another sorrel, was attractive but not nearly big enough, standing less than fifteen hands (five feet) at the withers. Jackson told Harman that he would take both sorrels, the big one for himself and the little one for his wife, who might need private transportation during the months of upheaval that likely lay ahead. He paid $150 in U.S. money for the two red horses.

The accepted story has been that the money went to the Confederate government, to which Jackson had consigned the confiscated horses. But newspaper articles a couple of weeks later reported that the original consigner, described as an Ohio drover, was "satisfied" with his payment for his load of livestock.

The seizure that provided Jackson with his horses contributed to a situation that infuriated Virginians and harmed the Confederate effort in the state. General Benjamin Butler, in command of Union forces in Maryland in early May, was greatly annoyed by the confiscation of the livestock train. A few days after the incident, Butler was sent to take command of Fort Monroe on the southeastern Virginia coast, still held by Federal forces. Soon after Butler's arrival, escaped slaves began appearing inside the lines, asking for freedom and protection.

Federal officials were not yet ready to turn the new war into a conflict over slavery. Washington's position was that secession was illegal and Virginia remained part of the Union. So Butler was told that the escaped slaves were still governed by the laws of the United States and should be sent back to their owners. Butler, a longtime opponent of slavery, believed otherwise. He retained the escapes slaves, calling them contraband of war who should be put into service working for the U.S. Army.

Thousands of escapees arrived and were put to work on construction projects and other duties around Fort Monroe. They, like Thomas Jackson's two new sorrels, never went back to their former owners.

The escaped slaves had a modest expectation of freedom after the fighting was over, but the horses, had they been aware of the history of their species in times of human war, would have been somewhat less hopeful. In May 1861, it was too soon to know just how hard the Civil War was going to be on horses, but the precedent was not particularly promising. On May 10, 1861, the two sorrels became part of a long and brutal history.

Human beings began to appreciate the value of horses in war not long after they realized that horses were good for something other than food. Although the final word is not yet in on the precise dates of horse domestication and the first use of the animals in warfare, we do know about the earliest surviving evidence of each step.

Horses and humans first encountered each other at least fifty thousand years ago. The acquaintance was neither close nor friendly, with horses providing meat and skins to Neanderthal and Cro-Magnon hunters.

There is a faint shadow of evidence that modern horses lived in close proximity to humans as early as 7000 BCE. Saudi archaeologists have discovered fractured statues of horses at al-Maqar in the center of the Arabian Peninsula and believe this discovery means that horses were first domesticated there nine thousand years ago. Other archaeologists point out that an artist might represent a wild animal as well as a domestic one, and they are not so sure about the al-Maqar date anyway.

Most scientists credit the Botai tribe of the Eurasian steppe with leaving us the earliest significant evidence of regular horse usage. By 3600 BCE the Botai were living closely with horses in at least three villages in what is now northern Kazakhstan, south of Russia. The Botai, named by modern anthropologists for one of their villages, hunted wild horses, as did other tribes on the broad, grassy steppe.

But they also learned how to use horses before eating them. Wear patterns on excavated horse jaws from Botai sites suggest the use of rawhide bits. The Botai horses were used in riding rather than driving. The wheel was in the process of being invented elsewhere as the Botai developed their horse culture, and they had no concept of wheeled transport.

These were modern horses, not now-extinct wild equids, because there is plenty of evidence that the animals were bred and raised, kept in corrals, and milked. The thought of milking a wild horse fully supports the concept of Botai domestication. The Botai were not known to relish war, but they faced inevitable conflict with other tribes of the steppe and may have had neighbors who coveted their horses. If there were battles, and there almost certainly were, the Botai would have used their horses, whose existence formed the vital center of their world.

The horses would not have provided platforms for fighting but rather quick transportation. The stone tools of five thousand six hundred years ago were simple and primitive and wouldn't have been especially dangerous to horses used in dashes toward hand-to-hand, dismounted battle. But danger is relative. The Botai happily ate their surplus horses, even the ones they had raised themselves, according to archaeological evidence of butchering on the equine bones that have been discovered.

Most horses used in war in ancient times went to battle hitched to vehicles. Excavated chariots and wagons as well as artistic depictions provide the next oldest evidence of horses used in war. Clay tablets from Iraq that date from three or four hundred years after the presumed date of Botai domestication portray animal-drawn vehicles. But horses aren't included, so we know very little about who or what pulled the vehicles.

Horses, or horselike animals, are clearly shown pulling war chariots in the Standard of Ur, an inlaid box discovered in a royal burial in northern Iraq that dates from about 2500 BCE. The Standard is the earliest surviving portrayal of horses in battle. But since it shows intricate trappings and an elaborate manner of deployment, the Standard depicts an already well-established practice. Somebody was using horses to pull war chariots in war well before 2500 BCE.

After the time of Ur, horses and their use in war spread rapidly through the Middle East and on to Egypt. By 1355 BCE there was a guidebook for the selection, training, and management of warhorses, written for the use of Hittite charioteers. Most chariots of the ancient world were designed to carry at least two warriors, one to drive and the other to wield javelin or sword.

In addition to the increased weaponry, the charioteers had another advantage over foot soldiers. A vehicle drawn by one or more horses, usually galloping, was far more intimidating than a warrior on foot. Unfortunately for the horses, being harnessed, whether singly, in tandem, or in fours, made them more vulnerable to accident and injury. It also turned them into large and often clumsy targets.

When officers realized that it was considerably more comfortable to go off to war with a horse, rather than marching with the foot soldiers, they helped change the way battles were conducted. The plumes, gold trappings, and other adornments guaranteed that enemy soldiers would recognize the value of directing a javelin or spear into the flanks of a horse carrying an important figure. An Egyptian pharaoh was impossible to mistake for a regular soldier, thanks largely to the decorations carried by his horse. Later, Roman officers made sure everyone was aware of their rank by their use of horse ornamentation, giving opponents big and tempting targets.

Mobility became the primary concern as the world moved into the Christian era. Tribes using their horses in a new way hurried along the disintegration of the Roman Empire. The Huns, from the western steppes of Russia, swept into Europe in the fifth century CE, destroying towns and exacting tribute from the surviving citizens. Under their famous chief Attila, the Huns traveled with herds of as many as sixty thousand horses. The spectacle of so many men moving so rapidly on horseback tended to demoralize the opposition even before the first spear was flung or the first arrow was released.

For the next several centuries, massed archers on fast-moving horses dictated the terms of combat. This method of warfare reached its peak in the thirteenth century with the rise of the Mongols, notably under their first great leader Genghis Khan. The Mongols, from a desolate country northeast of China, raised tough and fast horses, less than fourteen hands tall, that could live on poor feed and little water. These sturdy little horses were necessary for the Mongol nomadic lifestyle and proved ideal for war. The Mongol army was big and the horse herd was even bigger. More than two hundred thousand head traveled with the soldiers, first to China and Russia, then as far west as the eastern part of Europe.

The Mongols also used their warhorses in a new way. Mounted scouts preceded, paralleled, and followed the vast army to check terrain and look for enemy soldiers. Skilled riders on the very best horses acted as couriers to pass messages between sections of the huge army and back to Mongolia. The horse-based Mongol army was extraordinarily effective and would probably have devastated the rest of Europe as well if problems at home hadn't stopped the momentum. The Mongols returned to Mongolia, but Europe had learned a great deal from the invaders about horses and war.

Mobility and speed were hard on horses. Genghis Khan once moved his army one hundred thirty miles in two days, and he and other generals often demanded fifty miles a day from their mounted soldiers. This required a lot of grazing and water for the horses, resources often unavailable along the route. The Mongols lost many thousands of horses to hunger and thirst during a major campaign.

Mobility and speed also came mostly with small horses that were unarmored or lightly armored, a fact that ensured the deaths of thousands of animals in battle. After the Mongols left, European military leaders thoroughly understood the utility of light horses, but they also grew to understand that bigger horses would be required with new and heavier weapons and the trappings of war.

The number of equine fatalities in war went down briefly as horses and humans grew in height and weight. But as the horse grew stronger, so did the weaponry, making armor or other protection more important. Horse armor reached its apex during the Middle Ages, usually in the form of padding and hardened leather. But even when metal was added, armor provided limited protection against the increasingly deadly weapons of war.

The crossbow, known since ancient times, evolved into a portable all-metal device that launched an iron bolt capable of penetrating armor. It had a remarkable range of as much as three hundred fifty yards. This was followed by an even more deadly weapon. The longbow, with similar range but also the capability of launching a dozen projectiles a minute, became a more important weapon than the crossbow late in the fourteenth century. Both could kill an armored horse.

The gunpowder-based firearms that began arriving in Europe in the mid-fifteenth century would eventually supplant both. In each case, the soldiers who used the weapons soon discovered that it was easier to aim at the larger target that a horse provided. They also found that it was almost as effective to incapacitate a horse as it was to eliminate his rider. Later, when horses were hitched to artillery pieces, killing a horse became even more useful.

The long history of horses at war also proved that injury or death in battle was often the least of the hazards. In the nearly six thousand years that people had taken their horses off to war, they had found that the fundamental nature of horses often made it difficult to use them in military campaigns, as valuable as they might be.

Horses evolved to graze, eating a large volume of food over most of the day. Left to his own choice, a horse will graze sixteen or more hours a day, taking in at least a pound and a half of feed for every hundred pounds of his own weight. By that standard, a nine-hundred-pound light cavalry horse would need more than thirteen pounds of hay or other feed per day, while an eleven-hundred-pound artillery horse would require closer to seventeen. Multiply those figures by the size of the horse herd maintained by an army, and you have a staggering amount of feed to provide day after day.

Caretakers of warhorses also knew well that the phrase "strong as a horse" bore little relationship to reality. Horses were equally subject to contagious disease as human soldiers, with the additional problem of being unable to lie down for more than short periods without contracting pneumonia or colic, both often fatal. Serious wounds to the limbs were usually fatal to horses since amputation was not an option. Soldiers with amputations might have a modest chance of survival.

When, three weeks into the Civil War, Thomas Jackson took possession of his two new sorrel horses, the most likely predictor of their chances for survival was a war that took place five thousand miles away. The Crimean War had ended in 1856, and by 1861 it was already recognized as something new and terrible in the history of warfare. It was a good thing that the sorrels had not known what happened to the equine participants in that war.

The war, which featured Britain and France on one side and Russia on the other, resulted from the disintegration of the Ottoman Empire and the resulting conflict over who would control their client states in western Asia. It took place primarily on the Crimean Peninsula, an unwelcoming fragment of land that jutted from Ukraine into the Black Sea. The Crimea was sweltering in summer, deadly cold in winter, and covered by mountains that offered little grazing for horses.

The Crimean War was mostly a conflict of infantry and powerful new artillery, but enough cavalry was involved to raise the equine death toll to levels never seen before, particularly in terms of percentages. One British military historian figures 80 percent of the horses involved in the two-year conflict were killed or died of disease.

Here's an example. The Inniskilling Dragoons, part of a heavy cavalry brigade, fought well in the Crimea but brought none of its horses back with them. A fire aboard their transport ship *Europa* just a couple of days out of England in May 1854 killed all fifty-seven of their horses. After acquiring more in Turkey, the regiment performed admirably during the battle of Balaclava the same day in 1854 that the more famous Light Brigade made its doomed charge. Unlike the Light Brigade, the Heavy Brigade succeeded. But the result wasn't much better for the horses. Of the approximately four hundred heavy dragoon horses who took the field that day, nearly two hundred died in the charge, and many more were mortally wounded or lost.

Those figures pale in comparison to the losses of the supposedly more agile Light Brigade, which sent six hundred sixty riders into an ill-advised charge against entrenched Russian artillery. One hundred soldiers were killed, while more than four hundred horses died or were grievously wounded. Most of the rest suffered lesser wounds.

That terrible day was followed by a yearlong siege of the Russian stronghold at Sebastopol, a year that included nearly five months of a savage winter. Hundreds of the remaining horses died of starvation, and many that survived were then killed for meat anyway. All this happened just a few years before the outbreak of the American Civil War.

Nearly five hundred horses were lost in 1854's Charge of the Light Brigade.
PAUL AND DOMINIC COLNAGHI, LIBRARY OF CONGRESS

All things considered, the survival prospects of a horse pressed into military service in May 1861 were poor. Thomas Jackson's big sorrel, destined to be an infantry officer's mount, presumably had a somewhat better chance of seeing the end of the war than did the artillery horses rounded up by John Harman, but those chances were still not good. The little sorrel, intended to be a lady's mount, might have had an even better chance of surviving had he been sent to Anna Jackson. But as things turned out, he did survive quite well indeed.

CHAPTER 2

Horseman

Thomas Jackson was a man who loved horses. Throughout his life he would buy himself good ones as soon as he could afford to and then make sure that he and his good horses were noticed. It was not so much that his appearance mattered to Jackson—it certainly did not. Rather, it was recognition of his accomplishments that did.

He was an ambitious and complex man. Money was important to him, as was respect, but he often behaved as if neither was of any consequence. In the years leading up to the Civil War, Jackson barely held on to a teaching job at a small state military college, but he still managed to invest his way into a level of prosperity that brought him land, slaves, and bank accounts.

He dressed poorly and socialized with some reluctance but still admired good-looking and educated women. He was able to marry one with high social standing and, after her death in childbirth, won the hand of a second attractive young woman from a prominent family.

All in all, Thomas Jackson had a good opinion of himself. In May 1861 he may have predicted that he would come out of the war with a reputation as a singular warrior. He would have been astonished to know that he would also have a reputation as a bad horseman and that the fine little sorrel he took off the Baltimore and Ohio livestock car would be known as a poor horse.

Neither was true, no matter how many people talked and wrote about it during and after the war. The little sorrel was a good-quality horse and Thomas Jackson, the new major of Virginia troops, was a good enough horseman to know it.

It was true that the horse was different, not what an officer and a gentleman might be expected to ride, but that was no problem for Jackson. His own riding style was hardly that of an officer and a gentleman. Jackson came to war with a lifetime of familiarity with horses and from a family with generations of close contact with good ones. But his extensive experience with horses contributed to the reputation he was about to earn as an inferior rider.

Variations on the word "ungraceful" were used most frequently to describe Jackson's form on horseback. "He was an ungraceful horseman," wrote General Richard Taylor, who admired him otherwise. As a rider, "he was not a very graceful one," noted John George Gittings, Confederate soldier and distant relative of Jackson. The observation was voiced by almost everyone who saw him ride and others who based their opinions on hearsay.

Next came the nearly universal opinion that he rode with his stirrups far too short. Staff officer Henry Kyd Douglas described exchanging horses with Jackson during the Second Battle of Manassas and finding the stirrup leathers too short by a third of their length. The stirrups, Douglas noted, were "of no use to me." He claimed that he would have been better off riding bareback as he dashed away to deliver a message. Jackson, meanwhile, hiked up the leathers on the new horse by the same third.

Georgia volunteer W. H. Andrews hazarded a guess as to precisely how short Jackson's stirrups were. "Six inches too short," Andrews wrote, "putting his knees nearly level with his horse's back."

Many observers also noted that Jackson leaned too far forward in the saddle. John Esten Cooke, a Virginia poet and volunteer soldier, wrote the first full biography of Jackson shortly after the general's death in 1863. "The general rode in a peculiar fashion," Cooke wrote, "leaning forward somewhat."

A few commented on the position of his toes in the stirrups. Oddly, some suggested that his toes pointed too far out, while others remarked that the wayward toes pointed in. General Taylor was in the "toes turning out" camp, describing Jackson with "huge feet with outturned toes thrust into his stirrups." Indiana poet and artist Peter Fishe Reed, who cobbled together northern newspaper articles into one of the earliest books to mention Jackson, believed the opposite of Jackson's feet. Reed wrote in 1862 in his *Incidents of the War; or, the Romance and Realities of Soldier Life* that Jackson rode with "short stirrups, knees cramped up, heels stuck out behind."

To be fair, Reed almost certainly never laid eyes on Jackson, mounted or otherwise, but he said he was quoting a lady who had known the general well. That lady, according to Reed, claimed "that she has never seen him on horseback without laughing." Reed doesn't name the lady, nor does he explain the circumstances in which she laughed at Jackson.

These descriptions, probably somewhat accurate, manage to transform themselves into the widely held belief that Thomas Jackson was a dreadful rider, which was not accurate. Some of the early writers did recognize the difference between appearance and skill. John Gittings acknowledged that Jackson was a good rider, even if he was graceless. Edward Alfriend, a Virginia infantry officer, noted that Jackson's riding skills appeared to change under fire. "In battle he sat perfectly erect and seemed to grow taller," Alfriend wrote.

A man of Thomas Jackson's family background and personal history should have been a skilled rider. The first Jackson ancestor to arrive in North America was the future Confederate general's great-grandfather, a member of a famously horse-loving immigrant group known variously as Scotch-Irish, Scots-Irish, or Ulster Scot. That man was John Jackson, born in Northern Ireland in the early eighteenth century.

John Jackson would probably have called himself Irish without specifying further. He, like most Irish immigrants who came to America before the nineteenth century, was from the northern part of the island but rarely differentiated between the two sections.

The immigrants were people of lowland Scottish and border English descent whose ancestors had spent a few generations in the northern part of Ireland, thanks to the desire of King James I to turn Ireland into an English-speaking and Protestant part of his kingdom. In the early seventeenth century James established the Ulster Plantations, a scheme to provide land for Scots immigrants to settle the newly British province now known as Ulster.

The plan worked and Ulster remains mostly Protestant to this day. John Jackson's ancestors were among the lowland Scots who arrived early, but it's unclear where they settled. Most believe the site was Coleraine in County Derry, while others think the location was a village called The Birches in County Armagh.

Both villages were close to one of the great racecourses of the early years of Thoroughbred horse racing. This was the Down Royal course at Downpatrick in County Down, chartered by the king in 1685. The three-mile horseshoe-shaped course saw rich men match their great horses, including the legendary Byerly Turk, one of the three male line ancestors of all modern Thoroughbreds and most other horses of quality.

There is no record of the Jacksons having visited the course, but thousands of Ulster Scots did, and horse racing became part of the Scots-Irish culture that survived their later trip across the Atlantic. The

Ulster Scots may have enjoyed the entertainment provided by racing, but the farmland offered by King James in Northern Ireland proved insufficient. They began emigrating early in the eighteenth century with John Jackson among those leaving Ulster. Jackson, his father, and his brothers left around 1723 for England rather than North America, settling in London. The father and brothers disappeared from the public records, but John turns up in the criminal records of London's Old Bailey court. Jackson family tradition claimed that John Jackson was a house builder of substance, sailing to America with a contract in hand for a project in Maryland. In reality he was convicted of theft in January 1749 and sentenced to a term of servitude in North America. Jackson was sentenced to seven years as an unwilling indentured servant and shipped to Maryland, most likely on the sailing ship *Litchfield*, in May 1749. During the voyage he met a thief named Elizabeth Cummins. Jackson and Cummins became the great-grandparents of the future Confederate general. Family lore of a genteel ancestry was incorrect.

What became of the couple once they arrived in America is not recorded. Transported convicts were offered for the highest bid. Dr. David Ross of Bladensburg, Maryland, who in addition to his medical practice operated as a convict merchant, most likely was the person who sold Jackson and Cummins.

Ross's cargoes were well advertised and widely appreciated. In 1760 a planter named George Washington of Mount Vernon, Virginia, which was only fifteen miles from Bladensburg by boat, noted in his diary entry for January 25: "Wrote to Dr. Ross to purchase me a joiner, bricklayer, and gardner [*sic*] if any ship of servants was in." If Washington had needed a joiner eleven years earlier, Ross might have offered him John Jackson.

Ross, like Washington, was a very wealthy man who put much of his money into high-quality livestock, including horses, owning about a dozen of them at the time of his death. If he was interested in racing, he had only to walk across the street from his elegant brick mansion. One of the Maryland colony's twenty racecourses was in Bladensburg within sight of Ross's front door.

Cummins may have spent time in Bladensburg, but it's more certain that John was sold to Cecil County, in far northeast Maryland, while Elizabeth remained closer to where she arrived, either in Baltimore, Annapolis, or Bladensburg itself.

Cecil County had become an important location for racing and breeding fine horses at the time of Jackson's arrival in 1749. A racecourse in Charles Town was among the most important in the Maryland colony, attracting thousands of spectators, including George Washington, to annual race meets. When John Jackson's sentence was up, he married Elizabeth Cummins and the couple headed west. In 1758 they settled on a small farm near what became Moorefield, Virginia, across the rich Shenandoah Valley. This was true frontier, with little cleared land and few towns or villages. The Jacksons, like other Scots-Irish settlers, traveled west looking for land, and what they found was land that belonged to somebody else.

They probably owned an ordinary horse or two for work and transportation, but they lived close to far better horses. The Jackson homestead stood just a few miles south of the vast holdings of the famous horseman Thomas Lord Fairfax, who had inherited nearly a million acres of Virginia from his grandfather Lord Culpeper. Thomas Fairfax had ordered his property surveyed and, just in case, had young surveyor George Washington examine the neighboring land as well. So it turned out that Washington, also a fine horseman, surveyed the acreage used by the Jacksons.

Fairfax was not a racing man, even though his English ancestors had been instrumental in developing the Thoroughbred. But he was a fox-hunting man and he encouraged Washington to join him in this activity. They may well have galloped in search of fox through land that became the Jacksons' farm. Descendants of these first Jacksons, including Stonewall himself, came to enjoy fox hunting as well.

John and Elizabeth Cummins Jackson left the Moorefield area after ten years, moving several times farther west into what later became West Virginia, where horse racing was well under way. The first record of organized racing in the future state occurred in Charles Town in 1786. The site of the first racecourse was just seven miles from Harpers Ferry, where Colonel Thomas Jackson would choose himself a little sorrel horse off a confiscated railroad car seventy-five years later.

If the first two generations of American Jacksons did take advantage of their proximity to horse racing, they would have been typical immigrant Scots-Irish. As a group, they were exceptionally fond of matching horses for speed and did it from their earliest years on the North American continent.

Take as an example the Reverend John Hindman, whose fame (or infamy, depending on one's Presbyterian zeal) spread across frontier Virginia. The Londonderry-born Hindman had arrived in Virginia in 1742 to help organize Presbyterian churches in the frontier beyond the Blue Ridge Mountains. Hindman loved horse racing so much that he sailed back and forth across the ocean to better indulge himself.

The Scots-Irish settlers of Augusta County built race paths almost as soon as they had carved their homes out of the forest, and the Reverend Hindman quickly adapted, going so far as to serve as a jockey for John Stephenson, a leading landowner and racehorse breeder of the region. But the Presbyterian Church frowned on Sunday racing, an unfortunate situation given that frontier Virginians found Sunday to be the very best day for their favorite activity.

So John Hindman packed up, sailed back to the British Isles, took Anglican orders, and returned to Augusta County to race any day he pleased. The reverend lived only a year after his return to Virginia in

1748, but he managed to add several racehorses, a set of jockey silks, and other racing equipment to his estate.

Andrew Jackson, a second-generation Ulster Scot, was a famous lover of horse racing. The seventh president, probably not related to Thomas Jackson, even brought three of his best horses along to the White House in 1829, including the fast gray Thoroughbred Bolivar. Andrew Jackson himself managed Bolivar's training while he was president.

Thomas Jackson, born six decades after Andrew, was involved in racing, but his fondness didn't last a lifetime, as Andrew's did. Religious fervor burned more intensely than did any affection for racing. But at one point in his early life he was deeply involved in the sport and had close contact with outstanding horses. This period certainly affected his horsemanship.

Jackson's father, Jonathan Jackson, grandson of John and Elizabeth, was not known as a horseman, but he was an acknowledged and enthusiastic gambler whose interests lay mostly in card games. But it was inevitable that the occasional wager on a horse would be part of his life.

Jonathan was a frontier lawyer but not a very good one, and his fondness for gambling was part of his problem. He had settled in Clarksburg, Virginia, now West Virginia, to clerk for and later become a law partner of his first cousin John George Jackson, a prominent attorney and politician during the first decades of the nineteenth century.

Like all county seats, Clarksburg hosted monthly court days, so people with legal business could get it all done at once. They could file suit, collect debts, or face charges. They could also get a month's worth of entertainment during the two or three days court was in session. Among the entertainment at most court days in Virginia was horse racing. Since racing, and particularly gambling on racing, was illegal in many of Virginia's counties, courts in some towns found themselves prosecuting participants in earlier races while new races took place a few hundred yards out of town.

How much Jonathan Jackson might have wagered on racing as opposed to cards is impossible to know, but we do know he got himself deeply in debt, prompting his upright cousin John George to break up the law partnership. Jonathan died at thirty-six, leaving three small children and a mound of debt. The middle child was four-year-old Thomas Jackson.

Jackson had no real memory of his father. He did hear family stories about the debt and never became a gambler himself, although horses remained part of his life. After his father's death and his mother's subsequent remarriage and death, Thomas was sent to live with Jonathan's younger half-brother, Cummins Jackson. Cummins controlled hundreds of acres of family land as well as a thriving mill near Weston, Virginia.

Like Jonathan, Cummins was a gambler. But unlike his brother, he was a reasonably good businessman and could afford his losses. He could also afford to buy and keep racehorses and compete with them over his own racecourse. Undoubtedly he took in his orphan nephew because of family affection and responsibility, but he also realized the advantage of having a lightweight young boy to train as a jockey for his horses.

Cummins built his racecourse just to the west of the house and mill on the acreage that had been known for decades as Jackson's Mill. It was a grass course, as level as he could make it, designed to host four-mile competitions. Although there was quarter-mile racing elsewhere in Virginia, the longer form was gradually taking over. We know from memories gathered after Thomas Jackson became famous that Cummins favored the longer distances.

The course itself was most likely not four miles around. Typically, during the eighteenth and early nineteenth centuries, a racecourse was a mile or two miles in a round or oval shape. With anything bigger the spectators would be unable to see all the action. The horses would be required to complete two or more circuits to make up the standard four-mile distance. In important races, a horse would have to finish first in

Jackson's Mill in 1909. The racetrack was across the river in the left of the picture.
LIBRARY OF CONGRESS

at least two different four-mile heats to win a given race, which means a winning horse would be required to run at least eight miles in a day, sometimes as many as sixteen.

At a private course like the one at Jackson's Mill, races might consist of only one heat, known as a dash, to determine a winner. Dash is a misleading word. The race was still four miles long and even the fastest horses were unable to dash for that distance. The record is silent as to what kind of races Cummins Jackson conducted and Thomas Jackson rode, but most likely they competed in dashes, with wagers rather than prize money on the line.

Although Thomas Jackson's role as a jockey was well documented by people in a position to know about it, how early and how long he rode remains unknown. He arrived at Jackson's Mill as a seven-year-old who had done little riding. He soon learned his way around on horseback, riding into Weston to collect the mail, riding with Cummins and other uncles to inspect the property, even riding with them in informal fox hunts.

Cummins put serious money into racehorses, so Thomas was unlikely to have been allowed to race until he was twelve or so, old enough to control a thousand-pound animal galloping at thirty miles an hour. He continued racing at least until he reached fifteen because neighbors interviewed after he became famous remembered races taking place as late as 1839.

They also remembered the young Jackson to be a good rider. None suggested that he was ungraceful on horseback. They did recall in considerable detail that the combination of the lightweight Thomas and his well-to-do uncle resulted in a lot of races won and bets collected. They must have found the young jockey's form to be appropriate and typical because none of them mentioned otherwise. So Jackson may have learned early the forward-leaning, crouched style that so many observers criticized during the Civil War.

Nineteenth-century jockeys rode more upright than they do today, but they did lean forward farther than other riders of the time. The extreme forward crouch didn't appear until the end of the century. An American jockey named Tod Sloan is credited with revolutionizing race riding with the so-called monkey crouch that was as inelegant as it was successful.

What Thomas Jackson most likely did not do aboard his uncle's horses was ride with the unusually short stirrups so often mentioned. In the 1830s, jockeys in the kind of English-style long-distance racing that Cummins Jackson conducted invariably rode with long stirrups, much longer than jockeys do today. It was another sixty years before Tod Sloan and other American jockeys introduced the short stirrups to English-style racing along with their forward-leaning monkey crouch. Jackson's short stirrups came from somewhere else, although not from the next place he learned about riding. In 1842 he arrived at West Point, New York, to begin four years at the United States Military Academy. At the time, horseback riding was not a significant part of the education of future officers. Sixty percent of the cadets came from cities and towns and had ridden only rarely, but there was no equitation education at all until their final year at the academy.

Even then, riding instruction was limited to one hour every other day. Cadets learned to mount, ride at all gaits, and handle the saber on horseback. They also learned jumping, known as "leaping" in the nineteenth century. We know precisely the style they were taught because the equitation instructor during Jackson's time at West Point wrote a book on riding that was published while Jackson was there.

"The body should be erect," wrote Henry Hershberger, an experienced cavalry officer from Pennsylvania who arrived at West Point in

1881 Kentucky Derby winner Hindoo with the long stirrups used by nineteenth-century jockeys.
LIBRARY OF CONGRESS

January 1842. No leaning forward was permitted, except slightly and occasionally at the leap and even then leaning backward was preferred.

The rider's legs, he said in his *The Horseman: A Work on Horsemanship*, should be "hanging naturally." As for stirrup length, he was more specific. "When the rider stands erect in the stirrups the space between his fork or crotch should be four inches or the breadth of his hand." Some well-admired riders used stirrups so long that there was no distance at all between body and saddle. Fortunately for Cadet Jackson, riding instruction wasn't graded in 1845–1846, but other cadets did pay attention to his style.

According to Dabney H. Maury, later to become a Confederate general, Jackson was "singularly awkward and uncomfortable to look at upon a horse." He, Maury added, "seemed in imminent danger of falling headlong from his horse."

As far as anyone noted, Jackson never did fall headlong or in any other direction from a horse at West Point. Maury wrote about Jackson's riding long after their cadet years, having read decades of declarations that Jackson was a poor and ungraceful rider, and he may not have been totally accurate in what he remembered. Maury may also have failed to realize that a seat that appeared too forward and too short may have been nothing more than out of step with the mid-nineteenth-century riding ideal—not wrong, just different.

Jackson's next contact with a really good horse would have done nothing to cause him to lengthen his stirrups or sit farther back. In the summer of 1846, shortly after his graduation from West Point, Jackson was commissioned as a second lieutenant of artillery and sent with other young officers to Mexico in defense of the U.S. annexation of Texas.

Jackson received two brevet promotions as an artillery officer and found himself in possession of status and a good salary in Mexico City after the Mexican capital fell late in 1847. He promptly paid $180 for a beautiful horse, which he rode out in the evening to promenades

Gen. Joseph Hooker in accepted nineteenth-century military seat.
LIBRARY OF CONGRESS

frequented by the city's aristocrats. The horse, he told his sister, was worth at least $300. Jackson hoped he and the horse would impress anybody who saw them.

In the mid-nineteenth century most aristocratic Mexican horsemen, military and civilian alike, rode in a style called *a la gineta*. The method required stirrups noticeably shorter than those used in the older European military seat. It had been developed out of the style of the North Africans, who had invaded the Iberian Peninsula in the eighth century. A reconquest by the rest of Europe began almost immediately, but completion took nearly six hundred years. By the time all of Spain was again Catholic, the short-stirrup riding technique was firmly in control.

The *gineta* was transferred to Central and South America beginning in the late fifteenth century. Thomas Jackson would have seen it in full use on the Paseo, the wide boulevard over which he rode his expensive horse in 1848. He admired the ruling class of Mexico City, admired their good horses, and may have admired their *gineta* as well.

A good horse, he wrote his sister Laura, was important to him because "if an officer wishes to appear best he should appear well in everything." Everything would presumably extend to the length of his stirrups.

After the occupation of Mexico City ended in 1848, Jackson was transferred to Fort Hamilton in New York Harbor. He gave up the good Mexican horse but purchased another one in New York. This horse was named Fancy, presumably because of the animal's quality and good looks, and Jackson rode him daily, even though travel by horseback was rarely among his duties at the garrison. There are no descriptions of Jackson's riding from this time, but his style most likely included the forward lean from his racing years and the short stirrups from Mexico.

Jackson was proud and fond of Fancy. He was so upset by Fancy's brush with death at a stable fire at Fort Hamilton in March 1850 that he felt unable to visit his sister in Virginia that spring. A few months later he was forced to sell the handsome Fancy and travel to the wilds of Florida to search for Indians and help build Fort Meade.

Although he rode out from the fort in a fruitless search for Indians, he never wrote of acquiring another horse for himself in Florida. Either he borrowed one or the horse he did purchase proved unworthy of mention. In 1851, Thomas Jackson accepted a professorship at the Virginia Military Institute in Lexington, Virginia. He left the regular army but retained his love for good horses.

He left no record of specific horses he owned during his early years at the institute. After his second marriage, he decided it was time to own another impressive horse and acquired a bay carriage horse that he creatively named Bay. Anna Jackson remembered Bay as a particularly good-looking animal.

"His judgment of horses was excellent and it was very rare that he was not well-mounted," Mrs. Jackson said later. Bay was primarily a driving horse but could also be ridden. What became of Bay is unknown. Jackson rode out of Lexington on a horse on April 21 1861, leading a troop of volunteers off to Richmond to join the Confederate cause. But that horse, whether or not it was Bay, was returned to Lexington and Jackson continued his journey by train. After a few days in Richmond he was sent on to Harpers Ferry, again by train, where he began his war service and his march to fame. He also found the horse that would become famous along with him.

CHAPTER 3

Mystery Horse

The best evidence of the quality of the little horse is the fact that he was picked out of a load of livestock by two men who knew that while the undersized sorrel looked different from the mental picture that most Virginians had of the ideal warhorse, "different" and "bad" weren't the same thing at all.

Many of the individual characteristics of the horse eventually known as Little Sorrel weren't, at first glance at least, what a Confederate officer might pick if he could design his own mount. But much of what appeared to be negative proved invaluable for Thomas Jackson as well as for the horse, which first succeeded and then survived beyond all expectations.

The first thing that people noticed was this horse's coat color. In most equine activities, color is the least significant characteristic of a good horse. One of the oldest equine adages is this: there is no good horse in a bad color. But in warfare, color actually mattered. The rule of mounted warfare was that an officer should never pick a light-colored horse that will make him stand out, turning himself and his horse into a sizeable target. Although sensible, it was an often-violated rule, one regularly ignored at the very top.

George Washington himself owned a light gray warhorse known as Blueskin, but he preferred the more modestly colored chestnut Nelson as a battle mount. Artists have preferred Blueskin, though, and most equestrian portraits of Washington place him astride a light gray or white horse. But both Washington and Blueskin survived the Revolutionary War anyway.

Napoleon Bonaparte's white charger Marengo was celebrated during his lifetime and has remained famous ever since. Napoleon liked to be seen, admired, and feared. The prospect of making himself a target because of the color of his horse didn't worry Napoleon, and that attitude worked out well enough for him. He died in his bed in 1821 at age fifty-one from stomach cancer or poison, depending on whether you subscribe to conspiracy theories.

In one sense it worked out well for Marengo, too. The horse was captured at the Battle of Waterloo and taken to England, where he died at the remarkably advanced age of thirty-eight. His skeleton can still be admired today at the National Army Museum in London. On the other hand, Marengo probably considered himself a sizeable target, although in the end a lucky one, having been wounded eight times in battle.

Jackson's first cavalry chief, Turner Ashby, loved handsome and extravagantly colored horses, including the magnificent white stallion called Tom Telegraph. Ashby was fortunate to survive the death of the pure white horse in May 1862, when Tom Telegraph was targeted and shot to death. Ashby's luck didn't last. He borrowed a horse a few weeks later and was killed moments after the borrowed mount died of gunshot wounds.

Robert E. Lee's favorite and best-known warhorse was the gray Traveller, who turned much lighter later in life as all grays do. The most familiar photograph of Traveller was taken postwar and does show a tempting target of a horse. But during most of the Civil War, Traveller was iron gray and would have blended in well with the smoke of battle.

When John Harman and Thomas Jackson saw the new horse at Harpers Ferry, they observed an animal of an entirely acceptable color for an officer's mount, a horse that sported one of the most common equine colors. What they saw was a solid red horse with no white markings and with a mane and tail of a similar shade. Jackson and most likely Harman used the word sorrel to identify the color, but over the next few years, the horse would also be described as chestnut, dun, and claybank. Horse color was in the eye of the beholder in 1861. It still is, even though we now know about the genetic reasons for the hue of a horse's coat. What word you use to describe a solid red horse depends on the breed of the horse, where you happen to come from, and your own opinion of what you're looking at.

The same was true in 1861, except perhaps for breed. Horses then were identified mostly by type or use. A horse was either a saddle horse, a driving horse, a riding cob, or a racehorse. Although descendants of a particular stallion might be described as a member of his "breed," there were no strict requirements of ancestry and no color guidelines to qualify for membership in a breed registry for racing or for any other activity. Today, the choice of word for Little Sorrel's color is a function of breed and opinion. In 1861, it was strictly a matter of choice.

Today a solid red horse would be called chestnut if it's a Thoroughbred, Morgan, Standardbred, Saddlebred, or a member of most other breeds, especially those used in English-style riding activities. Some people might use the word "sorrel" for a particularly bright red horse, reserving chestnut for darker shades, but the registration papers will say chestnut.

If the horse is a Quarter Horse or a horse used in Western riding or sports, the same animal is also likely to be called sorrel, although the breed standard recognizes additional names for the red color, including chestnut. The registration papers will report the color, selected by the owner, as the closest to the breed association's recognized colors.

In 1861, in the absence of registration papers and breed requirements, the choice belonged entirely to the owner. With plenty of exceptions to be found, red horses in the northern states were chestnut and those used in the south and west were sorrel. The majority of memoirs and letters by people who saw him agreed with Jackson that Little Sorrel was indeed sorrel. But some persisted in calling him chestnut.

An even smaller number used the words "dun" and "claybank," highly subjective terms in the nineteenth century. A dun is a horse whose color, thanks to a gene variation, appears slightly faded, although the mane and tail are usually the primary color. A claybank was essentially the same as a red dun. Some horsemen reserved this name for a particularly faded-looking red horse, while others used it interchangeably with dun.

Today, a horseman can precisely identify the color of a horse through genetic testing. Chestnut and sorrel are genetically identical, each requiring two copies of a recessive gene for red. So what exactly was Little Sorrel? If the mount on display at the Virginia Military Institute is used as a guideline, he was a light but unfaded chestnut or sorrel, even though some people who saw him in life persisted in calling him dun. Little Sorrel's original taxidermist, Frederic Webster, as well as technicians who refurbished the mount over the decades, may have added coloring to brighten the coat color so he may really have been dun. Short of genetic analysis with any material that remains, we'll never know for sure.

Another characteristic of Little Sorrel may or may not have been important to Jackson, but it probably contributed to John Harman's selection. The little red horse was a gelding, having been castrated as a younger horse. Gelding a horse is an ancient practice, one that was somewhat less common before the twentieth century in the absence of equine anesthesia and antibiotics. But it was widely practiced in horses intended for nonsporting use. Stallions can be difficult to keep.

They are often aggressive with other horses, easily distracted by a mare or something they think is a mare, and sometimes hard for a rider to handle. They will be gelded if the owner believes the horse will concentrate better and show less aggression or if he expects little demand for offspring. Little Sorrel was so good natured later in life that it's unlikely he was gelded for behavior reasons. The operation was probably done because of his size. Then, as now, there was much less demand for small stallions than larger ones.

Little Sorrel was hardly the only prominent gelding among the famous warhorses of the Civil War. According to most records, Robert E. Lee's Traveller was a gelding, even though a few people remain convinced that his offspring exist. Traveller was well bred and well conformed, so he may have been gelded for behavior. Even as a gelding he was a horse who was known to kick and bite. The only one of cavalry general Nathan Bedford Forrest's most prominent horses to survive the war was the gray gelding King Philip, who was reputed to be quiet and good natured except in the presence of blue uniforms. Even gelding didn't limit King Philip's aggression toward the enemy.

Some officers didn't much like geldings, believing them to be too docile for war service. Jackson's first cavalry commander, the dashing Turner Ashby, preferred stallions, losing two magnificent ones, including the unfortunate white Tom Telegraph, to enemy bullets during the first year of the war. J. E. B. Stuart liked both stallions and mares, particularly mares. Stuart went through a lot of horses during the war and whether or not any were geldings has escaped the record.

John Harman certainly would have preferred geldings for heavy use in the family stagecoach business as well as for war. Little Sorrel's sex would have been a plus as Harman chose a horse for his commander.

But the horse's height might have made him think twice. Little Sorrel was most likely about fourteen hands, perhaps an inch or so taller, since his diminutive size was noted by almost everybody who wrote about him. In the mid-nineteenth century, a horse of sixteen hands would be described as tall and a horse of fifteen hands would have been average. The mount at VMI is on a plaster frame rather than the original skeleton. A measurement might not be entirely accurate, so most of our evidence comes from memoirs and journals.

The hand, a unit of measurement for horses and other livestock, is still in use today, centuries after it was standardized. A hand equals four inches, the presumed width of a human hand. Horse heights are expressed in decimal form, even though the measurement isn't actually decimal. If Little Sorrel were identified as being fourteen hands and two inches, his height would be noted as 14.2.

The measurement is taken on horses at the high point of the withers where the shoulder blades come together. Some other species are measured at the high point of the hip, a system that would have recorded Little Sorrel as even smaller than he was, since his withers were noticeably higher than his hips. Regardless of how he was measured, Little Sorrel was small for his rider. Stonewall Jackson was above average in height for a man of his time, a little over five feet eleven inches, and many observers noted that he looked far too tall for his horse.

Because of the height disparity it's probably true that Jackson intended Little Sorrel for his wife, who was much shorter at just over five feet. A taller horse would have been too big for her to mount and possibly too difficult to stay aboard. But Jackson soon discovered that height and the ability to carry weight were two different things.

A sturdy horse like Little Sorrel could have been expected to carry 20 percent of his own body weight, perhaps more with the conformation and gait characteristics that he possessed. Jackson was thin, weighing no more than 160 pounds during the war. Little Sorrel probably weighed about 850 to 875 pounds, making him fully capable of carrying the weight of Jackson, his saddle, and other equipment.

There was debate in the nineteenth century and plenty of discussion today about the soundness and health of small horses compared to larger ones. In reality, the lower body weight of a smaller horse means that there's less stress on bones and joints, and small horses often stay sound longer as a result. Small horses excel as endurance competitors. Arabian horses of no more than 15.2 hands dominate the lineups of one-hundred-mile endurance horse races. Other breeds are also used in endurance competition, but the horses tend to be smaller ones as well, including Appaloosas and Quarter Horses of less than sixteen hands.

More important in determining the potential soundness of a small horse is the circumference of the cannon bone in relation to his body weight. The cannon is the large bone that runs from knee to fetlock (the joint that looks like an ankle). If it's substantial in spite of the small body size, the horse is likely to be able to withstand a lot of work and enjoy both endurance and weight-carrying ability. The photographs of Little Sorrel show a horse with outstanding bone in the lower leg.

Jackson and Harman estimated the horse they picked to be eleven years old. That's older than ideal for an animal intended for heavy use, but far from elderly. The age does support the argument that Jackson always intended Little Sorrel for his wife since most horses mellow with age and become easier to ride.

At first glance eleven seems to be an odd estimate of a horse's age. A more likely choice would be "about ten" or "over ten." But horsemen of the mid-nineteenth century, in the absence of registration papers, were very good at equine age estimates. Eleven is in fact a key age in dental development. A mouth examination of Little Sorrel would have given a reasonably accurate calculation of his actual age.

At about eleven the shape of the lower incisors begins to change from oval or rounded to more triangular. Also at about age eleven, the corner incisors start to develop a subtle hook in the back, similar to one that appears and disappears several years earlier. The eleven-year-old hook remains in the mouth for a few years, until about age fifteen.

The surface of the teeth changes between ten and eleven years as well. At ten, back teeth still have remnants of cuplike indentations in the center of the teeth. By eleven, the cups are usually gone.

Finally comes Galvayne's Groove, a controversial method of equine dental aging in which the age of eleven is also key. The method was championed by Dr. Sydney Galvayne, who claimed to be an Australian veterinarian. His 1885 book on dental aging of horses declared that a trace of a narrow dark groove appears at the gum line in the upper third incisor just after the age of ten, becoming a noticeable groove at eleven, and eventually traveling down the entire tooth. Galvayne gave his name to the method well after Little Sorrel's age had been estimated, but good horsemen already knew about the groove. Some experts today dispute the accuracy of Galvayne's Groove, but they acknowledge that the groove exists, appearing after about age ten. They argue that the development rate varies among individual horses.

Horse aging by teeth isn't an exact science, but the age of eleven happens to be a milestone in several of the methods. All in all, the estimate that Little Sorrel was eleven years old at the time he was acquired by Jackson was probably accurate within a year on either side.

His conformation presented pros and cons to a man looking for a horse to ride to battle. There's only one photograph of Little Sorrel taken during the war, in May 1863, two years after Jackson acquired him. It shows a horse of an unfamiliar shape, at least to a Virginia horseman. A positive attribute was his short to medium-length back. This characteristic may not create an elegant appearance, but a horse with a shorter back can carry more weight with less discomfort and fewer injuries than one with a longer back.

The little red horse's large head might not have been visually appealing either, but an experienced horseman wouldn't have been unduly

The only wartime photograph of Little Sorrel, taken in May 1863.
RODENBOUGH, *PHOTOGRAPHIC HISTORY OF THE CIVIL WAR, THE CAVALRY* (VOLUME 4), 1911.

concerned. However, many would have objected to the steep, sloping croup—the area between the top of the hip and the root of the tail. As a result of the slope, the horse looked like he might be weak in the hindquarters. Little Sorrel did carry his tail fairly high, however, and that would have been a plus.

The pasterns—the section of leg between the fetlock and the hoof—were short and rather upright, considered a conformation flaw by many horsemen, but a horse with such pasterns is less likely to suffer ligament and tendon injuries. His hoofs were reasonably large for his size, although they look to have been trimmed a little too short before the 1863 photograph was taken. They appear to be big enough to stay sound, a vital characteristic in a horse destined for hard and steady work.

He was a horse with good and bad points of conformation, but it turned out that the good ones were very useful and the bad ones didn't matter at all. Little Sorrel proved to be a horse of remarkable soundness and endurance, despite his sloping croup, upright pasterns, and other flaws.

The question of beauty apparently didn't matter to either John Harman, who made the initial selection, or Thomas Jackson, who purchased and kept the little horse. Both must have realized that the horse wasn't classically handsome and they didn't care. Or perhaps they realized that he was perfectly good looking for what he was—a pacing horse of traditional American conformation. He was built exactly as he should have been to be a good pacer. Little Sorrel's pacing gait was noted by almost everyone who wrote about him. His gait was one of the reasons Jackson liked the red horse so much and decided against giving him to his wife.

The trot is a natural gait of most horses and almost all other four-legged animals. It's the intermediate gait between the walk and the canter in horses, or the walk and the run in other species. Members of a few species, the camel for one, always use a pace when they go faster than a walk but not quite as fast as a run. This gait is sometimes called an amble, although that term is usually reserved for a similar but distinct four-beat gait.

In horses, the pacing gait has been used by choice by a certain percentage of animals throughout recorded history. In this method of locomotion, the horse's legs on the same side of the body move forward and backward at the same time. In a trot, the legs at each corner of the body move forward and backward in unison—right rear and left front, right front and left rear, and so on. French cave paintings show horses pacing, as do medieval European woodcuts. The gait has been around for as long as people have used horses.

Three nineteenth-century harness racehorses demonstrating the pacing gait.
LIBRARY OF CONGRESS

Horse breeders have known almost as long that there's a genetic component to pacing. Offspring of pacing horses usually—but not always—pace, and offspring of trotters usually—but again not always—trot. That knowledge has allowed breeders to select for the desired gait. Centuries ago Europeans liked pacing horses for riding because it felt like rocking in a cradle to ride a pacer at speed. As roads improved, trotters became dominant because of the belief that trotting led to a more comfortable ride for people in wagons or carriages.

Today most horses trot, but many still pace, and the gait is desirable and selected for in several horse breeds. In Standardbred racing, pacers account for 80 percent of the harness racehorses in North America. They are faster than trotters, stay on the correct gait more consistently, and are more appreciated by bettors. The percentage of pacing racehorses is lower in the rest of the world.

There are horse breeds that feature pacing or ambling-like gaits, including the Tennessee Walking Horse, the American Saddlebred, the Paso Fino and other South American breeds, the Missouri Foxtrotter, the Icelandic Pony, and others. Most of these horses don't precisely pace. Instead, they have been bred and trained to use specialty gaits that are similar, usually featuring four separate and distinct footfalls rather than the unison steps that a true pacer employs.

Today we know why some horses pace. Swedish scientists have discovered a genetic mutation that appears in the genomes of all pacing horses. The gene, DMRT3, is now called the "gait keeper" and beyond question Little Sorrel possessed it. Scientists theorize that the gene resulted from a spontaneous mutation in an ancient equine ancestor and has been passed down through the centuries.

Oddly, trotting Standardbreds also possess the mutation, and scientists believe that in trotters it inhibits the tendency to break from the trot to the gallop, an important quality for harness racehorses since a break of gait requires the horse to be pulled to the back of the field. The mutation is also present in the genomes of members of the other so-called gaited breeds who exhibit pacing-like gaits.

There's a good reason that Little Sorrel and almost all modern harness racehorses possess the pacing gene. Most of today's gaited breeds in North America descend from a unique American horse breed. Little Sorrel appeared to have been so closely descended that he should probably be considered a member or near-member of that breed, the mysterious and marvelous Narragansett Pacer.

The Narragansett Pacer, now gone, was North America's first true horse breed. Although by the second half of the seventeenth century the mustang had already developed in the Spanish southwest, and horsemen in the southern colonies were breeding horses good at quarter-mile racing, these were types rather than breeds. The Narragansett did qualify as a breed well before 1700 since individuals could be chosen for specific physical characteristics, including appearance, and they almost invariably produced offspring that possessed precisely those same characteristics.

The three most obvious and most often reported characteristics of the Narragansett Pacer were color, gait, and size. The pure Narragansetts were invariably chestnut, they consistently paced rather than trotted, and they were almost always reported as being small. Other traits became known with use. Narragansetts were hardy, tireless, calm, and easy to keep. Journal after journal reported them as being able to travel incredibly long distances without discomfort.

The breed was named for the region where they first gained attention. The "Narragansett Country" was the southern half of what became Rhode Island, an area inhabited by the Narragansett Indians at the time of European contact. This tribe of Native Americans had no horses at contact, but their name lived on with the superb little pacing horses developed on farmland that had been their hunting territory.

The ancestry of the Narragansett Pacer is unknown. Theories about its origin abound, most of them contradictory and some of them much more grand than the truth. It's similar to literary scholars refusing to believe that a man of an ordinary background like William Shakespeare could have produced some of the most sublime works of the English language.

The Narragansett Pacer suffered from the same skepticism. The superb animal must have sprung from splendid roots, so the theory developed that an Andalusian stallion was lost in the shipwreck of a Spanish galleon off the Rhode Island coast early in the eighteenth century. The stallion, renamed Old Snip, swam ashore and produced a line of fine pacing horses that populated the farms of Rhode Island. An alternative story had Old Snip swimming away from coastal Spain or North Africa and being picked up by a Rhode Island–based sailing ship.

There are problems with the theory, including the fact that records exist of horses that were almost certainly Narragansett Pacers well before the supposed shipwreck or rescue. What's more, Andalusians are big and muscular, seldom chestnut, don't possess sloping croups, and primarily trot rather than pace. Even if some pacing blood had made its way into the

Andalusian gene pool, it's almost certainly untrue that an Andalusian stallion was the progenitor of the Narragansett Pacer. But much older Spanish and Portuguese genes may have contributed in a more roundabout way.

What is definitely true is that the man who supposedly found Old Snip was an enthusiastic user and breeder of Narragansetts. He was William Robinson, born in Rhode Island in 1691 and one of the largest landowners in New England. Robinson was politically connected, serving nine terms as a member of the colonial assembly of Rhode Island and two as deputy governor. But Robinson was at heart a farmer, although a very rich one.

Robinson didn't create the Narragansett Pacer but rather used, refined, and promoted it. The breed most likely grew from a shipment of livestock consigned to one of the earliest settlers of the Massachusetts Bay Colony. Francis Higginson brought nearly two hundred head of livestock, including sixty mares and stallions from his native Leicestershire, in 1629. These were saddle horses of unrecorded type and breed. The Irish Hobby and the related Scottish Galloway, whose ancestors first appeared in Britain in the thirteenth century, were popular for saddle use throughout the British Isles at the time, and the Higginson consignment certainly included horses similar to them.

These two extinct breeds were alike: small horses that developed from a cross of native British and imported Spanish bloodlines. The little horses paced rather than trotted and they featured physical characteristics typical of all pacers, including high withers and a sloping croup. They were said to be of all solid horse colors, including chestnut.

Robinson and other Rhode Island enthusiasts loved the Narragansett Pacers that descended from these imports, with the modest addition of other blood. By the beginning of the eighteenth century the pacers were almost exclusively chestnut. Only written descriptions remain of the remarkable little horses. There was no photography while the pacers prospered, and no positively identified contemporary paintings have been discovered.

Much of what we know of their appearance we owe to Dr. James McSparran, whose career nearly paralleled that of the Scots-Irish racing pastor of Virginia, John Hindman. Born in Ireland of Scottish parents, McSparran came to Rhode Island in 1718 as a Presbyterian minister, returned to England to take Anglican orders, then came back to America, where he remained for thirty-six years. He was a great admirer of the Narragansett Pacer, whose glory days coincided with his tenure as minister of St. Paul's Church of Narragansett. In 1752 his *America Dissected, Being a Full and True Account of the American Colonies* gave people in the British Isles an idea of the remarkable little pacing horse they had been hearing about.

Reverend James McSparran, admirer of Narragansett Pacers.
UPDIKE, *HISTORY OF THE EPISCOPAL CHURCH IN NARRAGANSETT, RHODE-ISLAND*, 1847

It wasn't unusual, McSparran wrote, to see people ride "ten, twenty, thirty, and more miles, to church." They had just the transportation to do it easily.

"They have plenty of a small sort of horses, the best in the world, like the little Scotch Galloways," he wrote, "and 'tis no extraordinary journey to ride from sixty to seventy miles, or more, in a day." He went on to describe their accomplishments.

"They are remarkable for fleetness and swift pacing, and I have seen some of them pace a mile in little more than two minutes, a good deal less than three," McSparran said of these little chestnut horses. He believed the pacers to be attractive, although other writers of the era referred to their own horses as "hideously ugly" or having "no beauty."

McSparran's descriptions, as well as others from the eighteenth century, could be of Little Sorrel. He was small, chestnut, possessed high withers and a sloping croup, and could pace remarkably fast.

Artillerist William Thomas Pogue, who fought with Stonewall Jackson in nearly a dozen battles, was fascinated with Jackson's horse. "Little Sorrel was a pacer and could make a mile in about 2-40," Pogue wrote. "Whenever we saw him it was at this tremendous stride or in a slow lazy walk." Pogue used racing shorthand for the mile time, meaning that Little Sorrel could pace a mile in two minutes and forty seconds, just about what McSparran said Narragansett Pacers could do a century earlier.

William Robinson and the other Rhode Island landowners used their Pacers to survey their massive plantations because they found the little horses tireless as well as comfortable. They probably called on their "slow lazy walk" for the farm work. The landowners also raced their pacers under saddle on beach courses along the Atlantic Ocean, sent them south to Virginia to compete in intercolonial races, and exported them to the Caribbean, where there was an insatiable demand for the hardy little animals. Robinson and his fellow lovers of Narragansett Pacers also sold them north, and the breed spread through Connecticut, Vermont, New Hampshire, and into Canada.

The new owners loved them too, finding them so useful that they contributed to the destruction of the breed. Narragansett mares crossed particularly well with a sturdy bay stallion of largely Thoroughbred ancestry who was offered at stud in Vermont at the turn of the nineteenth century. This stallion was known as the Morgan horse for his owner, a singing teacher named Justin Morgan.

The offspring of the Morgan horse and pacing mares mostly trotted and, after a few generations, the pace was bred right out of most of them, as were tendencies toward the sloping croup, high withers, and unusually small size. The chestnut color popped up occasionally, but the descendants of the Morgan horse were mostly bright bay, reddish horses with black mane and tail.

Throughout New England, road improvement made carriages and wagons practical, and stronger trotting horses were more suitable for harness work than little pacing ones were. Narragansett Pacers were used at stud, but they were invariably crossed with larger, primarily trotting, horses.

By 1800 pureblooded Narragansett Pacers were mostly gone and horsemen knew they had lost something special. The fact that several of the last pure- or nearly pureblood Narragansett Pacers were reported in the Hartford, Connecticut, area makes one of the most intriguing stories about Little Sorrel's origin a little more possible.

The Wadsworth family of Hartford used Narragansetts into the late eighteenth century, with Jeremiah Wadsworth, best known as George Washington's chief commissary during the Revolutionary War, offering a pacer named Whirligig for stud service in the 1780s. Wadsworth and others also offered the services of sons of Whirligig, including the handsome Young Rainbow, advertised as being seven-eighths Narragansett Pacer and one-eighth Arabian.

By 1787 the owner of the supposedly pureblooded Narragansett stallion Free and Easy, standing at stud in East Windsor, Connecticut, urged owners of Narragansett mares to "bring them that the breed so valuable may not be lost." In 1793, the owner of King Philip, "supposed to be the only one in the world of the Narragansett breed unmixed," stood in Berlin, Connecticut, but it was already too late. King Philip was a bright bay and must have had the blood of another breed in his veins.

All these Narragansett stallions, each mentioned as being one of the few or the only one left, served their stud careers within a twenty-mile radius of each other and of Somers, a small Connecticut town northeast of Hartford. Somers, a rural village of fifteen hundred people in 1850, today celebrates itself as the birthplace of Little Sorrel.

In Somers the story is accepted without question, but it's difficult to pin down its origin and it's even harder to determine the truth. The story goes back a very long way and was in circulation while many of the principal characters were still living and able to refute it if they chose to.

Somers, Connecticut, drawn four years before Little Sorrel was foaled.
JOHN WARNER BARBER, CONNECTICUT HISTORICAL COLLECTIONS

Somers's location, so close to the last few Narragansett stallions, was a place where a horse of the appearance and characteristics of Little Sorrel might well be expected to appear.

The story of Little Sorrel and Somers traces to a farmer by the name of Randolph Fuller, born in the town in 1827. Fuller's farm lay along the west side of Springfield Road, a well-traveled route between Somers and Springfield, Massachusetts. Directly across the road from the Fuller farm was property owned by Noah Chapin Collins, a sawmill operator who bred and owned horses and was active with the local Four Town Agricultural Fair. Fuller's mother and Collins's wife were sisters, but the two men were near contemporaries, with Fuller just thirteen years younger than Collins. Randolph Fuller and Noah Collins knew each other well both because of family ties and because they were near neighbors. Both bred horses and both competed with those horses at local fairs.

It's not clear when Fuller began telling a story of how Noah Collins bred Stonewall Jackson's Little Sorrel. Collins died in 1871, eight years after Jackson's death, but Fuller lived on until 1901. At some point, he gave details of the story of Little Sorrel's origin to Erwin Daniel Avery, a man who later took over Fuller's house and farm. Avery was born in 1845 and would have been an adult, twenty-six years old, at the time of Collins's death. In so small a town they would certainly have known each other.

From the written account left by Avery, the story appears to have come from Fuller and not from Collins himself. But Collins's widow, Elvira, Randolph Fuller's aunt, lived on until 1882 and at least one of Noah's children lived into the twentieth century. There was plenty of opportunity for members of the Collins family to contradict the story being told by their neighbor Randolph Fuller. None did.

In addition to the name of the breeder, Fuller gave another morsel of information to Avery—that Little Sorrel's original name was American Traveler. Noah Collins was indeed once involved with a horse named

American Traveler, who was reported to be the sire of a stallion that Collins stood at stud in Somers, presumably in the ten-year period between the start of the Civil War and his death. That stallion was named Ben Butler, probably for the Union general. Ben Butler was advertised as a seventeen-hand bay horse, an unlikely son of a chestnut of less than fifteen hands. If Little Sorrel's original name was indeed American Traveler, he probably shared that name with Ben Butler's sire. Names were so often reused during the nineteenth century that it was possible that there were two American Travelers in the same area a few years apart. The name Traveler was common for horses of all breeds in all parts of the country at the time. In addition, Narragansett Pacers were sometimes called Narragansett Travelers, either for their way of going or to identify a line of pacers descending from a horse named Traveler.

Somers's claim to Little Sorrel is on a historical marker in the center of town.
AUTHOR

The possibility that Noah Collins bred and owned the horse that became Little Sorrel has another point of support. The key figure in this part of the story is Noah Collins's brother, William Oliver Collins, who made his way from Somers to Ohio in 1833. William joined a long line of ambitious young Connecticut men making that trip. A strip of northern Ohio had been Connecticut's Western Reserve, land claimed during colonial times as part of the Connecticut Colony. After the American Revolution, Connecticut and other states relinquished their western claims, but there were private claims that lured Connecticut people west, and the attraction of a "western Connecticut" remained.

All we know for sure about where Little Sorrel came from before he was captured by the Confederates at Harpers Ferry in 1861 was that he had been loaded onto the Baltimore and Ohio livestock car in southern Ohio. William O. Collins was in southern Ohio then, having settled in Hillsboro in Highland County, Ohio, to practice law. He later became a railroad executive but remained in touch with his family's farming roots, becoming president of the Highland County Agricultural Fair. After the attack on Fort Sumter in April 1861, William Collins raised a company of cavalry and rode off to war at the head of the Eleventh Ohio Cavalry.

The Eleventh Ohio never saw action against Stonewall Jackson, and Collins never laid eyes on the horse the Confederate general was riding. But his friend William H. Trimble, also an attorney in Hillsboro, active in the Highland County Fair, fellow board member of Hillsboro's St. Mary's Episcopal Church, and Collins's occasional business partner, probably did.

Trimble, who judged pacing horse competitions at the county fair in Hillsboro before the war, was colonel of the Sixtieth Ohio Infantry. His regiment saw action during Jackson's Shenandoah Valley campaign in the spring of 1862. He may or may not have seen Jackson on Little Sorrel in the valley campaign—most likely not. But the Sixtieth Ohio was present at the Battle of Harpers Ferry on September 15, 1862, when the regiment

William H. Trimble may have carried the identity of Little Sorrel back to Ohio.
A BIOGRAPHICAL CYCLOPEDIA AND PORTRAIT GALLERY, VOL. 4, 1887

got a close enough look at Jackson to describe his attire and his horse. Trimble got an extra close look.

The Battle of Harpers Ferry was disastrous for the Federal garrison occupying the vulnerable little town where the Potomac and Shenandoah Rivers come together. After great success in northern Virginia in the summer of 1862, Robert E. Lee led his Army of Northern Virginia on an invasion into Maryland at the beginning of September. He sent Stonewall

Jackson, commanding the army's Second Corps, to capture Harpers Ferry and Jackson succeeded beyond all expectations. The capture of the garrison included the surrender of nearly twelve thousand five hundred Union troops, the largest haul of enemy soldiers and equipment of the war.

Among the captured regiments was the Sixtieth Ohio, whose soldiers watched Jackson ride into Harpers Ferry after the surrender. They were unimpressed.

"The head officer Jackson was riding a light colored dun," wrote Lewis Byrum Hull of the Sixtieth. He was, Hull wrote, "dressed very common." The horse was most likely Little Sorrel, who, as previously noted, was often called dun.

The *New York Times* correspondent who also observed the arrival of Jackson echoed Hull's opinion of Jackson's dress: "He was dressed in the coarsest kind of homespun, seedy and dirty at that; wore an old hat which any Northern beggar would consider an insult to have offered him." He didn't mention the horse.

When Colonel Trimble saw Jackson riding into Harper Ferry with his staff, he approached the Confederate general to ask that free black men from Ohio who had come with the regiment as servants be protected from seizure as slaves. After a brief discussion, Jackson agreed. That was apparently the extent of Trimble's relationship with Jackson, but if it was indeed Little Sorrel that Jackson rode that day, Trimble got a good look at him and may have recognized him as a horse that had belonged to his friend William O. Collins. There's no written evidence of Trimble saying anything to Collins, although the two men maintained their prewar friendship after the war.

Men from Hillsboro got an even closer look at Little Sorrel two and a half years later, after Stonewall Jackson's death. In April 1865 Union cavalry from General William T. Sherman's Division of the Mississippi swept through North Carolina to help apply pressure against civilians and seize livestock as part of the final push to end the war.

Among the horses confiscated was Little Sorrel, who, after a day in Union hands, was returned to Stonewall Jackson's widow. At least thirty men from Hillsboro were among the regiment that was involved in the raids near Mrs. Jackson's home. None can be identified as closely involved with William O. Collins in Hillsboro, but most probably got a good look at Little Sorrel and might have recognized him.

If indeed the story of Little Sorrel being foaled at Noah Collins's farm in Somers is true, this is the most likely scenario. Noah's brother, William Collins, received the horse sometime before the outbreak of war, possibly for racing use. Racing at the pacing gait was less common than at the trot, but sportsmen in southern Ohio were particularly determined to keep the sport alive. The first of the great pacing racehorses whose place and date of birth is known was Pocahontas, a chestnut mare foaled in 1847 in Butler County, Ohio.

Appreciation for fast pacers in Hillsboro was so great that in 1858 the local newspaper printed an extensive article on how to teach your trotter to pace "at a lively gait." The county fair, in which Collins and Trimble were active, featured annual awards for the "best pacer" and the "fastest pacer." If a little red pacing horse had been acquired by William Collins from his brother, Noah, in Somers, Connecticut, and had turned out to be not quite fast enough, he might well have been sold to a broker to be shipped east for possible war use. It's speculation, but it fits with the Somers story.

Unless some scrap of written information shows up, speculation is all we have. We may always have to wonder about where Little Sorrel came from before he stepped onto a railroad car in southern Ohio. Whatever his origin, he stepped off into the control of a Confederate quartermaster and his commanding officer in Harpers Ferry, Virginia, on his way to becoming a legend.

CHAPTER 4

Little Sorrel Goes to War

There was immediate work for Jackson's new horse in Harpers Ferry during the first weeks of May 1861. The major—soon to be colonel—proved to be a skillful organizer of fighting units and a capable supervisor of training. He wasn't necessarily popular with the troops since he was stricter than most of them felt he needed to be. He was also inclined to show up unexpectedly, riding up on his odd sorrel horses, the tall skinny one and, more often, the little rounded one.

The troops, all volunteers, had arrived in Harpers Ferry with their local militia units, for the most part commanded by brilliantly uniformed officers mounted on fine Virginia Thoroughbreds. Orders from Richmond had removed the high-ranking militia officers from their commands and nearly all had gone home in a huff, taking their extravagant uniforms and fine horses with them. Left in command had been Jackson, with his old military school uniform and his plain little horse.

Once Virginia's secession was completed, the new Confederate government took control of the Virginia troops, removing Jackson from command of the Harpers Ferry garrison and replacing him with the distinguished General Joseph E. Johnston. Johnston had been a brigadier general in the U.S. Army and was the highest-ranking officer to resign his commission to join the Confederate cause.

Johnston reorganized the units that Jackson had established, giving the former commander the First Brigade of what eventually became the Army of the Shenandoah. Jackson, freed from the paperwork of overall command, found himself even more active and more often on horseback as he trained the regiments under his immediate control. He also found himself more and more often using Little Sorrel, not caring what his troops thought about his appearance or that of his mount.

George Baylor was a member of the Second Virginia Infantry, one of the original units assigned to the First Brigade. He was unimpressed with his initial look at Jackson and Little Sorrel at Harpers Ferry. "He had rather a sleepy look and was a very unimposing figure on horseback," Baylor wrote of Jackson. Baylor later served under Jackson in his celebrated Shenandoah Valley campaign and developed a much more positive opinion of man and horse.

On June 16, Jackson rode out of Harpers Ferry at the head of his brigade. Johnston had decided that Harpers Ferry, surrounded as it was by elevations on all sides, was indefensible. He asked for and received permission to withdraw west, away from the Potomac River. Jackson, who would have preferred a more aggressive move, left Harpers Ferry with a growing reputation as a leader, at least at the brigade level. Little Sorrel had no reputation at all, except perhaps as the unfathomable choice of a mount of the brigade commander. Nobody recorded which horse Jackson chose to lead his troops out of Harpers Ferry. In the future, writers of diaries and memoirs would remember seeing Jackson aboard Little Sorrel and writing about it, but on June 16, 1861, they didn't know yet that they were looking at something special.

Johnston moved his army southwest to a spot near Winchester, forty miles from a possible Federal crossing of the Potomac. At Winchester a troop of young college men from Lexington joined Jackson's brigade. They called themselves the "Liberty Hall Volunteers," after the original name of Washington College, the alma mater of most of the seventy or so young recruits. Many of them had seen Jackson at the Presbyterian Church and public events in Lexington during his tenure at the nearby Virginia Military Institute, but they had never seen him as a commander of troops. They were puzzled by what they saw and surprised by his choice of a mount.

"A stranger would not have picked out the man in the faded blue uniform with no insignia of rank and riding around on a poor plug as the commander of the host," wrote Lt. John Newton Lyle. Nor would someone have predicted, Lyle added, that Jackson would become the greatest general since Napoleon. It goes without saying that neither Lyle nor anyone else predicted anything for Jackson's unimposing little horse either.

On June 19, Johnston sent Jackson's brigade twenty-five miles north to Martinsburg to destroy railroad equipment. Jackson, with the help of a cavalry contingent under J. E. B. Stuart, was also to watch for a possible advance of troops under Union General Robert Patterson. Jackson had about two thousand soldiers and was told to fall back if he found that Patterson, with his fourteen thousand or more troops, had arrived in force.

It's unclear if Jackson rode Little Sorrel the first time he faced enemy guns during the Civil War. That happened on July 2, when Stuart sent word that his cavalry had spotted Union soldiers crossing the Potomac River, heading south toward Martinsburg.

Jackson moved forward with one regiment, about four hundred men, and a single cannon under William Nelson Pendleton, a fifty-one-year-old clergyman from Lexington who had enlisted as an artillery captain.

As unlikely as the choice of Pendleton seemed to be, he was a West Point graduate who had served briefly as an artillery officer in the prewar U.S. Army. Pendleton's full artillery component included two small cannons donated by VMI, guns that had been used for cadet training under Jackson, as well as two other heavier guns. Under orders to do no more than test the strength and the intentions of any Federal advance, Jackson thought his limited force was adequate for his purposes.

But the Federal advance force included between two thousand and three thousand five hundred men, and Jackson was barely able to do what he was ordered. He made a brief resistance and then withdrew. The action occurred near a tiny village with a waterfall and a church, a spot with the serene name of Falling Waters. As the site was also near a stream called Hoke's Run, the battle is known by both names.

Jackson told Pendleton to delay the Federal advance as long as possible with his one cannon. Pendleton found his long-ago artillery training useful. He ordered his single cannon to aim at the legs of the approaching cavalry horses and the small six-pounder did its job.

"The effect was obvious and decided," wrote Pendleton to his wife four days later. "Not man or horse remained standing in the road, nor did we see them again." It would not be the first time in Jackson's Civil War that horses were the intended targets for artillery. Jackson's brigade withdrew safely to the protection of Johnston's full force in Winchester.

Johnston referred to the event in the road at Falling Waters as an "affair," while Jackson called it a "skirmish." Whatever the name, it ended with minimal casualties. Union General Patterson was sure he had won, with Jackson withdrawing in the face of his advance. But the Confederate side was pleased too, since Jackson had done precisely what was necessary. He had discovered the size of the Union force and determined it would be unwise to bring on a battle. Johnston was even more pleased when Patterson, convinced he had defeated a large force with an even larger one in the wings, not only didn't advance, he eventually retreated across the Potomac.

More is known about Jackson's choice of mount at the First Battle of Manassas, which took place three weeks after Falling Waters. That battle, also known as the First Battle of Bull Run, saw the first major combat of the Civil War. Jackson didn't use either of his sorrel horses, and there is no record of why not. Jackson did have a potentially serious incident on horseback in the weeks between Falling Waters and Manassas that may have affected his decision on what horse to ride, but it seems unlikely that the horse involved was Little Sorrel.

John Lyle claimed that he saw Jackson, while reviewing his troops, come galloping down the line "at top speed as if he were riding a race. His horse, we learned later, was running away with him." No harm was done. Lyle said Jackson "stuck to that horse like a tick."

The horse involved was probably not Little Sorrel. Lyle didn't know Little Sorrel by name or reputation in July 1861, but he certainly did later in the war. He first published his memoirs nearly forty years after the incident and surely would have named Little Sorrel in the account if the little horse were indeed the runaway. Besides, Little Sorrel may have been the least likely horse in the Confederate army to run away with anybody during a review of troops. If the horse that bolted was the big sorrel, that would explain why Jackson chose not to use him in battle. But it doesn't explain why he didn't use his calm little one.

According to early Jackson biographer John Esten Cooke, James Thomson, an eighteen-year-old volunteer aide and former cadet at VMI, loaned Jackson the horse he rode at Manassas on July 21. Thomson had just arrived to join the Confederate army and was an outstanding rider, owning excellent horses. Still, it was surprising that Jackson would choose an unknown horse if one of his own had been ready for action.

Jackson had been promoted to brigadier general after the action at Falling Waters and there is a faint possibility that he thought that neither of his sorrels looked imposing enough for a general to ride into battle. But since he hadn't bothered to replace his well-worn and slightly shabby blue VMI uniform with something more elegant, he wasn't likely to worry about conformation flaws of an otherwise capable horse.

It's more likely that Jackson's own horses hadn't kept up with him. He and his brigade began their trip from the Winchester area on July 18 when they received word that the Confederate forces at Manassas, twenty-five miles deep into Virginia from Washington, D.C., needed reinforcement in the face of a Union advance.

It was a challenging trip of nearly fifty miles to reach the front. The troops marched over mountains and then climbed aboard railroad cars to head to Manassas Junction, six miles from where the Union and Confederate troops had already begun shooting at each other. The railroad journey for Joseph Johnston's entire army had to be accomplished in waves because of undersized cars and an underpowered locomotive.

Jackson and most of his brigade arrived at the Manassas depot on the first train late in the afternoon of July 19. The rest of the soldiers pulled in on July 20. The cavalry and artillery traveled over land and Little Sorrel may have been among the late arriving horses. Soldiers by necessity took up the rail car space, and it's probable that Jackson's horses were either unavailable to him or unfit at three o'clock in the morning of July 21 when his day got under way, so he borrowed the Thomson horse. Jackson and the rest of what was now called the Confederate Army of the Potomac knew that battle was likely that day, although most thought it would begin with their own attack on the left section of the Federal line, the right of the Confederate line. Jackson's brigade was ready for action at five o'clock.

But the first shots came from the Union side, and when it happened Thomas Jackson was on a horse that he didn't know. The horse performed well throughout the day, first accomplishing a quick move under fire from the right, where Jackson had thought the action would be, to the left, where the Union attack had begun. The borrowed horse happened to be the one carrying him when he received his legendary nickname.

It was shortly after 11:30 AM that Jackson's brigade stood in wait just over a hill on the farm of the Henry family to be ordered forward. Jackson and the borrowed horse stood in front as a brigade of South Carolinians struggled beneath them to stop a Union advance. Brigadier General Barnard Bee spotted Jackson and his brigade of Virginians on the hill above.

"There is Jackson standing like a stone wall," Bee said, or something to that effect, as he urged his weakening line to stand strong. There's a school of thought that Bee meant his statement as criticism rather than praise, accusing Jackson of standing still while his troops were devastated by Union fire. But most people took it to mean that Bee intended that his men steady themselves and reach deep to hold back the Union forces. Bee suffered a mortal wound moments later, so nobody was able to ask him what he meant.

Bee may have been speaking of Jackson himself, or he may have been speaking of the First Virginia Brigade, but the description was soon applied to both. The First Virginia became the Stonewall Brigade and Thomas Jackson became Stonewall Jackson. Both performed magnificently during the remaining four hours of battle, holding fast against the Union troops, then rallying to drive them back toward Washington, D.C., in disarray. Jackson suffered a wound to a finger and James Thomson's horse was wounded slightly in the leg.

It was a brilliant victory for the Confederate cause, but not the decisive one that both sides had assumed the first major battle would be. The Union army escaped mostly intact because the Confederates felt too damaged themselves to pursue. Both sides now suspected they were in for a long and brutal war. Nearly five thousand casualties forecast a costly and painful conflict. The cost in the lives of horses was also going to be great. A young recruit in the Confederate army was stunned by what he saw. "Somehow I was especially moved by the sight of the battery horses on the Henry Hill, so frightfully torn by shot and shell," wrote Randolph

McKim. "The sufferings of the poor brutes, not in their own battle or by their own fault, but for man's sake, appealed to me in a peculiar way."

For soldier and horse, there was a welcome respite over the next few weeks. Stonewall Jackson returned his borrowed horse and soon was aboard Little Sorrel almost every day. As had already become his custom, Jackson was busy and active while others rested and waited. He drilled his soldiers, reported daily to army headquarters, and welcomed visitors. Soldiers and officers got their first glimpse of the newly celebrated brigadier general from western Virginia during this time of waiting, and the almost universal reaction was that he was poorly dressed and badly mounted. But Jackson was in no hurry to change either his worn blue jacket or his plain little horse.

Even a promotion to major general in early October didn't prompt a change to a more eye-catching mount. Jackson was then ordered west to take over the Department of the Shenandoah, a unit that came to be known as the Valley Army. He was to go without his Stonewall Brigade, to make use instead of the limited manpower he found in the Shenandoah Valley, taking with him only his staff and his horses.

If the thought dismayed him, he said nothing. He was aboard Little Sorrel on November 4 when he made a dramatic goodbye to his brigade. It was long remembered as a rousing speech of praise and tribute, one in which Stonewall Jackson showed unprecedented emotion and unusual trust in his horse. As he reached the climax of his oratory he dropped his reins and raised his hands toward heaven.

"You are the First Brigade in the Army of the Potomac," he told his troops, adding, "By your future deeds and bearing you will be handed down to posterity as the First Brigade in our second War of Independence."

With that exhortation he gathered up Little Sorrel's reins and galloped away to the cheers of the men. Jackson and a handful of staff rode directly to the station at Manassas Junction, where they dismounted and climbed aboard a train to the Shenandoah Valley. Little Sorrel was left behind.

The separation didn't last long. The day after Jackson's departure his Stonewall Brigade, consisting of five regiments of infantry and an artillery company, were ordered west to join him. It's not known whether Little Sorrel arrived earlier or traveled with the brigade, which arrived in at its new base of operations in Winchester on November 10. Jackson already had about sixteen hundred militia and a few hundred poorly controlled but effective cavalry under the flamboyant Turner Ashby. The Valley Army had formed its nucleus.

Shortly after his arrival in Winchester, Little Sorrel met the man who would become the second most important person during his career as a warhorse. If asked to pick a favorite, Jim Lewis may actually have been at the top of the little horse's list. Lewis was a black man, a resident of Lexington, a good cook, and an affectionate caretaker of horses. That's all that is known for sure about him.

Lewis is variously described as a slave, a hired slave, or a free black man. According to the best evidence available, Jim Lewis was indeed a slave, but he didn't belong to Jackson. Stonewall Jackson rented Lewis from his owner for $150 a year to fill a job variously known as body servant or camp servant.

By November 1861, that job had become well defined. Body servants were black men, mostly slave but some hired, whose basic duties were to clean, forage for food, cook, maintain the equipment and clothing of, and care for the horses of their white masters in the Confederate army. During the first year of the Confederacy, many officers and some wealthy enlisted men brought body servants to war. But food later became so scarce that most enlisted men sent their slaves home, leaving the use of black body servants to their officers.

Jackson did employ a servant, probably a black man, earlier in the war to perform at least some of the duties of a body servant. He reported to his wife after First Manassas that his coat was damaged during the battle, "but my servant, who is very handy, has so far repaired it that it

Jim Lewis is shown on the left in 1866's "Prayer in Stonewall Jackson's Camp."
J. C. BUTTRE, LIBRARY OF CONGRESS

doesn't show very much." It's not known if that servant did other duties, including horse care, or what became of him. Jackson also employed a black cook named George, probably not the man who repaired the jacket, but nothing is known of what became of him either.

High-ranking officers could also utilize soldier orderlies to perform some personal service, particularly horse care, but many Confederate officers came from a society where men were more comfortable with close personal service given by blacks than whites. Even Jackson, who grew up in the isolated mountains of western Virginia, had been around slaves most of his life and was a slave owner himself. He owned at least half a dozen during his lifetime, and he sold and hired out some of the men and women he owned. His will left four slaves to his wife Anna, who promptly freed them.

But Jackson also believed that slaves, like everybody else, should learn to read. He and his wife taught their slaves to read, in violation of Virginia law and Southern custom. Jackson also ran a Sunday school for blacks, free and enslaved, for several years, resolutely keeping it open in spite of pressure from friends and neighbors to close it. Jackson was a man of contradictions in many things, no more so than in his association with human slavery.

In Jim Lewis he chose a man who gave him steadfast service and who, in exchange, received trust and even respect. More important to Little Sorrel, Jackson hired a man who loved and protected his horses, even going so far as to occasionally challenge Jackson's orders regarding his horses. Jackson was known to be a strict slave owner, requiring absolute obedience, but he was so generous with Lewis that members of his staff sometimes complained about the servant's special and better treatment.

Census evidence suggests that Jim Lewis was a man in his early fifties when he arrived in Winchester, although some memoir writers described him as younger. Henry Kyd Douglas called him "a handsome mulatto in the prime of his life." The one illustration believed to show Jim Lewis does depict a man much younger than fifty.

Baltimore-based artist Adalbert Volck, a devoted supporter of the Confederate cause, drew "Prayer in Stonewall Jackson's Camp" after meeting the general and his staff in 1962. The scene is imaginary, but it does show a young black man close behind Jackson as he prays at a camp service. Volck either never met Jim Lewis or assumed he was much younger than he really was. J. C. Buttre, who changed some of the figures but left Lewis as a very young man, engraved a better-known version of this scene in 1866.

Jackson probably knew Lewis before calling him to Winchester. He wasn't likely to have taken on someone for such close and personal service sight unseen. Lewis may have been a student at Jackson's Sunday school, but no written evidence of that exists.

Lewis was a good rider, and that may have contributed to Jackson's choice since horse care was such an important part of the job. Later in the war Jackson allowed Lewis to ride his other horses, even his more valuable, better-looking ones, while he remained on Little Sorrel himself.

Lewis remained with Jackson until the general's death in 1863 and then continued in service with Jackson's chief of staff, Alexander Pendleton. The death of Pendleton late in the war was a second blow to Lewis, who returned home to Lexington. He died there shortly after the war ended.

In addition to reacquiring the Stonewall Brigade and his favorite horse, Jackson began eyeing other Confederate forces to the west. He asked for and received control of several thousand additional men assigned to other generals west of the Shenandoah Valley. Among them was Sam Watkins of the First Tennessee Infantry. The twenty-two-year-old Watkins was a close observer and colorful writer, and he was never more colorful than in his description of what he saw the day he arrived in Winchester. "This is the first sight we had of Stonewall Jackson," Watkins said, "riding upon his old sorrel horse, his feet drawn up as if his stirrups were much too short for him, and his old dingy military cap hanging well forward over his head, and his nose erected in the air, his old rusty saber rattling by his side."

Watkins didn't know it, but Jackson had already begun planning a hazardous winter campaign to drive all Union forces out of western Virginia. Sam Watkins was going to need every bit of his colorful language to describe what was about to happen.

CHAPTER 5

War in Winter

Some of the officers and men of the Valley Army suspected that Stonewall Jackson might be planning a dreaded winter campaign since he was unusually active riding among the brigades and studying the condition of men and animals. He wasn't telling anybody in Winchester anything, but he was negotiating privately with officials in Richmond. The men who would have to make the march weren't particularly concerned since the weather had been unusually warm that fall and early winter. On December 19 Charles Blackford of the Second Virginia Cavalry wrote to his wife, "The weather is the most remarkable I have ever known. It has been perfectly clear for a month and no colder than the average September."

The welcome warmth continued through most of December. An ice storm on December 21 should have been taken as a warning that winter wouldn't hold off forever, but when the troops were told to prepare for a march on New Year's Day, warm weather had returned. The day was beautiful, and many of the soldiers left their overcoats and blankets to be carried by trailing wagons. Most horses still wore smooth iron shoes. There had been so little snow and ice during the season so far that the footing was fine.

The leading units of Jackson's army got under way just after 9:00 AM on January 1, 1862. Some officers were convinced that their goal was the Federal garrison at Romney, a small but strategic mountain town forty-two miles west of Winchester. They were surprised when they were directed north by staff members of the notoriously closed-mouthed Jackson, but the day was so pleasant and the troops so well rested that nobody questioned the order.

Jackson himself was late joining his column. He spent a few hours making arrangements for lodging for his wife Anna, who had traveled north to join her husband during the weeks of late autumn. A few hours later, personal business taken care of, he hopped aboard Little Sorrel and the pair paced quickly along the column, reaching the lead before nightfall.

Something else arrived along with the commanding general. A cold northern wind was already blowing hard as the troops stopped for the night, less than ten miles from where they started. They found the supply wagons badly strung out and most of the soldiers were unable to reach either their blankets or their dinner. Hunger as well as frigid rain and snow made sleep nearly impossible.

Once snow had covered the ground there was also very little for horses to eat, except for the limited supplies of grain their riders or drivers had the foresight to carry. The cold and snow bothered the horses less than it did their humans, but their hunger was just as real.

The next day officers and some of the soldiers realized they were headed to a second Federal garrison at the resort town of Bath, north of Winchester. The occupying force there was small and the town was less strategically important than Romney, but Jackson believed it had to be subdued to protect his column from an attack from the flank as it approached the more desirable Romney, farther to the south and west.

Alternating layers of mud, ice, and snow covered the road by morning and travel became excruciatingly slow. Private Marcus Toney of Tennessee was one of the late additions to Jackson's army. He described in his memoirs the road conditions on the second day of the march. "After a few companies had passed over the snow became as slick as ice," Toney wrote. "Skating would have been good if a fellow had had skates." Toney was speaking of soldiers rather than horses, but the animals had equal difficulty keeping their balance. Those pulling wagons and artillery pieces had the additional problem of mud so deep that the road was nearly impassible in places, further delaying the food for soldiers and feed for horses.

John Lyle's company had been ordered to remain at the rear with the headquarters wagons to guard Jackson's archives of orders, reports, and other papers. He got a close-up view of what was going on. "The grade was not only steep but was cut into holes, axle-deep," Lyle wrote later. He was amazed by the variety and volume of the oaths from the frustrated teamsters who struggled to extricate the wagons. "But the mules and horses hitched to the wagons were hardened to it and their sensibilities were untouched," he added.

On January 3, as the column continued to inch its way to Bath, heavier snow began falling, adding to the misery of man and horse. That night, snow covered the sleeping soldiers, leaving behind "white mounds in the shape of graves" on the morning of January 4, according to John Lyle. One by one, the mounds burst open and "live men popped out of them."

On January 4, the fourth miserable day of marching, the leading elements of the column had reached Bath. As they set up in a line for possible attack, Marcus Toney got his first glimpse of his commanding general. It was the best thing he had experienced on the march, and Jackson's little horse was part of it.

"General Stonewall Jackson rode up on Old Sorrel," Toney wrote in his memoirs. "The General wore a skull cap, a blouse, gray jacket, and the reins hung loosely on Old Sorrel's neck. He looked more like a plow horse than a warrior."

The Federal forces withdrew across the Potomac River to Hancock, Maryland, leaving Bath to the Confederates. Jackson ordered a bombardment of Hancock, demanding the Union surrender. The Federal commander refused and, after a couple of days of cold, snowy siege, Jackson gave up and continued on to his original goal of Romney. His troops did manage to destroy railroad and telegraph equipment and acquire some greatly needed supplies before their departure.

The weather didn't improve as they headed southwest. A massive snowstorm struck the mountains just after the column moved out of Bath, piling snow on top of ice. Soldiers and horses slipped and fell, several suffering fractures. A leg or arm fracture was occasionally fatal to a soldier, if it was severe enough and infection set in. A limb fracture was always fatal to a horse.

Stonewall Jackson and his horse remained unscathed. Little Sorrel might have been shod with cleats, but the army's farriers may not have bothered because of the warm weather in early winter. His pacing gait was the primary source of his secure footing, but his short-bodied conformation helped as well. He probably suffered far less from the slippery conditions than other horses on the march.

His comfort may have been greater as well. Little Sorrel's ancestors, both immediate and distant, were from the north and he inherited a predisposition to grow a thick winter coat that would have been well grown by the first week in January. Photographs in later life show Little Sorrel with a remarkably furry coat, no matter what time of year the picture was taken. Elderly horses often have long coats that shed slowly, so the photographs may be somewhat misleading. But he certainly had the genes for an ample hair coat in January 1862.

He would have had little shelter during the nightly bivouacs, but some horses, given a choice, will remain outside twenty-four hours a day, year-round. Even those who seek shelter are often satisfied with a canopy of trees, something they found in good supply during the Romney expedition. A horse with a thick hair coat can tolerate temperatures well below freezing, even with limited shelter.

Exposure to cold and snow might not have been much of a problem to Little Sorrel and any other horse lucky enough to have lived in the north, but all horses would have suffered from a continued shortage of feed and water. Heavy snow cover made grazing impossible, and all their feed had to be supplied by wagon. As the expedition wore on and road conditions worsened, food for soldiers and feed for horses became increasingly scarce.

Water was also a problem for the horses in the column. In normal weather with grazing available, a horse of Little Sorrel's size would require about eight gallons of water a day. That figure increases in winter, with no moisture absorbed from grass. A horse experienced in winter living might get some of his water needs from eating snow, but most domesticated horses can't do that effectively. Ponds and streams had frozen over by the second week of the expedition to Romney and some of the horses in the column began to show the illnesses typical of water shortages. The tough Little Sorrel remained healthy.

Jim Lewis traveled with the wagon trains and was available for horse care when the column stopped at night. He would have done only minimal grooming, but nightly hoof care would have been vital. In snowy weather, shod horses are vulnerable to the formation of hard little snowballs in the concave underside of their hoofs. These packed balls can extend beyond the rim of the hoof and may cause slips and falls as well as an irregular gait that can lead to lameness. Hoofs must be cleaned of ice nightly, and Stonewall Jackson, a horseman from the mountains, would have known it. Little Sorrel carried Jackson throughout the entire Romney campaign and remained sound.

Other horses had worse luck. John Casler of the Thirty-Third Virginia Infantry was among the soldiers assigned to the wagons and caissons to help them around turns and keep them from going off the road. He was also involved in a mostly losing effort to keep the horses and vehicles upright. "The horses were smooth shod," Casler wrote in his memoirs, "and in going up a little hill I have seen one horse in each team down nearly all the time. As soon as one would get up, another would be down, and sometimes all four at once."

Eventually the teamsters figured that unshod horses would fare better than smooth-shod ones. So soldiers and farriers pulled shoes from many of them, preventing most of the little snowballs and allowing for some suction with each footfall. The one hundred sixty supply wagons that had survived now did a little better at keeping up with the soldiers. After a cold and wet rest along the road south to Winchester, the column turned west toward Romney.

The weather had warmed a little and the thick layer of ice changed to deep slush. The horses and soldiers found the traveling less slippery but only marginally more comfortable. By the time Jackson reached Romney on January 14, he discovered that the Federal garrison had escaped, providing the Confederate troops with a bloodless capture of the town. Bloodless didn't mean absence of injury and death, though. Dozens of men had lost fingers and toes to frostbite and many more had fallen ill.

The Federal troops had left so quickly that the Confederates were able to supply themselves with tents and food stores, so the soldiers weren't quite as cold and hungry during the time they spent in the tiny town. But conditions didn't improve much for the horses. Artillery officer William Pogue wrote in his memoirs of the wretched time spent in Romney. It was, he said, a period of particular misery for horses. "Horses tied to the hitching rope had to eat what little feed they got in the mud," Pogue wrote. "No boxes or nosebags were to be had." The horses, Pogue added, stood in mud so deep that they found it difficult to change their positions to make themselves comfortable.

As the commanding general's horse, Little Sorrel lived a little more comfortably than the others. Jim Lewis began to make his reputation as an outstanding forager for humans and horses during this expedition. Little Sorrel also began to make his reputation as a horse who could survive equally well on "a ton of hay or live on cobs," as Jackson aide Henry Kyd Douglas said. Little Sorrel, according to Douglas, always looked the same, regardless of condition. In truth, Little Sorrel did lose weight at several points during the war, but he continued on with good appetite and good energy in spite of the shortages, never more severe than in the Romney expedition.

Jackson was convinced that chasing the Federal occupying force out of Romney constituted a fine victory and briefly thought of continuing the expedition to push Federal forces farther away from the Shenandoah Valley. But the illness of so many soldiers and the loss of so many horses from the artillery and wagon trains made that a questionable move. Instead, he chose to leave his newly acquired troops in Romney and head back to Winchester with his own Stonewall Brigade.

The new troops were dismayed at the prospect of being left behind in what they considered a dangerously exposed pigpen. Snow had turned back to rain shortly after the column's arrival and the mud was like nothing the soldiers had ever seen. What's more, Federal troops in considerable numbers were only about twenty miles away. But Jackson's brigade was overjoyed as it marched out of Romney on January 23. The soldiers and officers left in Romney seethed with anger.

William Pogue was thrilled to be leaving with Jackson for the forty-five-mile trip across the mountains to Winchester, which now seemed like a sophisticated metropolis rather than the town of less than five thousand residents that it was. Even a night spent in the open under a heavy snowfall failed to dim the excitement of being on the road back. The air was fresh and the surroundings clean, Pogue reported, and "the horses also ate and rested in some comfort."

Jackson himself decided to make the trip in one day. Although most of them rode big Thoroughbred-type horses, staff members struggled to keep up with the rapid pacing gait of Little Sorrel. Anna Jackson hadn't expected to see her husband quite so soon, having heard stories of the troubles the column had faced on the expedition. After their early reunion, the couple settled comfortably into what turned out to be a quiet six weeks of winter quarters. Anna heard much of what had happened during the expedition from her husband. Among the topics was the performance of Little Sorrel.

"In making the trip from Romney, he was more than ever charmed with Little Sorrel, whose powers of endurance proved quite remarkable," Anna wrote years later. "After bearing him along with so much fleetness and comfort, he said the horse seemed almost as fresh and unwearied at the end of the journey as at the beginning."

She probably knew by this point that Jackson had intended Little Sorrel to be a gift for her. If she hadn't figured it out before, she also now knew that she wasn't going to get her gift, at least as long as her husband was at war. But troubles over the Romney expedition arose quickly and it appeared for a while that Jackson's war might end before either of them expected, turning Little Sorrel into a lady's mount after all.

Some of the problems emerged among the soldiers of his own brigade, the lucky men who had set up winter quarters just outside Winchester. Jackson approved almost no furloughs, even though much of the brigade came from the Shenandoah Valley. The grumbling arising from the no-furlough rule plus complaints from sick soldiers who were told to return to the ranks as soon as they were mobile contributed to tension in the town. If it bothered Jackson, he said nothing.

But the complaints coming from Romney could be heard throughout Virginia and even Jackson couldn't miss them. By the end of January, the situation in the little town had deteriorated well beyond the terrible conditions of mid-month. Streets were now filthy as well as muddy. The captured Federal food supplies had rotted and rats had converged on the storage sites. Union troops remained within a short march, although they had shown no signs of trying to retake the town.

On January 31, Jackson received a telegram from Secretary of War Judah Benjamin in Richmond ordering him to recall the Romney troops to Winchester. Jackson was stunned by the order, which he knew must have come from Confederate President Jefferson Davis. What he didn't know yet was that officers and even some enlisted men in Romney had been bombarding Richmond with letters complaining that they had been arbitrarily assigned to a place that was unhealthy and impossible to defend.

Jackson was convinced it was neither. If Romney remained unhealthy, he believed, it was the result of the officers there failing to enforce sanitary standards. Defense, he thought, was no more difficult than at any other place in western Virginia where loyalties were decidedly mixed.

The fact that officers under his command had gone around him to government leaders was the most infuriating aspect of the whole incident. Jackson immediately sent word to Benjamin that he had sent the recall notice to Romney as ordered and that he would now resign his commission and return to teaching at the Virginia Military Institute. But Jackson had friends in high places as well, and Little Sorrel was saved from a career as a lady's horse, at least for a while.

Two friends, Virginia governor John Letcher and former U.S. congressman and newly elected Confederate congressman Alexander Boteler, swung into action immediately. They confronted both Judah Benjamin and Jefferson Davis and stirred up public opinion against Jackson's departure from command. Jackson was persuaded to withdraw the resignation and Little Sorrel remained a commanding general's favorite mount.

Wartime Virginia governor John Letcher was an important ally for Jackson.

But the Confederates left Romney anyway, giving up the fruits of the miserable winter campaign, and Federal forces soon retook the town. Union General Nathaniel Banks gained further ground. By the end of February, his troops were within twenty miles of Winchester. The Romney brigades had been dispersed rather than returned to Jackson's control, and the Valley Army had been so weakened that army engineers told him he might not be able to hold Winchester either. He asked Richmond for more troops but was refused.

On March 7, Banks and his soldiers had reached a point just five miles from Winchester. The Union general was convinced that Jackson had many more men than he actually did, a common failing in the Union high command during the early years of the war, and was slow to advance farther. But even the aggressive Stonewall Jackson had to face reality. Winchester, the first city of his Shenandoah Valley campaign, would have to be abandoned.

CHAPTER 6

Into the Valley

Stonewall Jackson left Winchester shrouded by a cloud of bitterness. He'd thought about taking the war to Banks in a bold night attack, but the reality of weather, timing, and the size of his little army thwarted him. To protect his army he opted instead for retreat. It was a painful decision.

Jackson chose Little Sorrel on the night of March 11, 1862, since the little red horse had become his clear preference during the difficult winter. Jedediah Hotchkiss, mapmaker and important chronicler of Jackson, wasn't present on March 11, but he thought it was important enough to mention the horse as Jackson's mount that night in his chapter in *Confederate Military History*, published nearly forty years later.

It made perfect sense for Stonewall Jackson to ride his best horse on what he felt was the worst day of his war. He assumed that he faced many days on the road, possibly including one or more battles against an enemy with far superior numbers. There was no question that Little Sorrel was ideally suited for long miles under saddle and Jackson suspected by now that he was equally ideally suited for battle.

What's more, his quiet good nature provided an antidote to a sour mood and his easy, rocking chair gait didn't get in the way of a rider's complex thinking. In the best of times, Stonewall Jackson kept his own counsel. Now, after an atypical backward step in the face of terrible odds, an easy amble was the perfect companion for serious thought.

The first leg of the trip was brief. A few miles out of town Jackson found a suitable fence corner, dismounted, and went to sleep on the ground for a couple of hours with his favorite horse stretched out right next to him. He was more cheerful in the morning as he followed and then led his marching army southwest, deep into the Shenandoah Valley. By local tradition, Jackson's forces were moving *up* the Shenandoah Valley as they headed southwest, since the elevation of the landscape increases north to south.

Much of the time he walked as his soldiers did, leading Little Sorrel by the reins. Nobody is quite sure why he completed some of the dozen miles of that first full day's journey on foot. His horse hadn't been heavily used for a few months, so there was no need to rest him. As usual, Jackson felt no need to explain his actions.

The pace was slow but steady. Jackson was determined to think of his movement south not as a retreat but rather as a tactical repositioning. By the evening of March 13, he and his army of forty-five hundred had reached Strasburg, where they stayed two days. Union troops were following at an even slower rate, eventually stopping in Strasburg themselves on their slow-speed chase. But by then Jackson was long gone.

He had led his troops farther south to Woodstock and finally stopped them in the Mount Jackson area, more than forty miles from Winchester. Little Sorrel probably carried Jackson for most, if not all, of these miles.

The time was tense for Jackson but easy for his horse. The weather remained cold and damp with occasional snow showers, so spring grass wasn't yet up and the occasional grazing the horses managed provided little nutrition. But Mount Jackson was a reasonable distance by good road from a Confederate supply base at Staunton, especially convenient since Staunton was Quartermaster John Harman's hometown. The agricultural bounty of the rich Shenandoah Valley provided food for soldiers and sufficient cut hay and grain for horses.

But Little Sorrel wasn't idle. He carried Jackson on daily inspections into Camp Buchanan, as the troops named their campsite. He used the time to check on their training and organization and, particularly, to see how newly arrived militia members were settling into their regiments. Governor John Letcher had called up these militiamen just before the Confederates abandoned Winchester, and they now joined in the defense of the Shenandoah Valley.

One of those militia members was Jedediah Hotchkiss, the former schoolmaster and self-taught topographer whom Jackson immediately seized upon as a valuable addition to his engineering staff. Today, more than a century and a half later, the maps Hotchkiss drew at Jackson's request remain works of art and history, and they would form a vital link in the coming Confederate campaign in the Shenandoah Valley. But the personal journals Hotchkiss kept during his time with Jackson, as well as his assiduous research after the war, are even more important for historians as they try to understand Stonewall Jackson and figure out what happened to his favorite horse.

Some militia members, although not Hotchkiss, saw almost immediate action. On March 21, Jackson learned that Union General James Shields, commander of the six-thousand-man detachment that had remained in Strasburg, was preparing to leave and rejoin Banks near Winchester. Since Jackson's standing order was to force as many Union troops as possible to remain in the valley, he became convinced that Banks had been ordered east to join in a possible Union assault on the Confederate capital of Richmond.

That meant immediate action for Jackson and his troops. He intended to turn around and reach Shields quickly, before the Union general had a chance to join Banks and the rest of the Union soldiers. The next two days saw the first forced march of Jackson's little army in the Shenandoah Valley, the lightning-fast movement that got the Confederate troops to places nobody, especially the Union commanders, believed they could possibly be.

On March 22, Jackson, riding Little Sorrel as always, led his forty-five hundred soldiers twenty-five miles down the valley, adding another sixteen miles by mid-day on March 23. This was an improbably quick pace, one that left fifteen hundred men straggling behind along the way. There were perhaps three thousand soldiers available when the column reached Kernstown, just a few miles short of Winchester. In the meantime, Jackson's cavalry commander Turner Ashby had fought a minor skirmish against a handful of Shields's troops. Ashby then assumed that only a small number of Shields's division was there and the rest of Banks's corps was gone. Ashby passed that word on to Jackson.

That assumption was matched by an assumption by the Union commander. Nathaniel Banks was convinced that Jackson was either forty miles south or somewhere along the way, and he personally took off from Winchester just about the time the Confederate troops arrived south of the town. Banks figured that Shields's division, commanded by Nathan Kimball because of an injury to Shields, was present in full and could handle anything that might come along.

Still aboard Little Sorrel, Jackson acted on his misinformation and ordered an attack. But Shields and Kimball had been wiser than Banks and had hidden most of their troops between Kernstown and Winchester. Jackson realized quickly that there were many more than a thousand or so rear guard Union soldiers.

The three thousand Confederates had challenged as many as ten thousand Union troops. Short of ammunition and badly outnumbered, Jackson's men fought hard but were forced to withdraw from the field. It was a first-ever battlefield defeat for Stonewall Jackson.

Jackson was unprepared for the number of Union defenders at Kernstown.
HARPER'S WEEKLY, APRIL 12, 1862

William E. Caffey, an English-born Confederate artillerist who wrote under the pseudonym "An English Combatant," took his first note of Stonewall Jackson at about this time. He noticed Little Sorrel as well. "As for uniform, he has none—his wardrobe isn't worth a dollar," Caffey said of Jackson. "His horse is quite in keeping, being a poor lean animal of little spirit or activity."

But Jackson realized that Little Sorrel performed just fine in what may have been his first experience under musket and artillery fire. Jackson was displeased with his army's performance at Kernstown, but he was highly pleased with Little Sorrel. He rode the horse in all of his remaining battles.

William Caffey had second thoughts about Little Sorrel as well. Later in his *Battle-fields of the South from Bull Run to Fredericksburg,* he gives a different picture of the horse. "The old sorrel war-horse is well known throughout the army," he wrote. "With head down, it seldom attempts more than a trot, but stands fire well, and that may be the reason why the General prefers and always rides him."

As it turned out, the excellent performance of Little Sorrel wasn't the only good thing to come out of the Kernstown defeat. Generals Shields and Kimball told everyone for years that they were the only generals to defeat Stonewall Jackson in battle, but officials in Washington, including Abraham Lincoln, were disturbed by the fact that Jackson had appeared at Kernstown quickly and unnoticed. They now wondered if he might suddenly show up at the outskirts of Washington itself.

Lincoln and the War Department persuaded themselves that Jackson had many more soldiers than he did. Banks was told to return with his full corps and officials began concentrating Federal forces in the Shenandoah Valley. As Jackson and the Confederate government had hoped, troops were taken away from the planned Federal assault on Richmond.

This was, by any standards, a victory, though the defeat on the battlefield at Kernstown remained an embarrassment to Stonewall Jackson for the rest of his life. The fact that he had relied on someone else for observation and assessment of the enemy led him in the future to conduct his own reconnaissance. Little Sorrel would almost always be his companion in this risky business.

Jackson's troops headed back up the valley to regroup and train. For Jackson, a man who liked to attack, it would be a time to figure out how to fulfill his mission to occupy as many Federal troops as possible, by attacking, defending, or just biding his time.

He began planning immediately, as soon as he set his troops in motion. The day after the battle, observers noticed him riding at the front of his column, lost in thought, reins dangling. He trusted Little Sorrel to find his own way and get him to where he needed to be. Little Sorrel did just what he hoped.

It was a leisurely withdrawal up the valley, made possible by a Union pursuit that was again even more leisurely. A cautious Shields couldn't believe that Jackson would have attacked as he did without considerable support behind him, so he was reluctant to provoke a new battle. But there was regular skirmishing between Union and Confederate cavalry as the infantries marched. At one point Jackson found good ground to defend, halted his troops, and had them prepare for battle, should General Shields want it. He didn't, and the retreat continued.

"It was the boldest retreat I ever saw," wrote John Worsham of the Twenty-First Virginia Infantry years after the war. "If the enemy did not hunt for us, General Jackson would hunt for them."

The lethargy of the retreat perplexed the soldiers, but it was much easier on men and horses than the trip down the valley had been. Worsham noted that it had taken them only two days to march nearly fifty miles before Kernstown and eighteen days to march one hundred miles after the battle.

On one level it was an awkward time for both Jackson and Little Sorrel. Shortly after the firing stopped at Kernstown, Jackson relieved Brigadier General Richard Garnett from his command for telling his brigade to retreat when it ran out of ammunition. It was the Stonewall Brigade, Jackson's old command, that made their withdrawal even more painful to contemplate. Jackson thought the soldiers could have succeeded with bayonets alone.

The soldiers involved believed that they might have all died if Garnett hadn't pulled them back. For weeks the brigade stood silent when Jackson rode among them on inspection, as he tried to do with every section of his army daily. Little Sorrel had already become accustomed to cheers from the troops on these inspection rides and he would habitually raise his head, increase his speed, and look altogether livelier as soon as heard the ovation. He must have been puzzled by the silence now.

But Jackson had more to worry about than the lack of applause. He now realized that he was going to have to know a great deal more about the valley than his opponents did if he was to have any chance of success against staggering odds. He knew within a couple of days of the battle that Union strength was mounting rapidly. It was what he wanted, to be sure, but his troops were already greatly outnumbered and the disparity was growing. He called for Jedediah Hotchkiss.

"I want you to make me a map of the valley," he told his new cartographer. He wanted every hollow, every mountain, every pass, and every road within the valley's full one hundred forty miles accounted for, and he got exactly that. Hotchkiss became close to Jackson and was trusted with duties well beyond mapmaking. He acted as a courier, scout, bridge-destroyer, and sounding board.

But for the next month and a half it was the mapmaking that was most important. With the help of Hotchkiss, Jackson moved his army around like the pieces on a chessboard, using Ashby's cavalry to screen its movement. Nathaniel Banks was alternately convinced that Jackson was running away, hiding in place, and leaving the valley to join the Confederate forces protecting Richmond.

By late April, Jackson's army was at Swift Run Gap—strictly speaking, outside the Shenandoah Valley—waiting for promised reinforcements. Banks knew in general where he was but couldn't see him and figured the little Valley Army was finally off to Richmond. That was a mistake.

Because of the report that Jackson had left, Shields's division was sent out of the valley too, off to Fredericksburg to be in position to either defend Washington or attack Richmond, leaving Banks in place to defend against any new Confederate troops that might appear.

What concerned Jackson more in his role as defender of the Shenandoah Valley was the movement of another Federal army. Two brigades of General John C. Frémont's Mountain Department had crossed the Allegheny Mountains on the western border of the valley. The controversial but widely celebrated Frémont, still known as the "Pathfinder" for his expeditions in the west, rose to command less than two months earlier. He was not one to stand still, so he sent six thousand men under General Robert Milroy east across the Allegheny Mountains to see what could be done about the Confederates in the valley. Jackson and Richmond officials assumed that Frémont planned to unite with Banks, creating a huge army that even Stonewall Jackson couldn't handle.

The move wasn't unexpected, and there were some Confederate troops already in place. The small Confederate Army of the Northwest was commanded by a man as colorful as Frémont but much less self-important. General Edward "Allegheny Ed" Johnson, a former frontiersman and Indian fighter, was waiting with nearly three thousand men near Staunton in the far south of the valley. Jackson, fifty miles to the east, saw the Frémont-Milroy move as an opportunity to take care of the smallest of the Union armies threatening him. He figured Banks and his nineteen thousand men weren't going anywhere for now, and that army could wait for later. Besides, Jackson hoped to pull off a march that would have befuddled the best of military minds, which Banks did not possess.

So Jackson, Little Sorrel, and the rest of the Valley Army headed due south on April 30. The column moved out first, getting under way in a pouring rain that, after weeks of showery weather, immediately turned their line of march into a morass of mud. Jackson and his staff, including careful observer Jedediah Hotchkiss, hurried past the marching soldiers to reach the front of the column.

Hotchkiss later described Jackson riding Little Sorrel at full gallop through the mud around the column, pursued by staff members on fancier horses struggling to keep up. He doesn't say who won what he called a "ludicrous" race, but he did note that the soldiers cheered their general as he galloped past. They had forgotten their anger over the dismissal of the admired General Garnett. It was now adulation as usual for Jackson and Little Sorrel.

The twelve-mile march south took two and a half days, thanks to roads that were soon like quicksand. Wagons and artillery became bogged down beyond the ability of their horses to pull them out. Soldiers were forced to stop marching to help pull, and at one point on May 1, Jackson himself jumped off Little Sorrel to help extricate a cannon from the mud.

Once the army reached the little town of Port Republic, Jackson ordered it to head due east, and his own army now also assumed they were going to Richmond. But at Mechum's River Station, on the other side of the Blue Ridge Mountains and out of the valley, the men climbed aboard rail cars that were actually headed west. They were soon back in the valley, and by May 5, Jackson's army was at Staunton, six miles from Allegheny Ed. Jackson, still on Little Sorrel, made the trip on horseback with his staff and a few troops over a treacherous mountain pass.

Jackson was pleased with the efficiency of the leg of the journey from Mechum's River Station, and the men were pleased that the heavy rains of the last several weeks had finally let up. Thanks in part to the relentless rain, the shabby blue uniform coat from VMI that Jackson had worn for the entire first year of the war had finally reached the end of its road. He replaced it with a simple homespun gray wool jacket, and now, his staff officers thought, he looked somewhat spiffier. If they thought he should replace Little Sorrel with a more elegant mount, they kept that thought to themselves.

The respite in Staunton didn't last long. Milroy had been confused about the direction of Jackson's move until May 7, but he now realized the Confederates' intentions and saw that they were uncomfortably close. Although he didn't believe the two Confederate armies had yet combined, Milroy soon understood that the armies of Johnson and Jackson would total nearly nine thousand men and greatly outnumber his brigade when they did unite. He withdrew back toward the Allegheny Mountains, calling on his commander, General Frémont, to send help in the form of a brigade headed by General Robert Schenck.

The chase was on. Jackson, still aboard the tireless Little Sorrel, placed his army in line behind Allegheny Ed's troops as all nine thousand headed west to confront Milroy and, with any luck, more of Frémont's army. Before Jackson took his place at the front of his column, he tried to deceive any Union loyalists who might be watching. He and a few of his staff officers headed south on the Lexington road, thereby starting the rumor that the army was actually headed south. According to Hotchkiss, Jackson turned after a few miles onto a connecting road to catch up with his westbound army.

Late arriving staff members, having heard the rumors, rode much too far south and went twenty-five miles out of their way before they caught up with Jackson. As usual, only the humans complained.

A surprise assault by Union artillery on Jackson's column was handled, but it left the leading regiments of his column a full five miles behind the end of Johnson's. Early on May 8, his forward-most regiments came under fire from skirmishers as they approached the little village of McDowell. Jackson hurried to the front of the column, accompanied by only Jedediah Hotchkiss, to see for himself what his troops faced. Captain Edward Alfriend of the Forty-Fourth Virginia Infantry was shocked by Jackson's willingness to expose himself to enemy fire. He urged the general to move out of range.

"I wish to look forward here," Jackson told Alfriend curtly and that was that. He looked while Alfriend's company did their best to protect him. Jackson and Little Sorrel survived uninjured.

A few minutes later Jackson caught up with Allegheny Ed Johnson. The two generals, accompanied by Jedediah Hotchkiss and other staff members, rode to the top of a rocky ridge where they could get a good view of Milroy's troops arrayed before them in the town of McDowell. The Union soldiers got a good view of them too and began firing. In spite of the firing, Jackson concluded that Milroy wasn't going to attack that day and sent most of his staff down the other side of the ridge to rest in preparation for possible action the next day. He and Little Sorrel remained, having survived another close call.

For the rest of his war Jackson would continue to take terrible chances with his own and his horse's safety. It was mostly the lesson learned from his defeat at Kernstown that led him to a behavior that, while brave, was risky to all, including the survival of the Confederacy. He didn't trust other people's observations and wanted to make his own whenever possible.

Jackson's Calvinist beliefs almost certainly played a part. Like most fundamentalist southern Presbyterians of the time, Jackson believed John Calvin's teachings from three centuries earlier: nothing happens except what God has decreed, and "fortune and chance" play no role in what occurs. He may have felt he was taking no chance at all by exposing himself to fire. What was decreed would happen. Of course, Calvin was talking about human beings and Little Sorrel hadn't been consulted.

Although Jackson had convinced himself that there would be no Union attack, Milroy, believing that the action on the ridge was part of a Confederate effort to post dangerous artillery on high ground, did launch an attack a couple of hours later. That began the short, bloody, and indecisive Battle of McDowell. General Johnson's troops, first in line, did most of the fighting, with Allegheny Ed directing the action until he suffered a severe leg wound. When darkness fell a couple of hours later the firing stopped and the Battle of McDowell was over. The Confederates suffered two-thirds more casualties than the well-directed Union force, leading Milroy to claim a victory.

But by morning Milroy was gone, headed back to the safety of Frémont's army. Again, Jackson had managed to fashion an important strategic win out of less-than-ideal material and most historians consider McDowell to be the first of the string of successes in Stonewall Jackson's Shenandoah Valley campaign.

Jackson ordered a pursuit of the retreating Federal brigades, stopping only when Milroy made a stand at a narrow and easily protected mountain pass a few days later. By then it was obvious that Milroy posed no immediate threat and Jackson turned his army around to head back to the Shenandoah Valley. He wasn't convinced that Frémont wouldn't make an effort to unite with Banks again soon, so he ordered Hotchkiss to locate and construct barriers in the mountain passes that might allow the Federals to sneak back into the valley under the cover of the mountains.

Jackson turned his attention back to Banks and the troops under Confederate general Richard Ewell, who had been sent by Richmond to reinforce the Valley Army. Ewell had been waiting impatiently in the camp vacated by Jackson's army when it took off on its western adventure. Ewell wrote of Jackson as an "enthusiastic fanatic" who kept his long-term intentions to himself. In the meantime, Ewell's job was what Jackson's had been, to resist any movement within the valley by Banks and prevent Banks from moving out to join in the threat on Richmond. That movement began to happen in mid-May.

Banks seemed to be moving north, possibly detaching some of his troops, but Ewell had received orders from the east that contradicted Jackson's to stay put. Joseph Johnston, commander of the forces protecting Richmond, told Ewell that every man was needed there. Waiting for word from Jackson caused Ewell to explode in anger at his commander. "I tell you, sir," he raged at a subordinate, "he is as crazy as a March hare!" Later, after repeated successes under Jackson, Ewell changed his mind, noting that the secretive Jackson "just knows how to keep his own counsel." He became Jackson's most trusted subordinate general until his severe wounding at Chantilly four months later.

Jackson, having taken care of Frémont at least temporarily, had big plans for his enlarged Valley Army. As his troops marched back into the valley he met with Ewell on May 18, revealing some, but not all, of his strategy to his second-in-command.

On May 20, Jackson was joined by part of Ewell's nine thousand men. Soldiers in Ewell's division were eager to see Stonewall Jackson, who had become increasingly celebrated in the army, thanks to the victory at McDowell. General Richard Taylor, who commanded a Louisiana brigade assigned to Ewell, was among the curious soldiers who linked up with Jackson.

General Richard Taylor of Louisiana was critical of Little Sorrel's appearance.
LIBRARY OF CONGRESS

Taylor was a celebrity himself. He was the only son of Zachary Taylor, Mexican War hero and twelfth president of the United States. Richard Taylor had also been briefly the brother-in-law of Jefferson Davis, whose first wife was Richard Taylor's second-oldest sister. That sister had died of yellow fever in 1835 after only three months of marriage to Davis, making the relationship distant, as was Zachary Taylor's presidency. But Richard Taylor still mentioned family whenever it might be helpful.

More than a trace of snobbery is apparent in Taylor's war memoirs, published in 1879. His descriptions of Jackson and Little Sorrel date from the day his brigade of Ewell's division joined Jackson's army and Taylor first laid eyes on Stonewall Jackson. Jackson wore, he said, "a pair of cavalry boots covering feet of gigantic size, a mangy cap with visor drawn low, a heavy dark beard, and weary eyes."

As for Jackson's transportation, the general was "mounted on a sorry chestnut with a shambling gait." Perhaps he had never seen a pacer before. He got a better look later when he rode alongside Jackson as commander of the lead brigade of the Valley Army, at sixteen thousand men finally large enough to do honor to the name. Although he remained full of opinionated observation, Richard Taylor was never critical of Little Sorrel again.

On May 22, the army began a northward march in search of Nathaniel Banks or any of the elements of his command that he had foolishly scattered around the valley. The tedium of the march was broken when Jackson passed the column to reach the front. J. William Jones was marching with the Thirteenth Virginia Infantry.

"Hearing loud cheering in the rear, which came nearer and nearer," he wrote years later, "we soon saw it was Stonewall himself, mounted on that old sorrel we afterwards came to know so well." Jones said his regiment "gave a hearty greeting to the great captain who had come to lead us on to victory."

Victory came quickly to the three-thousand-man segment of the army that reached the outskirts of Front Royal on the afternoon of May 23. The troops were mostly from Ewell's division, but Jackson and Little Sorrel led them in person. The Union garrison at Front Royal was small, only about one thousand men, with the rest of Banks's troops to the northwest in Strasburg.

Front Royal itself was both important and not. It stands at the northern entrance of the Luray Valley, a smaller valley that parallels the larger

Shenandoah Valley. Just north of town the two branches of the Shenandoah River come together. In 1862, the town provided twenty-five miles of good train and road access to Winchester, the town that commanded the northern approach to both valleys. However, Front Royal was almost impossible to defend since high peaks surrounded it. But the railroad trestle and the bridge on the Winchester road were vital, and Jackson had to act quickly to prevent the Union troops from burning them. He was so impatient that at least once he rode Little Sorrel in front of his own troops, risking himself and his horse to bullets from both Confederates and Federals.

The Union contingent in Front Royal was overwhelmed. The hour-long battle turned 90 percent of the Federal soldiers into casualties, including nearly seven hundred captured. But they won the footrace to the bridges, placing hay on the ties and setting it on fire by shooting into the hay. The hay burned, but the rain-soaked wood of the bridges didn't, and the Confederates had time to pitch the burning hay into the water. Jackson and Little Sorrel, along with four cavalry companies, chased the Union soldiers down. By late afternoon, Jackson's army was in full possession of Front Royal. Winchester stood twenty-five miles away to the north. Just nineteen miles away to the northwest of Front Royal, Nathaniel Banks and his six thousand soldiers in Strasburg had no clue what had just happened.

The next day, hearing news of the disaster at Front Royal, Banks started his troops northward to his base of supplies at Winchester, more easily defended than Strasburg. He wasn't surprised that Jackson had attacked, but he was stunned that the Valley Army had gotten so far north undetected. At first, the Union troops moved out slowly, assuming again that Jackson couldn't move quickly enough to reach them before they got to Winchester.

It was true that the Confederates were farther away from Winchester than Banks was. Jackson began a march on May 24 that he kept up day and night, hoping to prevent Banks from reaching his supply base.

Jackson was determined that nobody stop to rest as they headed north. Henry Kyd Douglas observed the general moving around on Little Sorrel to make himself more comfortable. The trustworthy little animal marched onward, protecting his rider from a fall in spite of the dark and the sleepiness that everyone, man and horse, was experiencing.

After failing on the field at Kernstown and being less than fully engaged at McDowell, Jackson was determined now to be at the front for all of the action. He was in front at Front Royal and he remained in front through that night on the road to Winchester, even as his column approached the Union-held town they had abandoned two months earlier. There were sporadic brushes with Federal troops along the route, including occasional musket fire coming at them from the darkness.

"I quite remember thinking at the time that Jackson was invulnerable, and that persons near him shared that quality," Richard Taylor wrote later. He might well have added "horses" near Jackson to his observation about invulnerability. Little Sorrel was also untouched that tense night.

Elements of the Valley Army did manage to smash into the tail of Banks's long column, hitting primarily supply wagons and ambulances. The Federals abandoned the vehicles and hurried on to Winchester, assuming correctly that the underequipped and underfed Confederates would stop their march to loot.

As dawn broke on May 25 Ewell's portion of the army was less than two miles from Winchester, having taken a more direct route than Jackson himself. Most of Banks's six thousand five hundred troops had beaten the Confederates, and they prepared for attack. Banks was grateful that most of his command had reached safety and believed he had hours or days before Jackson could possibly be there. He was wrong on both counts. He wasn't safe, and Jackson was there.

Jackson directed a two-pronged attack, with Ewell from the southeast and Jackson himself from the southwest. Early in the battle, Jackson rode

Little Sorrel, accompanied by several officers, to the top of a small hill where he could get a firsthand look at the Union deployment against them.

"They were hit by a hail of grape and musket balls," wrote John Worsham of the Twenty-First Virginia Infantry. One of the officers was wounded and another saw a musket ball penetrate his sleeve.

"General Jackson sat there, the enemy continuing to fire grape and musketry at him," Worsham said. Jackson remained on that hill on a motionless Little Sorrel until he had assessed the situation and issued his orders. After a quick trip back to see that his orders were being followed, he returned to the hill to watch the effects of the advance by Richard Taylor's brigade. Jackson's invulnerability, and that of his horse, continued.

The Confederate attack smashed through Banks's army. After a briefly strong resistance, the lines crumpled and broke. Union casualties were more than two thousand men dead, wounded, or captured, while Jackson's losses amounted to only four hundred. As usual, equine casualties weren't carefully counted. One estimate had the Union forces losing five hundred horses and mules, some to capture but most to death. Even the coldly practical Jackson expressed regret later at the destruction of artillery and wagon horses during cannon attacks on the rear of Banks's column as it approached Winchester.

What was left of the Federal army dashed through the town and headed north to safety. Motivation gave the Federal troops speed, while exhaustion slowed down pursuing Confederates, so Banks had what was left of his troops crossing the Potomac River that night and early the next day. Jackson called his troops back from their pursuit.

Stonewall Jackson and Little Sorrel strode into the center of Winchester to wild cheering. Jackson was their savior, the residents believed, and Little Sorrel deserved adulation by association. It was in Winchester that the little horse first began to lose hairs from his tail, snatched from him as cherished souvenirs. Even today, museums and

Union General Nathaniel P. Banks was a victim of Jackson's lightning attacks.

archives across the south list such entries as "tail hairs from Stonewall Jackson's horse" in their databases.

Winchester didn't remain in Confederate hands for long. In addition to capturing thousands of dollars' worth of Federal food, equipment, weapons, and medical supplies, Jackson's army drew a massive response from Washington. The Confederates got exactly what they wanted. Washington canceled plans to reinforce the Union armies threatening Richmond. Federal officials feared that the natural extension of Jackson's expulsion of Banks from the Shenandoah Valley would be a march on Washington itself. Banks was still estimating Jackson's army at twice the size it actually was, so the fear seemed reasonable. Jackson was willing for Washington to be afraid, and he moved most of his troops north to the Potomac River to reinforce the perception that he might cross. The sides traded occasional artillery fire, but no serious fighting occurred and Jackson enjoyed the few days near Harpers Ferry.

Mid-afternoon on May 30, Jackson spent a few minutes observing an artillery duel between opposing batteries. Then, according to occasional staff member and full-time politician Alexander Boteler, "he dismounted from the old sorrel—his favorite war horse—and seating himself on the ground at the foot of a large tree, immediately in the rear of the battery, he presently resumed a more recumbent attitude and went to sleep." Boteler didn't mention whether Little Sorrel also lay down to sleep, but he often did, stretched out next to his master.

Abraham Lincoln himself made the next move. He ordered the reluctant John Frémont, recovered from his army's retreat at McDowell, to head east into the valley. The only slightly less reluctant Nathaniel Banks was told to head south again, and the highly annoyed Irvin McDowell was ordered to detach twenty thousand troops from his corps near Richmond and send them west. Jackson, Lincoln believed, would be tightly caught in a three-sided vise.

Jackson, while neither reluctant nor fearful, was sensible and made plans to withdraw from the banks of the Potomac River and head south, back into the heart of the Shenandoah Valley. Little Sorrel got a break. Jackson and some staff took the train as far as Winchester, leaving their horses behind. Jackson arrived late on the same day as the famous nap. By then, the Union troops from the east were almost at Front Royal and the chase was on.

Jackson called all his troops and horses back, climbed back aboard Little Sorrel, and hurried his army south, up the valley, toward safety. Frémont and McDowell, inexplicably, felt less urgency.

Perhaps it was the weather. The army was plagued by thunder, hail, and flooding rains during the trip up the valley. Unlike humans, horses usually don't mind rain, but most of them loathe slippery footing, whether from ice or mud. Little Sorrel was apparently not one of the mud-averse herd, and he carried Jackson steadily south without any problems. By now grass in the valley was fully in, so the horses had good grazing at the campsites chosen for the limited rest times. The soldiers may have been uncomfortable, tense, and often hungry, but Little Sorrel gained weight on the march.

Jackson decided to make his stand in the village of Port Republic, where two rivers join to create the South Fork of the Shenandoah River. His sixteen thousand troops began arriving in the area on June 6, just as the Union vise began to come together. He left six thousand men of Ewell's division near the Cross Keys tavern and moved a few miles southeast to the village of Port Republic to establish his headquarters.

His flamboyant cavalry commander Turner Ashby, whose exploits had alternately exasperated and delighted Jackson during the months they had been together, acted as the Valley Army's rear guard during the retreat from Winchester. His unit came under fire near the village of Harrisonburg late in the day of June 6 as Jackson and Ewell were establishing their campsites. After successfully fighting off a Union cavalry challenge, Ashby and his troopers faced a small Union infantry force trying to get between the cavalry and Jackson's infantry. Ashby's horse was shot and killed in the skirmish. Ashby continued leading his charge on foot, but a bullet pierced his heart almost immediately and he died instantly. It's not known if he was killed by the Union infantry or friendly fire.

Jackson had a connection to Turner Ashby's death that he might not have realized at the time. Ashby was not riding either of his famous stallions when horse and rider were killed at Harrisonburg. His most famous and best horse, the magnificent white Tom Telegraph, had been shot to death seven weeks earlier in the first days of the valley campaign. On June 6, Ashby had borrowed a horse from James Thomson, now an officer in his horse artillery. These batteries were designed for speed, using faster and better horses than the regular artillery batteries. Thomson liked horses and owned several good ones.

A year earlier, as a volunteer aide to Stonewall Jackson, Thomson had lent Jackson the very same horse to ride at the First Battle of Manassas. Both Jackson and the horse were wounded there, but each recovered quickly. The horse was not so lucky the second time.

Grieving troopers carried Ashby's body into Port Republic, where Jackson and his staff mourned his loss. On June 7, Jackson rode the handful of miles northwest to Cross Keys to maneuver troops, hoping to provoke action from Frémont's nearby force. Nothing happened and in the evening he returned to Madison Hall, the home of Dr. George Kemper, on the southern edge of Port Republic. The estate, standing on a hill overlooking the town, offered enough space for him and his staff and a large grassy paddock for their horses. Little Sorrel must have approved of the choice of headquarters.

Even though Jackson knew that two separate Union divisions totaling at least fifteen thousand men were close, with thousands more troops possibly moving south to join them, he felt safe at Madison Hall. The

estate stood at the end of the town, which itself lay on a peninsula connected by only one bridge to the mainland. The bulk of the Valley Army
remained on the mainland side in good, high position. But Jackson, his
staff, and their horses were in great danger of being trapped.

Jackson either didn't realize the peril or underestimated the inclina-
tions of the Union commanders. He was correct about John Frémont,
who would have had to go through Richard Ewell's six thousand soldiers
to get to Port Republic. But he was wrong about James Shields, the
Union general whose troops had defeated Jackson at Kernstown, the first
battle in the Shenandoah Valley, back in March.

Several days earlier Shields had sent out a squad of fast-moving cavalry and a handful of artillery pieces to capture Port Republic, which they
thought would be only lightly occupied by Confederates. They were right
about that, but the few Confederates there included Stonewall Jackson.

On Sunday, June 8, Jackson and staff members were enjoying a quiet
morning on a warm, dry day, standing on the porch at Madison Hall
watching their horses graze in the adjoining paddock. At 9:00 AM a
panicked Confederate cavalryman dashed up to report that Union cavalry was approaching Port Republic. Presumably Jackson realized at this
point just how vulnerable he had made himself.

Little Sorrel was grazing obliviously in a far corner of the paddock, so
Jackson set out on foot toward the main street of Port Republic, leaving
servant Jim Lewis to catch and saddle his horse. Aide Henry Kyd Douglas claimed that Jackson briefly borrowed his horse, then thought twice
about it. Within minutes, Jackson was mounted on Little Sorrel, rushing
to get across the only bridge that would prevent him from being trapped
on the peninsula.

Little Sorrel came through as usual, carrying Jackson on a dash
through the town and onto the bridge. Halfway across the river, a Union
shell struck the covered bridge just above their heads, but the two made
it through the onslaught of musket and artillery fire unscathed. They

also survived an artillery barrage aimed at them on the other side of the river. Jackson's army managed to fight off the invaders and save both their general and their supply wagons, although it was a near miss. The raiding party retreated.

One of the Union raiders later became famous in his own right, and part of his fame was due to another horse with a remarkable survival instinct. Irish immigrant Myles Keogh had joined General James Shields's staff as a captain in April 1862, and the fighting around Port Republic was the first action he saw during the Civil War.

At the end of the war Keogh remained in the regular army, saw duty in the west, and became one of the 268 soldiers killed with George Armstrong Custer at the Little Bighorn River in Montana on June 25, 1876. Keogh's horse, Comanche, whom he had acquired in 1868, is celebrated as the only U.S. Army survivor of Custer's immediate command. There were other horses that survived the battle, but they were euthanized during the cleanup, taken by the Indians, or simply forgotten. Comanche alone lived on. He survived until 1891, when he was believed to be about thirty years old. He was honored in retirement and mounted by a taxidermist after his death.

At nearly the same time that the Federal raiders arrived in Port Republic, the western part of the Union vise closed on Ewell's division four miles away in Cross Keys. Frémont, with nearly twelve thousand men, launched a half-hearted attack on the Confederate force of about six thousand, using only a fraction of his available troops. The Union attack was repulsed and defeated in a counterattack. The overmatched Frémont ordered a withdrawal from the battlefield, and Ewell was told to be ready to come to Jackson's support the following day rather than finish Frémont off.

That night, Ewell's aide Campbell Brown, who had suffered a shoulder wound during the battle, rode to Port Republic to carry a message to Jackson. Brown discovered just how useful an easy-gaited pacer could be in wartime. Brown's own horse was a trotter, whose gait he found unbearable as he rode alongside Jackson on Little Sorrel.

Brown thought he might faint from the pain and was forced to tell Jackson of his discomfort. He remembered for years the sight of Jackson riding comfortably along at the pace, while his shoulder was jarred by every step taken by his trotting horse. Jackson didn't offer to trade horses with the young officer, but Brown did write that Jackson looked "very compassionately" at him.

The advance regiments of Shields's army were now just to the north of Port Republic, and on the following day, June 9, Jackson and his army were on the move well before dawn. A day of attack, counterattack, and a second attack with Ewell's troops arriving from Cross Keys resulted in a lopsided Confederate victory.

Union forces lost nearly a third of their soldiers as killed, wounded, and captured, while Jackson's losses totaled 816 with an unusually high number killed. This was the largest single loss of troops during the valley campaign, but it did little to take away from the importance of Jackson's victory. After the battle, all Union forces withdrew and scattered, leaving Stonewall Jackson in control of the central and southern part of the Shenandoah Valley. Jackson was also left with a glowing reputation, North and South. Even his little red horse had become known beyond his own army. But most important, the two victories permitted Robert E. Lee, after giving brief thought to permitting Jackson to pursue the Union forces north into Maryland and Pennsylvania, to call the Valley Army east to help defend Richmond.

CHAPTER 7

River of Death

Port Republic turned out to be Stonewall Jackson's final battle in the Shenandoah Valley. The end of the campaign brought with it a few days of rest for the soldiers and horses. With Union forces scurrying north and west, some of the pressure fell away from the transportation routes for supplies. Soldiers ate better, but surprisingly, the horses began to experience shortages more typical of winter.

In a normal year, farmers would be cutting their first hay of the season at about the time the campaign ended. But hayfields in the Shenandoah Valley had been devastated by excessive grazing, early cutting, and damage done by marching and bivouacking armies. Little newly cut hay was to be had. Quartermasters found forage to haul in, mostly from Staunton to the southwest, but not as much or as often as Jim Lewis would have wanted for Little Sorrel and the other horses.

Little Sorrel had managed to keep on weight during a campaign that Jackson's chief of staff estimated to include four hundred miles of marching in addition to six battles. But he became thinner during the two weeks following Port Republic. When Jackson chose to take a long, difficult trip on horseback, he left Little Sorrel behind. Taking his own horse would have presented a logistical challenge, but Jackson may also have been concerned for the first time about the little horse's condition after nearly six months of near-constant travel.

Robert E. Lee, who took over command of the Army of Northern Virginia in early June, called on Jackson to hasten to a meeting with him and other generals at his headquarters near Richmond. The Federal Army of the Potomac had marched up the peninsula between the York and James Rivers and was now just a few miles from Richmond. Lee was always as much of an aggressor as Jackson, and he was making plans for a forceful response.

Jackson got his army in motion with a combination of railroad transport and marching, but he had to get himself to Richmond more quickly. He and a few staff members rode a postal car on the Virginia Central Railroad as far as Fredericks Hall, a small community that grew up around its railroad depot. Although the rail line continued to Richmond, Jackson chose to finish his trip on horseback, riding another fifty-two miles.

Jackson and his staff borrowed, commandeered, or purchased horses, depending on whose word you take, and rode them hard, changing mounts when needed. After fourteen difficult hours, the party arrived at a house less than two miles northeast of Richmond that served as Lee's headquarters. A four-hour conference followed, in which Lee outlined to his highest-ranking subordinates his plans to deal with the Union army under George McClellan that threatened the Confederate capital. Its exact size wasn't known, but Lee estimated that McClellan had between 100,000 and 150,000 soldiers. Lee's plan was bold and aggressive, but it was a highly complicated one that the exhausted Jackson may not have entirely grasped.

The conference ended as night fell on June 23, but instead of getting at least a modest night's sleep, Jackson climbed aboard his borrowed horse and headed back to his troops. The army had been in motion east-ward, so this leg of the trip was shorter. But Jackson was still forced to ride forty miles to reach the leading elements of his column, arriving at 10:00 AM on June 24. He had been ordered to be ready to attack the right wing of the Union army in less than two days, with the front of his badly strung-out column still a two full days' march away. It was a nearly impossible task, but Jackson seemed unconcerned.

The army made steady progress toward Richmond, Jackson again riding Little Sorrel, but progress was slower than it should have been. By nightfall on June 25, the day before Lee's planned assault, the vanguard of the Valley Army was still six miles short of where the entire column should have been to join the attack on schedule. Jackson remained sleepless and listless, although he probably managed a few brief naps aboard his steady little horse during the march.

By this point on June 25, George McClellan knew that Jackson was coming and he decided to strike first. The inconclusive Battle of Oak Grove involved only limited troops and did nothing to change Lee's mind about attacking McClellan, but it was the first of what became known as the Seven Days Battles, a series of encounters that were neither inconclusive nor limited. Jackson's army wasn't involved at Oak Grove, nor was he expected to be.

Very early on June 26 Jackson mounted Little Sorrel to lead his troops to what would become the second battle of the Seven Days. He soon met up with J. E. B. Stuart, whose cavalry had been assigned by Lee to protect Jackson's marching column. The meeting between the two major generals gives us a picture of what both Jackson and Little Sorrel looked like that day as they approached battle.

Lt. William W. Blackford of Fredericksburg, Virginia, had recently joined Stuart as an engineer and aide and had been looking forward to his first glimpse of the now-famous Stonewall Jackson. He was disappointed. Jackson wore, Blackford said, a "threadbare, faded, semi-military suit," in pitiful contrast to the splendid appearance of Stuart. Blackford saved some of his criticism for Little Sorrel. Jackson's horse was a "dun cob of rather sorry appearance," although Blackford admitted that the little horse was well built. The word "cob" is still used to describe a horse taller than a pony but shorter than a full-sized horse, usually fourteen to fourteen and a half hands and stocky. Blackford's depiction was accurate.

Blackford's description of Little Sorrel as "dun" does suggest to some that Jackson rode a different horse that day, but others who knew Little Sorrel well said he was indeed Jackson's mount, with one witness describing him as a "chestnut sorrel."

It was slow going for Jackson's men as they approached McClellan's line. The Army of the Potomac lay just a few miles east of Richmond along the sluggish Chickahominy River, a tributary of the James. It was swampy, muddy, mosquito-infested country that was terribly hard on man and horse. The Union army had suffered thousands of cases of what they called Chickahominy Fever, a disease that combined the worst symptoms of malaria and typhoid. One surgeon referred to the Chickahominy as "the river of death" for the epidemic of fevers among the Union soldiers.

The Confederates who had been waiting in the area for McClellan to act seemed a little less affected by fever, but hundreds of them became debilitated too. Most modern medical historians believe that Chickahominy Fever, which isn't recognized today as a specific illness, was a variant of typhoid, although a few hold out for simultaneous infection with malaria and typhoid. But identification doesn't matter. The bottom line was that the swamps of the Chickahominy lowlands were deadly, quite apart from the effects of musket balls and artillery shells.

Horses don't get either malaria or typhoid, but they do get other quite similar mosquito- and water-borne diseases and, more important in the short run, their hoofs suffer badly from the kind of deep, sucking mud that covered the bottoms of the wetlands that made up the Chickahominy swamp. Horses often became stuck and the movement of artillery and

The Chicahominy River swampland brought misery to soldier and horse alike.
JOHNSON AND BUEL, *BATTLES AND LEADERS OF THE CIVIL WAR, VOL. 2*

supply wagons was agonizingly slow. If the horses were forced to spend
more than a short time in the thick mud, they could suffer the rotting and
subsequent breakdown of the hoof wall, making them lame and useless.

In the case of Jackson's Valley Army, the change from the cool mountain weather of the late spring left them unprepared for what they found
in the swamps. A long march following three months of fighting up and

down the Shenandoah Valley made their condition even worse as they approached a rendezvous with Lee's army.

Jackson himself was unwell and unready for battle, for reasons that people still debate. The consensus is that he suffered from exhaustion and sleep deprivation growing out of the valley campaign. His smooth-gaited little pacing horse did allow him the occasional catnap on the march, but catnaps don't compare with deep sleep. Besides, nearly one hundred miles of Jackson's travel had been on borrowed trotting horses, most likely not nearly as comfortable as Little Sorrel.

He was also ill. According to his wife Anna, he wrote her later that he had been suffering from intermittent debilitating fever during the week of the Seven Days Battles. Jackson had never spent much time in the Chickahominy region, but he had contracted malaria as a child on an Ohio River adventure. He was also stationed in Florida a decade earlier and was almost certainly exposed to malaria then. Many regular army soldiers who were stationed in the South before, during, and after the war suffered malaria attacks off and on for the rest of their lives.

Whether it was exhaustion or illness, Jackson's performance in command on June 26 was not what it had been in the Shenandoah Valley. He was hampered by a lack of maps and poor directions from guides, unclear orders from Lee, and difficult travel conditions. A good horse could do only so much to help. Even Jackson admirers find it hard to explain his actions on that day.

The fast-moving, always-aggressive Jackson was slow and curiously passive. His troops were six hours behind Lee's schedule, which had called for them to strike McClellan's right wing early in the day. The delay prompted General A. P. Hill, who had been waiting impatiently for word from Jackson that his army was ready, to launch a premature attack in mid-afternoon. The resulting Battle of Mechanicsville (Beaver Dam Creek to the Union side) resulted in disastrous losses for the Army of Northern Virginia. Jackson failed to come to Hill's support even though he could hear the sounds of battle from the spot where he stopped his troops.

Oddly, Jackson did succeed in spite of his failure to act. McClellan knew the Valley Army was on the scene and Stonewall Jackson's fearsome reputation prompted McClellan to begin an immediate withdrawal of an army that had now swelled to 150,000. McClellan moved south, calling it a "change of base" rather than a retreat. But his southward move showed that he had lost confidence in his plans to take Richmond. McClellan never again regained the offensive.

On June 27, Lee's army, with Jackson now in place but still sluggish, began a slow pursuit of the huge Union force. Jackson was most likely aboard Little Sorrel, although aide Henry Kyd Douglas, who was often mistaken, said Jackson rode the other horse he had acquired at Harpers Ferry, the animal alternately known as Young Sorrel, Gaunt Sorrel, or Big Sorrel.

Other people on the march that day disagreed. John William Jones of the Thirteenth Virginia Infantry, who later became a prolific writer on his experiences in Jackson's army, knew Little Sorrel well. Jackson wore his "dingy uniform . . . his faded cadet cap tilting on his nose, mounted on his old sorrel." Jones and others noted the contrast when Jackson and Lee met in the late morning at Walnut Grove Church as the Confederates converged on the departing Union column. Lee, that "king of men" as Jones described him, rode his handsome gray charger with grace and calm, while Jackson, he thought, seemed "to be in a very bad humor" as he rode his unimpressive little horse away from the meeting.

Lee planned for a multipronged attack concentrating on the Union corps that had been left behind to protect the larger army as it withdrew. He expected Jackson to strike the Federal right and rear as the rest of the Army of Northern Virginia advanced on the Union front. If the plans worked, Lee would attack with 57,000 men, the largest force he would ever put together in the war. This was to be the Battle of Gaines's Mill, named for a local landmark, or the First Battle of Cold Harbor, named for a nearby crossroads, or the Battle of the Chickahominy, named for the slow, dark river that meandered through the area. The Gaines's Mill name is most commonly used.

Lee's attack began shortly after noon without Jackson. Lacking the services of Jedediah Hotchkiss, who had been left behind in the Shenandoah Valley to draw maps, Jackson had been led down an incorrect road and had been in no hurry to fix the problem. After the Valley Army's delayed arrival, Lee's coordinated assault didn't get under way until late in the afternoon. It was a disjointed attack, but the Confederates broke the Union lines and earned a hard-fought and expensive victory. More than 15,000 men on both sides were killed, wounded, or captured, and well over half the casualties were Confederates.

Gaines's Mill was a Confederate success and recognized as such. McClellan hurried his retreat and the Confederates were eager to claim their victory, although most of them realized they had lost, at least temporarily, a chance to destroy an important segment of the Union army by their late advance. Jackson got little credit for the victory even though his men had been involved in the final assault.

On June 28, action continued to the south, but it was a day of reorganization for Jackson and his troops. It wasn't a day of rest for Little Sorrel, though. Jackson still hadn't had much sleep, but he moved around the Confederate camps anyway. John Hinsdale, a young Lieutenant from North Carolina, was supervising a burial detail when he noticed the cheers of his men. Jackson hurried by on his "ugly horse," acknowledging the ovation by raising his cap. "He was evidently in a hurry," Hinsdale wrote in his diary. What Jackson was in a hurry doing is unknown, since memoirists and letter writers were understandably more interested in the battles of the Seven Days than the days of inactivity. Lee spent June 28 developing an elaborate plan to pursue the still-retreating Army of the Potomac.

McClellan had concentrated his army at Savage's Station on the Richmond and York River Railroad, which consisted of a house and out-buildings that had already been turned into a supply depot and military hospital complex for the Union army. On June 29, Jackson's army, after rebuilding a key bridge, was to march south and link up with another segment of the Army of Northern Virginia to strike a massive blow against Federal forces at Savage's Station. Lee hoped for a chance to decimate the entire Army of the Potomac at a site that appeared ideal. But a combination of slow bridge building, confusing orders, and possible lethargy meant that Jackson never arrived at the chosen battlefield before the fighting ended.

Only a portion of Lee's army went into battle at Savage's Station, greatly outnumbered by Federal defenders, but they did manage a stale-mate on the field. They were unable to stop the continued retreat of McClellan's forces, but each day saw the Federals leave Richmond farther behind. Lee was ready to pursue the next day and hoped to bring on a major engagement at a position of his own choosing.

On the morning of June 30, Jackson and Lee met at dawn. Robert Stiles, a young artilleryman who had been waiting for a good look at Stonewall Jackson, spotted a lone horseman riding well in advance of half a dozen other mounted men. It was Jackson, having this time arrived early for a meeting with Lee. Stiles was unimpressed. "Jackson and the little sorrel stopped in the middle of the road," Stiles wrote. "Horse and rider appeared worn down to the lowest level of flesh con-sistent with effective service."

A few seconds later, Stiles saw Lee and his "magnificent staff" appear. Now Stiles was full of admiration. Jackson and Little Sorrel were thin and dirty, he noted, while Lee and Traveller were flawless. "That morning every detail of the dress and equipment of himself and horse was absolute perfection," Stiles said of Lee. The difference between Lee and Jackson, he thought, could not have been more striking.

Some of Stiles's description of the meeting between the two generals was probably misremembered or fabricated. The artilleryman described Jackson as drawing a triangle with his toe in the dust in front of Lee and the commanding general studying the primitive map. No triangular movement was planned or happened that day, and enough dust to draw upon would have been hard to find after a night of heavy rain. But the description of Little Sorrel's condition sounds accurate.

The horse went into the Seven Days plump and sturdy but probably got little to eat and much work over the first five days. More than 200,000 troops, plus thousands of horses and their wheeled vehicles, were squeezed into an area of less than a hundred square miles. Good grazing was now limited and the almost constant fighting, skirmishing, and marching had ensured that little cut forage had been shipped in. A horse can lose condition dramatically in a week with too little food and too much movement, which is most likely what happened to Little Sorrel.

Lee's plan for the day was to trap McClellan's army at Glendale, where a crossroads formed a bottleneck to the Federal army as it hurried south to the safety of the James River. Lee hoped either to cut the Union army in two or destroy a big part of it.

The Confederates did catch up with the rear of the Union column, but the Federals had time to set a strong defensive line near Glendale. Only part of the advancing Confederates arrived, not including Jackson, and the resulting battle was at best a draw. Both sides suffered heavy casualties at the Battle of Glendale, the fifth or sixth battle of the Seven Days, depending on how you count, but the Army of the Potomac was able to save most of the column and continue its retreat south. Just three miles away was a location they believed would be provide a perfect position to stand and fight.

The next morning the Confederates discovered that McClellan's army, but not McClellan himself, who was safely aboard a gunship on the James, had securely settled itself on Malvern Hill, a fifty-foot

Malvern Hill is shown on the left of this contemporary drawing.
JOHNSON AND BUEL, *BATTLES AND LEADERS OF THE CIVIL WAR, VOL. 2*

plateau ideally suited for artillery placement. July 1 saw a battle that one eyewitness called "closer to murder than war" and Little Sorrel was right in the middle of it.

Two miles to the south side of the plateau, the James River allowed Union gunboats to hide, ready to move into position to fire on any Confederates who broke through. Steep slopes on the east and west made assault unlikely there. Lee believed that the defenders could be broken with massed Confederate artillery from the north, and then exploited with infantry. But he underestimated the dominance of the Union position and was unable to mass his own artillery to overcome it.

As Jackson led his infantry column toward Malvern Hill, they came under heavy artillery fire. After a quick deployment of his infantry, Jackson began directing the placement of artillery pieces. But Union shells blasted individual Confederate guns and gunners before they got their second shots off.

Jackson and Little Sorrel survived several near misses at Malvern Hill, most of them leaving them typically unruffled. Early in the battle, as Jackson conferred with General Richard Ewell, an artillery shell whistled by, missing Little Sorrel's head by inches. Jackson took no notice and the horse "kept on with its shambling gait," according to Ewell's aide Campbell Brown. Ewell noticed the close call, though, stopping his horse before they headed farther into artillery range. Jackson, Little Sorrel, and the others were covered with dust from the explosion of the shell on the ground in front of them.

Shortly afterward John Gittings, a distant relative of Jackson's from West Virginia, marched by with his unit. He watched Jackson direct the placement of an artillery battery that had already come under heavy fire. "He sat on his horse under this hurricane of canister and grape," Gittings remembered years later. He described how the men of his column would keep looking back at the general and his horse, "as if for the last time." But neither Stonewall Jackson nor his horse were finished quite yet.

A few hours later Little Sorrel realized even before Jackson did that some chances may not be worth taking. At another meeting with Ewell, the two generals dismounted. While they conferred in the company of several aides, a fragment of a Union shell blew a hole in the head of a courier's horse right next to them. The surviving horses shrieked and bolted, Little Sorrel for once joining in the equine alarm. Jackson held tightly to the reins, controlled the little horse, and calmly remounted. He directed the now perfectly composed Little Sorrel to a location farther to the rear.

After hours of lopsided artillery dueling, Lee ordered infantry to advance, but that movement led to even greater loss of life. By nightfall, the assault was over. More than five thousand Confederate soldiers were killed or wounded. Union losses, while substantial, were much less. There was no count of horses killed, but the figure rose well into the hundreds. Even though an effort was made to remove the artillery horses to the rear once the guns were placed, Union shells found many horses anyway.

The Battle of Malvern Hill was a resounding and devastating defeat for the Army of Northern Virginia, but it was hard to convince the soldiers of either side of that fact. McClellan abandoned the hill in the night, hurrying his army to his new and safer base at Harrison's Landing on the James. His campaign to capture Richmond by marching up the peninsula between the York and James Rivers was officially over.

In spite of the terrible loss at Malvern Hill and a couple of the lesser engagements of the Seven Days, Lee's army had succeeded in its primary goal. The Confederate capital was safe and, while Lee lost several chances to destroy McClellan's army, soldiers and civilians alike saw the week of battles as a great victory.

Lee was now a hero of the Confederacy and Jackson had lost none of his luster, even though his performance was less than stellar. Little Sorrel was also expanding his reputation. The word among the soldiers was that Stonewall's little horse might not be a beauty, but he was brave and tough and steady, everything you could possibly want in a warhorse.

Jackson gave the soldiers of the Army of Northern Virginia a good look at his horse during a march toward Harrison's Landing in pursuit of McClellan three days after Malvern Hill. Artillery officer William Pogue enjoyed the sight and sound of Jackson "bareheaded on Little Sorrel at his best speed" sweeping by the marching column, drawing cheers so loud that they echoed long after the two were out of sight.

A few days later, Lee, fully convinced that McClellan presented no immediate threat to Richmond, withdrew most of his troops, including Jackson's army, to the west. He had already proved that he believed in the adage that the best defense is a good offense, and his instinct to attack moved to the forefront. In this, Stonewall Jackson agreed completely.

CHAPTER 8

Risk and Redemption

Stonewall Jackson left the Chickahominy swamp as he had arrived, riding his easygoing little pacing horse. After Malvern Hill, Jackson was ill, exhausted, and not particularly pleased about what had happened. The summer of 1862 wasn't yet at its halfway mark and the soaring temperatures had already taken their toll on man and horse alike. The swampy ground on either side of the Chickahominy had contributed to the misery.

But the still unwell Jackson now faced many more miles in the saddle. The prospect of hours aboard the rough-gaited Big Sorrel was unappealing, so Jackson again chose Little Sorrel, even though the horse had been heavily used for weeks. Jackson and his staff left their camp twenty-five miles from Richmond just after nine o'clock on the night of July 8. Most of his fourteen thousand men were already well under way. Henry Kyd Douglas was one of the sleepy staff members who rode along with Jackson, noticing the general nodding off and trusting Little Sorrel not to let him fall.

Jackson was known throughout the war for his naps aboard the sure-footed Little Sorrel.
RANDOLPH, *THE LIFE OF GEN. THOMAS J. JACKSON*, 1876

After two days of marching, Jackson's troops arrived at the farm of Hugh Augustus Watt, a cousin of the Hugh Watt on whose farm the Battle of Gaines's Mill had taken place. This Hugh was most likely unhappy to see an army arrive, even though he was quickly assured that no battle was in the offing. Jackson set up his headquarters tent in the Watt front yard and Little Sorrel enjoyed his first good grazing in two weeks. The weather remained hot and humid, but it was delightful by comparison to the dismal swamps of the Chickahominy River bottom.

Hugh Watt was the uncle of Hugh A. White, a young officer of the Stonewall Brigade, who was permitted to enjoy meals in his uncle's farmhouse. It was a welcome quiet time for Little Sorrel. The Watt farm was less than three miles from Richmond, but Jackson spent most of his time in camp. He called on the services of Little Sorrel only once during the long weekend near Richmond.

Jackson and Little Sorrel traveled the three miles to the capital on Sunday, July 13, on what Douglas called "official business." The business was momentous. The day before Lee had received word that John Pope, commander of a newly reorganized unit of the Federal army now known as the Army of Virginia, had begun moving some of his troops south. Lee responded with a reorganization of his own, giving Jackson the left wing of the Army of Northern Virginia. Jackson was told to head north and west to try to intercept the leading Union forces, while Lee retained the larger part of his army near Richmond.

After a stop in the city for church services, Jackson remounted Little Sorrel and took off at a gallop, according to Charles Blackford, a cavalry officer borrowed from J. E. B. Stuart for courier and scouting duty. The road back to camp was clogged with wagons. Jackson, becoming impatient to get back to his troops, led his staff on a shortcut across a farmer's field of ripe oats.

The hoofs of the hurrying Little Sorrel and the other horses cut up the crop. The infuriated farmer, already on hand to keep a wary eye on the military wagons passing his property, swore loudly at the group of riders, Sunday or not. "I intend to have every damned one of you arrested!" the farmer shouted, according to Blackford. The oaths stopped when Jackson revealed his identity. The farmer immediately gave the horses permission to travel wherever they wanted to in his oat field. Little Sorrel would have certainly preferred to sample a little of the crop rather than gallop across it.

But orders were out and a more pressing duty was at hand. The left wing was to move toward Gordonsville, a vital road and rail crossroads in Orange County north of Richmond. Later that day, Stonewall Jackson's wing of the Army of Northern Virginia, with Jackson and Little Sorrel in front, marched out of the camp at the Watt farm and into an immediate future that all knew would include battle. The goal was the new Union army that Lee believed was consolidating in central Virginia. Jackson was to prevent them from moving against Richmond at the least and, at the best, drive them back to Washington.

The trip began in chaos. Jackson had planned to transport his troops to Gordonsville by train, but a break in the line sent some of the regiments to Richmond to take a different line and others on a march to a point on the rail line beyond the break. Some made the sixty-mile trip on foot, with regiments arriving in Gordonsville over the course of several days.

Jackson himself appeared on July 19 and remained in the area for three weeks, first in Gordonsville itself and then south of the town. He needed the respite after his illness and exhaustion.

Mapmaker Jedediah Hotchkiss, who had spent the weeks of the Seven Days battles in the Shenandoah Valley, observed that Jackson looked poorly after his time on the Chickahominy. Hotchkiss doesn't mention Little Sorrel, who presumably looked pretty much like he always did.

But he and the other horses enjoyed their three weeks in Orange and Louisa Counties, where they found plenty of grass and recently cut hay. Little Sorrel soon became his usual rotund self, and memoirs that cover this period never refer to him as "gaunt."

The change of calendar from July to August brought more of the same in terms of weather. Temperatures in the upper eighties and into the nineties every day of the first week of the month caused suffering to man and horse alike. Even Hotchkiss, who was inclined to refer to every clear summer day as fine, began to describe a "warm fine day" and finally "a very warm day" on August 5. Two days later, Jackson moved his headquarters to the north and east. As usual, only Jackson knew exactly where they were headed, but most assumed it was to meet at least part of John Pope's army.

Now they faced dust as well as heat as they marched to battle. What Jackson had hoped to be a lightning march in the manner of the Shenandoah campaign turned into nearly two days of dust-clogged misery and painfully slow progress. Jackson had himself as well as the weather to blame. He failed to inform the commander of his largest division, a late coming addition to the Confederate left wing, of a change in plans for the order of the march.

That was Major General A. P. Hill's huge six-brigade Light Division, almost the size of an army corps, which made no progress at all on August 8. The two smaller divisions, slowed by their own supply trains, traveled only a few miles themselves. Jackson was still uncharacteristically lethargic himself. But he knew his only hope of success was to attack a small advance portion of John Pope's massive Army of Virginia before Pope was able to get his much larger segment up to join the leading brigades.

The Union vanguard was held by an eight-thousand-man corps headed by Nathaniel Banks, the still-angry target of Jackson's accomplishments earlier in the year in the Shenandoah Valley. Because of the slow forward progress of the Confederate troops, the Union cavalry quickly and easily spotted the movement. Banks, who had moved south in person, was well aware that Stonewall Jackson was on the way.

Fortunately for Jackson, he remained aboard the quick Little Sorrel and was able to maintain some contact with his strung-out column. After a long and frustrating day, the least successful march he had ever led, Jackson and his staff spent the night of August 8 at a farmhouse owned by James Garnett, a spot near the center of his scattered brigades.

"The grass in the yard was very long and nice," noted Jedediah Hotchkiss, who was referring to its suitability for comfortable camping. Jackson himself didn't sample the comforts of the grass, opting instead to spend the night on the front porch of the house. He maintained his reluctance to stay inside civilian homes while on the march, but the lawn apparently didn't appeal to him. Little Sorrel and the other staff horses enjoyed the untrimmed grass for other reasons.

The leading regiments moved out after dawn. Jackson mounted Little Sorrel and headed to the front of a wing that now totaled twenty-two thousand men. He was preceded by only a modest cavalry unit—not including Stuart—and hoped they would give him plenty of advance notice when they ran into Nathaniel Banks's division. He was unhappy with the cavalry commander and had already asked Stuart to join him from his assignment with Lee around Richmond.

The temperature had reached well into the eighties when Jackson stopped Little Sorrel at a farmhouse to wait for word from the cavalry and pull nonessential wheeled vehicles out of the line of march. The marching column continued on a northeast course toward Culpeper, still nearly eight miles away. Jackson remained convinced that Culpeper was the place where Union General John Pope planned to concentrate his Army of Virginia.

While waiting at the farmhouse, Jackson and Little Sorrel took a detour to lead the staff on a trip up a hill half a mile to the east. Jackson hoped to get a better idea of what was happening ahead, realizing that much activity would be hidden in the undulating hills in this section of the piedmont of Virginia. In spite of the hazy heat and the dust kicked up by his own column, he saw Union cavalry, which he had expected, and he believed he saw evidence of enemy infantry and artillery, which he did not expect, at least not yet.

By now, at mid-day, Jackson already suspected that the vanguard of Pope's army was already somewhere south of Culpeper. He had heard sporadic firing from cavalry skirmishers since early morning and some soldiers thought they had heard artillery. At nearly the exact moment that Jackson began to believe that a division of the Union army was here and not at Culpeper, artillery fire broke out, and suspicion suddenly became certainty. The staff urged Jackson to withdraw from his hill.

"[S]everal shots were fired at the General before he got back to the Culpeper Road," wrote Charles Blackford in a letter to his wife a few days later. It was the first of many times that day that Jackson and, by association, Little Sorrel escaped death.

The battle variously known as Cedar Mountain, Cedar Run, Slaughter Mountain, and Major's Gate was under way. The highest point on what was to become the battlefield was known locally as both Cedar Mountain, for its vegetation, and Slaughter Mountain, for the family that lived on the slope. Cedar Run was a shallow, marshy stream that meandered over the territory, and Major's Gate was an entrance to a lane that at first appeared to Confederate officers be an important landmark but proved not to be as the battle unfolded. Historians have mostly settled on Cedar Mountain to identify the battle, although many of the participants thought that Slaughter Mountain better described what happened there.

Cedar Mountain, shown in 1865, provided both a good view and dangerous exposure.
ANDREW J. RUSSELL PHOTOGRAPH, LIBRARY OF CONGRESS

The duel between the artillery of Stonewall Jackson's wing of the Confederate Army of Northern Virginia and that of Nathaniel Banks's corps of the Union Army of Virginia raged for more than two hours, and Jackson spent most of that time in motion on the back of his indefatigable little horse. He arranged his infantry into a position to advance once the artillery had done its work. He sent messages, the most important to the still-trailing Light Division of A. P. Hill. He rechecked the disposition of the regiments at the front. He again searched for high ground to take a look at the lay of the land and the location of the Union forces.

Although any man or horse on the battlefield was in danger from flying shells, Jackson put himself and Little Sorrel in extra jeopardy halfway through the artillery duel. John Blue, a cavalry lieutenant from western Virginia, had been assigned to Jackson as a courier and was amazed at what he saw of the famous general's actions. Lt. Blue was among the officers Jackson led up the northern slope of Cedar Mountain, barely within the lines of the Confederate right.

Blue noted that Jackson sat there on Little Sorrel, "immobile as a statue," as he watched the artillery battle through his binoculars. Shells exploded around the group, killing one horse and severely wounding two others. Jackson seemed not to notice, and Little Sorrel remained stationary as well.

Jackson eventually agreed to a timid suggestion from a staff member that he leave such an exposed position, leading the group a short distance down the hill. He stopped, then sent the others on their way.

"They will hardly fire at a single horseman," Jackson said as he calmly continued his study of the Union forces within their full view and cannon range. Little Sorrel seemed not to mind that the other horses were permitted to seek cover while he was not.

John Blue developed an admiration for Little Sorrel as well as for Stonewall Jackson that afternoon. Jackson sat alone on the slope of Cedar

Mountain for just a few minutes after the other riders left. When he finally came down to his waiting staff he received word that Brigadier General Charles Sidney Winder had been incapacitated by what proved to be a fatal wound. Winder, commander of Jackson's old Stonewall Brigade, had just been promoted to division command and was a vital link in the line of battle. He was an old Lexington friend of Jackson's and that, as well as the fact that his division was assigned to the very front of the Confederate infantry line, shook Jackson.

Jackson and Little Sorrel raced half a mile north to the scene of Winder's wounding, the staff struggling to keep up with the pair. Blue observed that Jackson and his little horse jumped two fences to reach the forward-most infantry, now trying to adjust to a sudden change in leadership. He noticed nothing wrong with Jackson's form at the jump, although fellow West Point cadets had years before loudly criticized the young Jackson. Blue mentioned neither too-short stirrups nor a seat too far forward.

Blue was apparently impressed enough with the jumping prowess displayed by Little Sorrel to mention it in his memoirs, printed in a West Virginia newspaper near the end of the century. But he would have been even more impressed if he had known that pacing horses, especially those with the sloping croup and high withers of Little Sorrel, rarely have the strength in the hindquarters to jump really well.

Jackson spent only a few minutes at the far left before returning to a more central position. He seemed not to have noticed mistakes in the disposition of his line of battle, although he couldn't have missed the confusion that resulted from Winder's wounding. He presumably didn't realize that he had misread the position and intentions of the Union troops.

The result was near disaster. Just as Jackson attempted to deal with the flaws in the Confederate line, Union infantry struck a stunning and unexpected blow. A full brigade hit the side and back of the Confederate left, staggering the Stonewall Brigade, which was thrown first into disarray and then into terror. The famous unit staggered and partially broke, hundreds of soldiers rushing to the rear.

Then came one of the iconic moments of Stonewall Jackson's military career, and he was—appropriately—with Little Sorrel when it happened. Seeing the disintegration of the Stonewall Brigade and the catastrophe it might mean, Jackson dashed to the site of the break and drew his sword. Or, to be accurate, he tried to draw his sword but found it impossible to remove from its scabbard. The blade may have rusted or it may have caught on something in the leather, but Jackson was unable to get it out. So he unbuckled the scabbard and raised the sword over his head, scabbard and all. For emphasis, he grabbed a Confederate battle flag from a startled color bearer.

"Rally, men," he shouted. "Where's my Stonewall Brigade? Forward!" There are different versions of Jackson's exhortation, but the stories all show the same effect.

"As he dashed to the front," wrote Charles Blackford to his wife two days later, "our men followed with a yell and drove everything before them." He added that Jackson was usually "an indifferent and slouchy looking man," but now "his whole person was changed."

Blackford claimed the men would have followed Jackson into the jaws of death itself, which seemed not out of the question here in the shadow of Cedar Mountain. And Blackford gave some of the credit to Little Sorrel. "Even the old sorrel horse seemed endowed with the style and form of an Arabian," he told his wife.

The Confederate line regained its composure, reformed, and drove Banks's corps back from whence it came. How much was due to Jackson's inspiration and how much to the fortuitous arrival of A. P. Hill's massive Light Division could be debated.

Exchanges of artillery fire continued. But except for a foolish and futile charge by a Pennsylvania cavalry battalion that killed a few dozen troopers and even more horses, the Battle of Cedar Mountain was over. Pope liked to think he had a victory, since Jackson's march north was stopped, at least temporarily. But Jackson was left in control of the field, and that was the ruling definition of victory at the time. Admirers of Stonewall Jackson were convinced that the dominant Stonewall of the valley had reemerged, overlooking mistakes that so nearly led to disaster.

If it had been possible to ask the surviving horses of Cedar Mountain battle, they might have singled out Little Sorrel as the hero. As he often did, he performed well beyond what anybody might expect of a little pacing horse, facing without flinching what even a horse should realize was mortal danger. Again he was tireless, covering a dozen or more miles under fire over the course of a very long day. Jackson and Little Sorrel

The first public look at equine carnage in the Civil War came from Cedar Mountain.
TIMOTHY O'SULLIVAN PHOTOGRAPH, LIBRARY OF CONGRESS

slept well that night, lying down with the rest of the staff and their horses on long grass just beyond the battlefield.

Jackson had ordered the troops to camp in place, not knowing whether Banks had been reinforced enough to renew the battle on August 10 or if he himself would be in a position to pursue the Union army. But J. E. B. Stuart arrived in the night, did a proper reconnaissance, and told Jackson that Banks was being heavily reinforced. Jackson received information from another source, a captured Union sergeant with good sources, that Pope was likely to withdraw north.

Charles Blackford, who had captured the talkative sergeant, brought his prisoner to Jackson's headquarters, where staff members stood waiting with their horses outside the headquarters tent. As Little Sorrel waited in front for Jackson to emerge, Blackford noticed the sergeant caressing the horse's rump and running his left hand through his tail.

Little Sorrel, as usual, didn't mind the attention, but Blackford soon noticed that each of the prisoner's left-handed strokes took away a handful of the horse's tail hairs. Jackson emerged and looked at the scene with surprise. "Why are you tearing the hair out of my horse's tail?" Blackford quoted Jackson as asking. The sergeant told Jackson that each of Little Sorrel's hairs would bring a dollar in New York. Blackford reports Jackson as being both amused and pleased.

Henry Kyd Douglas told an almost identical anecdote about a prisoner and Little Sorrel that supposedly took place a month later, but Blackford's was the first and almost certainly the most accurate, since it was included in a letter written just eight days after Cedar Mountain, not in memoirs completed decades later. It's possible that both stories are true, but tail hairs of Little Sorrel are commonly found in museums today, so somebody pulled plenty of hairs out of his tail at various points during his long life. The Union sergeant was sent off to prison still in possession of his valuable red hairs.

By that night, Jackson realized that John Pope's Army of Virginia would number more than fifty thousand when consolidated. He began to withdraw the Confederate troops from the Cedar Mountain area, returning to his previous campsites near Gordonsville, where there was better access to provisions for men and grazing for horses. The next move would be up to Robert E. Lee.

Over the next ten days, Lee put together as much of his army as he dared give up and sent it to Jackson's wing. Lee was convinced that the recalcitrant and exceptionally slow George McClellan would eventually be prodded out of his comfort zone and move to join John Pope, creating a Federal force of well over one hundred fifty thousand, a figure that Lee couldn't begin to match.

A quick move was vital, but various problems with logistics made that impossible. A restless Jackson slept poorly and did some personal scouting. All evidence suggests that he continued to ride Little Sorrel during this period even though the horse certainly deserved a rest. Jackson may have had no other horse of his own available.

Aide Henry Kyd Douglas, in memoirs written years later, described an incident that took place during Cedar Mountain that would have affected Jackson. Anna Jackson's younger brother, Joseph Morrison, had joined Jackson's staff shortly before the battle. During the fighting young Morrison, according to Douglas, had joined his brother-in-law in an attempt to rally the troops. According to Douglas, Morrison, riding one of the general's horses, was sprinkled with blood from a wound in the jaw suffered by the horse.

The horse may have been Big Sorrel, the only other horse Jackson was known to own at this point. If so, the horse survived the wound, which must have been minor. A serious injury in the mouth or jaw would have made it impossible for the horse to eat for weeks, and we know Big Sorrel survived the war.

There are other possibilities. The wounded horse may have been an animal purchased by or given to Jackson but not noted in letters or memoirs. The wound, or even the horse itself, if not Big Sorrel, may not have existed at all. Douglas was a colorful and engaging writer, but he exaggerated, embroidered, and occasionally invented incidents. No other memoir writer mentions the wounded horse, nor does Jackson's widow, who would certainly have known about her brother being aboard a wounded horse owned by her husband.

Whether Big Sorrel was injured or not, Jackson chose the trustworthy and unflagging Little Sorrel for transportation as the Army of Northern Virginia prepared to attack John Pope's army again. Sometimes Little Sorrel proved more tireless than his rider.

On the night of August 19 Jackson decided to conduct a cavalry scout himself. He led a party of two dozen men on horseback along dark narrow roads and by-paths, looking for something that nobody but Jackson had any idea about. "It was one of those freaks which sometimes seize him," noted Captain Blackford, "and which make many people think he is somewhat deranged."

It was fortunate that night that Jackson was on Little Sorrel's back, since once again he fell asleep in the saddle and safely emerged from the scout anyway. The party found nothing along the hidden by-ways, but at daybreak they reached the top of a mountain and were treated to a view of John Pope's entire army camped for several miles in each direction around Culpeper.

The view was useful, but the route Jackson took was not. A marching army couldn't use the narrow paths taken by the small party on horseback. Blackford concluded that Jackson was "wandering in another world." It was fortunate that he was aboard Little Sorrel as he wandered.

Jackson's wing began a steady move north the next day as Pope and his army continued their own march. During the following days, the two bodies sent out cavalry to scout and skirmish and occasionally trade fire. On August 22 Jackson's wing approached the Rappahannock River and came under artillery fire from the other side. A cannonball struck and killed a horse whose nose was alongside Little Sorrel's rump. Both Jackson and Little Sorrel saw the other horse fall dead but paid no attention.

Charles Blackford commented on both Jackson and Little Sorrel in a letter home. He told his wife that it would take half a dozen bombshells to wake them up, but "when once roused there is no stopping either one of them until the enemy has retreated."

Jackson and his wing completed their fifty-five-mile march on July 26 when they pulled into Bristoe Station on the critical Orange and Alexandria Railroad. As far as anyone reported, Little Sorrel carried Jackson the entire distance. After damaging trains and tracks, Jackson sent two infantry regiments and Stuart's cavalry on to Manassas Junction, four miles away, which had become the main supply depot for John Pope's army. They were followed by more troops.

The hungry and poorly clothed Confederates gorged on Union supplies at the lightly defended depot. Union headquarters, receiving word that the Manassas station had been attacked, sent four New Jersey regiments by train to take care of what they thought was a small raiding party. They were shocked to find the terrifying Stonewall Jackson there with a huge force.

It was a rout, but one that turned into another near miss for Jackson and Little Sorrel. Jackson, who rarely felt sorry for anybody, must have experienced some remorse for what was happening to the New Jersey soldiers and pulled out a pocket handkerchief. He rode forward on Little Sorrel and waved the white cloth, calling for the Union soldiers to surrender. They refused and Jackson and Little Sorrel were fired upon. "I heard the minie [ball] as it whistled by him," wrote nineteen-year-old cannoneer Edward A. Moore from Jackson's own Lexington, Virginia.

Jackson called for his troops to resume full artillery attack, devastating the four Union regiments, killing their general, and forcing the surviving soldiers to retreat. But it became obvious that the railroad depots couldn't be protected for long from a Union force that already could include seventy-five thousand men even without the addition of McClellan, if he ever got there. Jackson ordered his men to pack what they could and set fire to the rest of the supplies.

He led his men on a perilous night march north, moving to a position from which he could both monitor Federal army movement and escape, should something go terribly wrong. If he was fortunate, he might also draw John Pope into battle on a favorable ground. Jackson's wing marched right out of the view of even the best scouts from Pope's army. Pope convinced himself that Jackson had disappeared because he was retreating to the Shenandoah Valley.

Jackson settled his men on a hidden ridge along an unfinished railroad embankment just northwest of the field of the First Battle of Manassas. There they stayed, near a little crossroads named Groveton on a farm owned by the Brawner family, until the afternoon of August 28. At mid-afternoon Jackson received word that a Union column was marching east below his hidden troops. He decided to take a look himself and, to the horror of watching staff members, rode Little Sorrel onto a rise within plain view and easy musket range of the passing Union regiments. It was one of several times he had exposed himself and his horse to great danger and again successfully challenged fate.

Abner Doubleday, leading a brigade of New Yorkers in the Union column, claimed later that he suspected the shabby rider on the odd little horse was a Rebel officer, but he was overruled by other officers in the column, who thought it was just a poor farmer. Doubleday said they later learned from Confederate prisoners that it wasn't just an officer but "Stonewall Jackson reconnoitering our movements."

Jackson exposed himself and Little Sorrel to Abner Doubleday's troops on the ridge in the rear of the drawing of Groveton Crossroads.
JOHNSON AND BUEL, *BATTLES AND LEADERS OF THE CIVIL WAR, VOL. 2*

Jackson and Little Sorrel turned suddenly and returned to the safety of a stand of trees, where he ordered his men to attack the passing column. It turned into a strange and brutal battle in which both sides suffered terrible losses and neither could press an advantage. Jackson rode near the front lines for most of the two and a half hours of the battle, but he and Little Sorrel again emerged uninjured.

Jackson's most important division commander, Richard Ewell, wasn't so lucky. He suffered an injury that led to the amputation of a leg and his absence from the army for nearly a year.

Little was gained and much lost in this brief battle known alternately as Groveton and Brawner's Farm, but one thing did result. The Second Battle of Bull Run was under way, a battle that would become one of the great accomplishments of the Civil War careers of both Stonewall Jackson and Robert E. Lee.

Jackson's troops remained in place the night of August 28, and on August 29, Pope began repeated assaults on the Confederates. Each was stopped, with heavy losses on both sides. Pope apparently failed to notice when James Longstreet's right wing came up later in the day. When Pope renewed his attack on August 30, his troops were first struck by a massive show of artillery force. Then, Jackson and Longstreet began a counterattack that drove Pope's troops east, across the old battlefield, and all the way across Bull Run. Only a better-organized Union army prevented a repeat of the disaster of the First Battle of Manassas.

Jackson apparently rode Little Sorrel on August 29, but it's unclear what happened after that. The horse disappears from the record sometime after August 29 and stays gone for a little more than a week. Some of the memoirists who were most closely associated with Jackson were away themselves during this period and not in a position to report on their general's horse. Charles Blackford went home with a fever. Jedediah Hotchkiss was on duty but spent little time with Jackson on the second and third days of the battle. Henry Kyd Douglas was there and is the only source for the idea that Little Sorrel was not used the final day.

Douglas wrote after the war that on August 30 he was asked by Jackson to exchange horses with him as the battle raged. Jackson, he said, was riding a small bay horse captured the previous day from the Union army, a horse who refused to go forward and was otherwise misbehaving. Douglas, who had been ordered to carry a message to Longstreet asking for help, made the change and then had trouble himself with the bay. He doesn't say why Jackson was riding a captured horse or what happened to Little Sorrel.

But there is some evidence that Jackson used Little Sorrel for at least some of August 30 after the incident described by Douglas. Infantryman Gus McClendon of the Fifteenth Alabama claimed in his memoirs to have seen Jackson riding his famous horse that day as Jackson and Longstreet began their counterattack against Pope. "He came on top of the railroad embankment, mounted on Old Sorrel at a slow gallop followed by one courier," McClendon wrote. He went on to describe in great detail

Jackson's "dusty, dingy, faded gray uniform" and the "legs of the pants stuffed into the legs of an old pair of boots." Both writers offer convincing detail, so it's possible that both were right and Jackson switched horses during the battle. But one of the two may have been wrong. McClendon didn't really know Jackson but had seen him many times. Douglas knew him much better, but his memoirs include plenty of embroidery and some apparent falsehoods.

In later writings Douglas says that Little Sorrel was temporarily lost or stolen at about this time, a situation he claimed lasted more than two weeks. Other observers reported Jackson aboard his favorite horse much sooner than two weeks after Second Manassas. Douglas wrote often about and was fond of Little Sorrel, so his word has to be taken seriously. Other writers who were involved with Jackson at the time did note the horse's absence at various points, but none of them refer to Little Sorrel being lost or stolen, including Anna Jackson, who would probably have been told the truth by her husband. Many later writers have taken Douglas at his word and repeated the "lost or stolen" story.

John Newton Lyle of Lexington, who had served under Jackson since the previous summer, wrote in his memoirs that "there was rejoicing in the heart of the General's military family when Old Sorrel was stolen." But Lyle released his memoirs in 1903, well after the Douglas story appeared in print. It's unclear whether he remembered it independently or was repeating Douglas's version.

There are several possibilities for Little Sorrel's absence from August 30 (or August 29, if McClendon was wrong) to the first or second week in September. Being stolen is the least likely. There were more impressive and less identifiable horses to be had, including dozens of captured Union mounts.

There is a slight chance that Little Sorrel was wounded on August 30, leading to the switch to the recalcitrant bay. Survivors of the Black Horse Troop, a cavalry company assigned to provide couriers for Jackson during the battle, remembered that one of their troop, Private Erasmus Helm Junior, suffered a mortal wound while holding Stonewall Jackson's horse during the fighting on August 30. It's possible that the horse was hit as well. Nobody mentions a wound to Little Sorrel, and that would surely have been worth noting unless it was extremely minor. But a wound doesn't explain why Gus McClendon saw Jackson on Little Sorrel after Douglas claimed he had switched horses with the general.

Little Sorrel's absence probably happened because somebody, possibly not Jackson, believed that Little Sorrel had finally had enough. He had been in almost constant use for months, carried Jackson in a dozen battles, and been fed irregularly.

The most likely scenario is this: someone either convinced Jackson to give the horse a break or independently arranged for him to be misplaced to the rear. The culprit may have been Jim Lewis, who was known to be solicitous of the little horse, but that would have been an extreme step for a slave to take, even one as well treated as Lewis was. A staff officer would have been a more likely perpetrator of the disappearance if it were a deliberate act.

Why he stayed missing so long is harder to figure out. Little Sorrel may have become mixed up in the baggage trains after being sent to the rear during the day or at the close of action on August 30. Although the major fighting ended at sundown and the battle turned out to be over, it was hardly a time of calm. Heavy rain began to fall, adding to the inevitable confusion brought by darkness.

The Confederate commanders thought that Pope might regroup and attack the next day. If not, they intended to pursue the Union army to try to block it from reaching the protection of Washington, D.C. There was unavoidable disorder in the rear and no time for Jackson to order someone to find his horse or go looking himself.

Pope began to pull his troops away from the field on the night of August 30, but he was soon urged by Washington to renew the attack within the next few days. He didn't want to, but he did begin preparations for a direct assault. The Confederates acted first. On August 31, Lee had sent Jackson and Longstreet on a circular route to prevent Pope from reaching Washington. At sunset, still in the pouring rain, Jackson's wing reached Ox Run in Fairfax County, near a plantation named Chantilly, where they settled in for blocking action. But the Union army attacked on September 1, initiating the brief and bloody Battle of Chantilly. What horse Jackson used that day is unreported.

Jackson failed in his attempt to stop Pope from reaching Washington, but the battle is considered a Confederate victory since the Army of Northern Virginia was left in control of the field. It was enough of a victory that Lee was emboldened to do what Jackson had been urging him to do for months: invade the North.

The army left Chantilly for its northern adventure with Little Sorrel in an unaccustomed position. He was out of contact with Stonewall Jackson, apparently trailing behind with the supply wagons. Jackson would soon realize how much he had come to rely on his little horse.

CHAPTER 9

Invasion

Stonewall Jackson rode to battle in the North aboard borrowed horses. Two members of the Black Horse Troop loaned him fine black mounts and somebody gave him a cream-colored horse to ride across the Potomac River on September 5. Several observers noted the different horses but didn't consider it curious that he wasn't riding his now-famous sorrel. It may have been common knowledge where the little sorrel was, or perhaps everyone thought there was nothing significant in the general giving a heavily used horse a rest.

But the absence of Little Sorrel, whether mysterious or not, led to a potentially serious problem for Jackson. After crossing the Potomac, the column marched ten miles north, stopping for the night of September 5 at a place the memoir writers identified as Three Springs, a few miles south of Frederick, Maryland. This was probably the Three Springs Farm of Thomas N. Harwood, a wealthy landowner whose son William Thomas Harwood served in the Thirty-Fifth Virginia Cavalry, a partisan

Jackson crossed the Potomac aboard a borrowed horse with Little Sorrel some-where to the rear.
ALFRED WAUD DRAWING, LIBRARY OF CONGRESS

unit that included men from Maryland. They had seen heavy service in the Shenandoah Valley campaign.

During the afternoon or evening of September 5, a wealthy local man presented Jackson with a magnificent gray mare. The Confederate sympathizer may have been Thomas Harwood, the owner of the farm where Jackson set up headquarters. The general was pleased to receive the handsome horse. Whether it was because, as Henry Kyd Douglas claimed, Little Sorrel was missing or, as Anna Jackson later wrote, he was happy to have a good-looking mount, Jackson gratefully accepted the gift. There are differing stories of what happened next.

Douglas's version is most often repeated. He doesn't mention Jackson trying out the mare on the night of September 5 but believed she was saddled the following morning as the troops were ready to continue their march. "The next morning," Douglas wrote in *Century Magazine* in 1886, "he mounted his new steed, but when he touched her with his spur the loyal and undisciplined beast reared straight into the air and, standing erect for a moment, threw herself backward, horse and rider rolling on the ground." Douglas says Jackson lay still for several minutes before he could be carried to an ambulance for the day's march. He remained in his tent for a full day after camp was set up just south of Frederick.

Samuel Bassett "Chester" French was a military advisor to Confederate president Jefferson Davis and an occasional volunteer aide to Stonewall Jackson. He was fond of horses and his gossipy memoirs give a lengthy version of what happened to Jackson and the gift mare. French's version is similar to Douglas's, except French gave no reason for Little Sorrel's absence. French wrote that after the accident Jackson immediately gave the gray mare away to a cousin from his mother's side of the family recently arrived from western Virginia. Jed Hotchkiss said he gave the gift horse away after the Maryland campaign when the young cousin left to join a newly formed mounted infantry unit.

William E. Caffey, who wrote about his Confederate artillery service under the pseudonym "An English Combatant," claimed that Little Sorrel was available for use at the time of the accident and Jackson learned a lesson with the gray mare. "The old sorrel was again brought forward and the General ambled off," Caffey wrote, "never essaying to mount 'fine' horses again." Caffey was with the Army of Northern Virginia during the Maryland campaign, but it's unclear whether he saw the accident or just heard about it. Most versions put Jackson in an ambulance after the event, not on horseback, but Caffey's story suggests that Little Sorrel was at least present and available by the morning of September 6.

Jackson spent the night of September 6 and three days and nights thereafter in a beautiful grove of oak trees, known as Best's Grove, three miles south of Frederick. Jackson and Little Sorrel were certainly reunited, if not on September 6, then at some point during the encampment near Frederick, which ended on September 10. William Caffey wrote of the intense interest in Jackson aroused among Marylanders: "Hundreds traveled many miles to see the great original Stonewall . . . and imagined that angelic spirits were his companions and counsellors." But then the visitors got a closer look. "It was not until the great man had mounted his old horse and frequently aired himself in the streets, that many began to think him less than supernatural," Caffey wrote. "His shabby attire and unpretending deportment quite disappointed the many who had expected to see a great display of gold lace and feathers."

By "old horse" Caffey may have meant a horse Jackson had used previously or a horse that was presumed to be old, but there's little doubt that he was referring to Little Sorrel. Caffey's reference to having "frequently aired himself in the street" suggests that Little Sorrel was carrying Jackson through the streets of Frederick throughout the period of encampment.

While in Frederick, Jackson and Robert E. Lee worked out plans to capture Harpers Ferry. The primary goal was to protect the Confederate supply line from the Shenandoah Valley, with the added benefit of preventing the huge Federal garrison there from being sent north and east to reinforce the main Union army in Maryland. John Pope's failure at Manassas was more recent than George McClellan's at the Seven Days, so McClellan had been restored to the command of the Army of the Potomac. Pope's Army of Virginia was no more.

Lee gave Jackson three of four Confederate columns of the Army of Northern Virginia. His columns were to march on Harpers Ferry from three directions, with Jackson's personally led column of fourteen thousand men to approach from the west. Harpers Ferry would be surrounded and choked.

On September 10, Jackson's column moved out of the Frederick camp. He rode at the front of his marching soldiers, presumably on the trustworthy and comfortable Little Sorrel. Jackson intended to make a loop to the northwest to disguise his intentions to any Union sympathizers and spies who might be watching.

He stopped fifteen miles short of his destination. As the column made camp at the farm of southern sympathizer John Murdock, a mile southeast of Boonsboro, Maryland, Jackson ordered Douglas and part of his escort from the Black Horse Troop into the mostly Union-favoring village to see what was going on. There are several versions of what happened next, including those of Douglas and members of the cavalry troop.

According to survivors of the Black Horse Troop, twenty of the cavalrymen went into Boonsboro to picket the village and provide early warning of any Union approach. According to Douglas, he rode into town with a single cavalryman, while Chester French said *he* was the companion. The two were attacked by a strong contingent of Union cavalry that had ridden through the pickets, if indeed there were any pickets. Douglas, according to him, and Alexander D. Payne of the Black Horse, according to his colleagues, tried to stand their ground against the Federals, then turned to hurry back to camp.

According to both accounts, they saw Stonewall Jackson himself on foot, heading out of the Confederate camp toward Boonsboro, leading his horse. Douglas gave himself credit for holding off the cavalry while the Black Horse troopers said the key figure was Payne. It was probably both. Jackson was able to mount the horse, most likely Little Sorrel, and gallop back to the safety of the Confederate camp. The Union cavalry turned off. It was a near miss, but Jackson and Little Sorrel were saved from capture.

"The only allusion he [Jackson] made to the incident," Douglas wrote later, "was to express the opinion that I had a very fast horse."

Two days later, the column arrived in Martinsburg, Virginia (now West Virginia), the second-largest town of the Shenandoah Valley. The twenty-five-hundred-man Federal garrison had just abandoned the town, heading east to Harpers Ferry and the protection of a much larger Union contingent there. With the Confederate line of supply from the valley now protected as far as Martinsburg, Jackson could turn his attention to planning the assault on Harpers Ferry, but planning took a while to get to.

Jackson and his horse suffered from the burdens of hero worship as soon as they arrived in Martinsburg. The general lost most of the buttons from his coat to keepsake-hunters and his horse lost chunks of hair.

"As a penalty of sharing his master's fame, poor Little Sorrel lost many locks from his mane and tail," Anna Jackson wrote years later in her biography of her husband. Henry Kyd Douglas wrote that the horse who lost his hair wasn't Little Sorrel, who was, Douglas claimed, still missing.

Anna Jackson wasn't there and Douglas may have been, but Anna has come down with a better record of accuracy than Douglas has. The visit to Martinsburg came well after other people reported seeing Jackson back aboard Little Sorrel. Douglas, like many other Civil War veterans, wrote much of his work well after the war and his inaccuracies may have resulted as much from foggy memory as from his love of a good story.

Jackson began his final eighteen-mile march to Harpers Ferry early on September 13, as the two other columns also moved to encircle the Federal garrison. The one arriving from the northeast under General Lafayette McLaws had to fight its way into possession of Maryland Heights, one of the three prominences overlooking the town. General John Walker's column had an easier time securing Loudon Heights to the south.

Jackson approached Bolivar Heights on the western edge of the town and spent September 14 planning an assault on the Federal garrison, expecting to have to send substantial infantry to subdue the town. On September 15, the infantry advanced, but a massive artillery attack from Maryland and Loudon Heights subdued the Federal garrison quickly. Within ninety minutes, a white flag of surrender waved in the village.

The commanding officer of the Union garrison was brought to Jackson's position on Bolivar Heights.

Henry Kyd Douglas was struck by the difference in appearance between the generals and their mounts. He told his *Century Magazine* readers about the appearance of Union General Julius White. "General White, riding a handsome black horse, was carefully dressed and had on untarnished gloves, boots, and sword," he wrote. "On the other hand, General Jackson was the dingiest, worst-dressed and worst-mounted general that a warrior who cared for good looks and style would wish to surrender to."

Later in the morning, Jackson rode down into the center of Harpers Ferry to take a look at the site of his first command and the place where he and Little Sorrel had come together. Most of the once prosperous town lay in ruins. Many of the 12,500 Union troops captured in Harpers Ferry lined the streets to catch a glimpse of the Stonewall Jackson they had heard so much about. Some cheered, but others were unimpressed by horse and rider, including Lewis Hull of the Sixtieth Ohio Infantry, who referred to Jackson's mount as being a dun.

He was apparently referring to Little Sorrel, the horse that Douglas criticized a few hours earlier, but there is a chance that Jackson changed horses to go down into the city. One observer claimed he was on a "cream-colored horse," and yet another called his horse "dark brown." At about this same time, Colonel William H. Trimble of the Sixtieth Ohio met Jackson to ask for protection for the regiment's black servants. Trimble was the close associate of William O. Collins, brother to the man who supposedly bred Little Sorrel in Connecticut.

Jackson's troops left Harpers Ferry within hours of their victory, rushing to meet up with Lee's force sixteen miles north in Sharpsburg, Maryland. A night march was treacherous for man and horse alike, but the column safely reached Sharpsburg by late morning on September 16, 1862. Almost certainly, Jackson chose the sure-footed Little Sorrel for this trip.

Jackson rode Little Sorrel into the town of Sharpsburg on September 16, 1862, to meet Robert E. Lee and prepare for the Battle of Antietam.
ALEXANDER GARDNER PHOTOGRAPH, LIBRARY OF CONGRESS

Stonewall Jackson and Robert E. Lee met on the main street of the little town. Before receiving word of Confederate success at Harpers Ferry, Lee had initiated plans to pull out of Maryland. A battle the day before at South Mountain, the northernmost remnant of the Blue Ridge Mountains, had been a costly failure for Lee's invasion force. But Lee, buoyed by Jackson's success, decided to make a stand at Sharpsburg. His South Mountain troops arrived first, and he was relieved to see Jackson show up a little later. If McClellan had attacked before Jackson's arrival, the Army of Northern Virginia might have been doomed. Even so, the Confederates were outnumbered nearly three to one.

Lee and Jackson believed Sharpsburg to be acceptable if not ideal ground for a battle, protected by the Potomac River to the west and the steep-banked Antietam Creek to the east, with a ridge west of town allowing for effective placement of artillery. During the daytime hours of September 16 the united Confederate army set up for battle, knowing that McClellan and the Army of the Potomac were on their way.

Lee ordered Jackson to the left of a four-mile line that more or less paralleled the Hagerstown Pike, a north-south road that lay to the west of Antietam Creek. During the afternoon, Jackson deployed his troops, then he allowed himself and his men a little rest. They had had all been awake for the better part of two days and needed sleep desperately. Jackson had a headquarters tent erected behind his line but chose instead to sleep next to a tree, using its exposed roots as a pillow.

Little Sorrel most likely got a little sleep as well, almost certainly near the spot where Jackson slept. As much as the horse enjoyed stretching out on the ground whenever he was given the opportunity, he probably dozed standing up when surrounded by too much activity. He, like all horses, possessed an attribute called the "stay apparatus," an arrangement of muscles, ligaments, and tendons that allows a horse to lock his front legs and hips so he can sleep upright. The mechanism can be disengaged instantly in the face of a threat, which is useful for a prey animal menaced by fast-moving predators, and equally useful for a horse about to be called to battle. Standing-up sleep isn't as deep or restful as the lying down kind, but it's a good second best for a horse who hadn't had much rest for thirty-six hours or more.

Jackson soon resumed placing his regiments. He expected attack primarily from the north, but he had to be prepared for an advance from the east. By nightfall on September 16, he knew that Union troops were in place both north and east. Skirmishing and light artillery fire ensured that neither soldiers nor horses got much more sleep that night.

The always-aggressive Jackson preferred attacking at a moment of his choosing rather than waiting for the enemy to attack at an unknown time, but he was ready with a forceful response to any assault, whenever it came. The time came just before dawn, at five o'clock, on September 17.

The attack came, as Lee and Jackson expected, on the Confederate left. Jackson and his men were already awake and ready to go.

A thunder of cannon fire broke the edgy silence as Union artillery opened on Jackson's line. The guns of General Joseph Hooker's First Corps, along with long-range artillery from the east bank of Antietam Creek, struck first, but Jackson's batteries answered quickly. Shortly thereafter, Hooker sent his three divisions, more than eight thousand men, marching toward Jackson's line.

Four hours of desperate battle followed with charge and counter-charge and devastating loss of life, human and equine, on both sides. Jackson and Little Sorrel spent the first part of the battle behind the lines, primarily on an elevation known as Hauser's Ridge. They then became actively involved in the fighting. His first authorized biographer, his former chief of staff Robert Dabney, believed Jackson felt even more invulnerable than usual that day. "During this terrible conflict General Jackson exposed his life with his customary imperturbable bravery," Dabney wrote, "riding among his batteries and directing their fire, and communicating his own indomitable spirit to his men." He apparently also communicated his lack of fear to his horse, who was his usual composed self amid the most appalling loss of life of the war.

The outmanned Confederates were bolstered by the late arrival of Lafayette McLaws's division from Harpers Ferry. McLaws was hurried north to reinforce Jackson's beleaguered wing, meeting up with Jackson at Hauser's Ridge three hours into the battle. The two generals sat on their horses within easy range of Union artillery, which hadn't let up for more than a few minutes since the opening volley. As the two discussed deployment of McLaws's division, a shell struck a nearby courier. Just seconds later another shell fell directly in front of the forelegs of their horses. The shell failed to explode, saving the two generals and their two horses from death.

"The enemy, it seems, are getting our range," Jackson said, according to McLaws's aide, who wrote about the scene later. Much to the relief

Union troops crossing Antietam Creek. Hauser's Ridge is directly ahead.
JOHNSON AND BUEL, *BATTLES AND LEADERS OF THE CIVIL WAR, VOL. 1*

of the aide and McLaws, Jackson turned Little Sorrel's head and moved out of range.

Jackson's soldiers managed to push back a final Federal charge, and by nine o'clock in the morning the sides were where they had been when the first cannon opened fire. It was an expensive return to the status quo. About five thousand soldiers of both sides lay dead or wounded, a casualty rate of more than 30 percent. Jackson's wing alone suffered nearly 40 percent casualties. Nobody counted the horses, but many died that morning.

One of the most evocative images of the Battle of Antietam was the Alexander Gardner photograph taken a few days later of a dead but unburied white horse, the mount of a Confederate colonel also killed in the battle. The horse looks peaceful, as if he were quietly napping. He probably lay down in pain and died of his wounds, untended because there were so many soldiers in need of help that terrible day.

The Gardner photograph of a dead Confederate horse became famous throughout the North.
ALEXANDER GARDNER PHOTOGRAPH, LIBRARY OF CONGRESS

The battle moved south and Jackson saw no more significant action that day. But Little Sorrel got no rest. Jackson immediately began to search for a way to attack the Union left as the battle exploded at the center. Lee wanted the attack from the left wing to lessen the pressure on the center. Jackson wanted it because attack was what he always wanted to do.

The assault never happened. The Union artillery remained strong on the left and Jackson's losses had been too heavy to launch an effective attack on artillery. He spent the remainder of the twelve-hour battle riding Little Sorrel up and down his line, searching for openings and looking for ways to attend to his wounded.

As evening approached, the battle had shifted far south of Sharpsburg itself, with the Union troops steadily gaining the upper hand. The very late arrival of the division commanded by A. P. Hill, finally finished with dealing with the captured Federal troops at Harpers Ferry, saved the Army of Northern Virginia from destruction at Antietam.

More than twenty-three thousand soldiers were killed or wounded during the battle, making it the single bloodiest day in American history. The Union side lost two thousand more men than the Confederates, but Lee's army was less than half the size of McClellan's and had lost a much greater percentage of its total force. Even so, Lee chose not to withdraw overnight. He was prepared to defend against a Union advance if necessary, and he spent the next day supervising aid to the wounded and removal of the dead from the field.

But Jackson remained eager to attack, at least until he realized that the horrific losses suffered by the Union army hadn't prompted McClellan to withdraw. General John Bell Hood, whose division had played a key role in stopping a particularly robust Union attack, described meeting Jackson and Little Sorrel the morning of September 18.

"That morning I arose before dawn and rode to the front, where, just before dawn, General Jackson came pacing up on his horse," Hood wrote in his memoirs. Jackson asked him if McClellan's troops had pulled out overnight. When told they hadn't, Jackson told Hood, "I hoped they had," and paced away on Little Sorrel.

That night, under cover of darkness, Lee withdrew his troops from Sharpsburg and headed back across the Potomac River to Virginia. The withdrawal made the Union army the technical victor, although the battle had resulted in nothing more than a return to the status quo. But the overall effect of the Battle of Antietam was momentous. Jackson and Lee had both been eager to invade the North and that invasion was over for now. In Washington, Abraham Lincoln had been eager to make a move to emancipate the slaves in the rebellious states, and that process had now begun. Within weeks, Lincoln issued a tentative Emancipation Proclamation, and shortly after that the British government rejected a long-standing Confederate hope that Britain would help end the war in the South's favor.

Jackson's troops provided the rear guard for Lee's retreating army. He expected McClellan to follow and thought an attack likely. To Lincoln's great disappointment, McClellan, possessed of the delusion that Lee was retreating with a hundred thousand troops, failed to pursue. In reality, Lee had fewer than thirty thousand men fit to fight, while McClellan could have overwhelmed them with his sixty-five thousand.

The army took hours to cross the Potomac in the dark, with Jackson's wing last to leave Maryland. According to his early biographer Robert Dabney, Jackson watched every man cross. "For hours, he was seen seated upon his horse in the middle of the river, as motionless as a statue, watching the passage of his faithful men," Dabney wrote shortly after the war. "Nor did he leave this station until the last man and the last carriage had touched the southern shore." The final man crossed at 10:00 AM on September 19.

That night McClellan did try to pursue, crossing the Potomac near Shepherdstown, now in West Virginia but then still Virginia. A brief violent clash resulted, and McClellan decided that the pursuit would be too dangerous. Simultaneously, Lee decided that his Maryland adventure was truly over, giving up any immediate hope of returning to Maryland. Jackson and Lee had dreamed of a success that would force the Union to the bargaining table, and that dream was lost.

The brightest spot of the Maryland campaign had been Jackson's capture of Harpers Ferry and twelve thousand five hundred Union troops. But the success had been fleeting. The Union soldiers had now been paroled, and Harpers Ferry was soon back in Union hands. The Maryland invasion, while not a total failure, was near to it.

The return to Virginia brought two months of reorganization and rest. In October, Stonewall Jackson was promoted to lieutenant general and in November his wing became known as the Second Corps of the

Army of Northern Virginia. The army, devastated by its losses in Maryland, began to grow again. Stragglers who had failed to cross the Potomac to fight in the North began drifting back, and recruiting picked up in the wake of the fears produced by Lincoln's announcement of the Emancipation Proclamation.

For Little Sorrel, October and November were comfortable months. He was used, but not excessively, and there was a reasonable supply of feed for the horses of the army. The invasion may have failed in one respect, but it did take pressure off farmers in the Shenandoah Valley and elsewhere. Hay came in, grain was harvested, and Little Sorrel ate well.

Jackson moved headquarters several times in the autumn of 1862, including a stay at Bunker Hill, a tiny community in Berkeley County near the battlefield at Falling Waters where he had first seen action fifteen months earlier. Jackson established his headquarters at Edgewood, the home of John Boyd. Early biographer John Esten Cooke said Jackson and Little Sorrel were especially busy during the Bunker Hill stay. Jackson "was often seen moving to and fro among his troops on his old sorrel horse with the old uniform," Cooke wrote just after the war. "He was always greeted with cheers by his men."

During the stay in the Bunker Hill camp, J. E. B. Stuart sent his Prussian aide Heros von Borcke with a gift uniform coat he had ordered for Jackson from his Richmond tailor. Stuart's gift was a magnificent creation of gray wool, gilt buttons, and gold lace.

"I was heartily amused at the modest confusion with which the hero of many battles regarded the fine uniform from many points of view, scarcely daring to touch it," von Borcke wrote in his memoirs. Jackson at first said he would keep the coat as a memento but eventually agreed to try it on. "Having donned the garment," von Borcke remembered, "he escorted me outside the tent to the table where dinner had been served in the open air. The whole of the staff were in a perfect ecstasy at their chief's brilliant appearance."

He later put the coat away, refusing to wear it for several months. Stuart was one of many Jackson friends and admirers who thought he also deserved a better-looking horse, but Stuart knew better than to suggest that Jackson replace Little Sorrel. Jackson did accept a fine new bridle and martingale from an admirer in Winchester. Little Sorrel, with a natural balanced head carriage and the outstanding balance of his gait and breed, may have been an unlikely candidate for a martingale, a strap designed to prevent a horse from throwing his head around. One photograph taken later in his life shows an uncomfortable Little Sorrel with a far-too-short martingale.

In late November, Robert E. Lee noticed Federal activity on the northern side of the Rappahannock River in Fredericksburg. He sent a message to Jackson, asking him to prepare his corps to move east. A few days later, Jackson decided to hurry ahead of his corps and, along with Little Sorrel and a small staff, headed toward Lee to learn about the next chapter of their war.

CHAPTER 10

Defending the Rappahannock

Stonewall Jackson liked very little about what he knew of Lee's plans to defend against the coming Federal offensive. The weather was terrible on November 29, with relentless snow and sleet, reminding Jackson, his aide James Power Smith, and four couriers that they were facing another winter campaign. But winter fighting hadn't much bothered Jackson twelve months earlier and it was unlikely to trouble him now.

Nor did the prospect of another battle against the massive Army of the Potomac. Jackson came alive under fire. The hotter the fighting, the more his unique skills came to the fore. Jackson's problem was the location Lee had chosen to make his stand against the Federal army and its new commander Ambrose Burnside.

Jackson preferred to make a stand farther south on the banks of the North Anna River, but Lee thought the Rappahannock River town of Fredericksburg, with hills providing ideal siting for artillery and opportunities to hide infantry, was a better choice. Jackson also knew that the

Confederate position in Fredericksburg would be utterly defensive, and Jackson was always a soldier who preferred offense to defense.

Little Sorrel had been the natural choice to make a long, fast ride to get to Lee. He was quick and comfortable and did what every good horse does. He tried his best to respond precisely to what his human partner wanted. The five other horses struggled to keep up with Jackson's fast-pacing mount. With his secure pacing gait he fared better than the trotting horses of the staff on the dirt-chinked wood of the Orange Plank Road.

As for the prospect of battle, the horse might well have assumed battle would be just ahead. Nineteen months into his war, Little Sorrel had participated in nearly a dozen marches that resulted in battle. Like his rider, he may have been eager to get started. Years later, he was known for his excitement at the sound of martial music and artillery salutes. At any rate, it was clear that he would never shy from battle, so he paced willingly toward Fredericksburg.

At noontime the group was about halfway to Fredericksburg and took a break at one of the few houses in the tangled second- and third-growth woodland known locally as the Wilderness. It was a former tavern, now the home of clergyman Melzi Chancellor. Jackson and the others were given lunch and the horses were fed before they continued the long day's ride.

As the group drew closer to the city in the late afternoon, snow began falling heavily. They began to appreciate just how close battle might be.

"One of the most dismal sights of war was presented to us," said James Power Smith, writing half a century later. "The road was quite filled with wagons and carts and people on foot, unhappy refugees from Fredericksburg."

The goal of Jackson's party was not Fredericksburg but Lee's headquarters, five miles south of the city on Mine Road. After a warm welcome by Lee, the group found lodging for the night at a nearby estate. At first they were refused, but Smith told the owner that it was Stonewall Jackson himself asking and the group received a warm welcome. Smith, who remembers that his own dinner was very good, fails to record whether Little Sorrel and the horses were stabled or tied outside. They were, presumably, fed and watered after their trip of nearly forty miles.

The next morning, Sunday, November 30, Jackson and Smith rode north into Fredericksburg, where they were surprised and saddened to realize that they could hear no church bells. After sitting on their horses for a few minutes in the center of town, they moved down to the river. A small brigade of Mississippi infantry formed a thin picket line along the west bank, knowing that as many as a hundred thousand Union solders waited to cross the river. Little Sorrel and the other horses drank from the Rappahannock before turning back south toward Lee's headquarters.

Jackson established his own headquarters on the grounds of Fairfield, Thomas Coleman Chandler's plantation. Fairfield had once consisted of twenty-five hundred acres of rich farmland surrounding an impressive brick house as well as dozens of outbuildings, all maintained by an army of slaves. But Fairfield had lost dozens of slaves during the early years of the war, thanks to nearby Federal occupation, and the plantation was no longer particularly prosperous. Still, Fairfield was big enough for Jackson's corps when it arrived, in addition to being close to Lee's headquarters. Jackson chose to remain in a tent with his staff rather than taking up the Chandlers' offer of a room in the main house.

Little Sorrel was probably not stabled, but he must have appreciated another important attribute of Fairfield. It was less than half a mile from Guiney Station, a stop on the Richmond, Fredericksburg, and Potomac Railroad, the primary supply depot for the Army of Northern Virginia. By December 1, there was almost no grazing available for any horse, not even for the mount of a corps commander. All hay and grain had to be shipped in, and proximity to the depot gave Little Sorrel an advantage. As a small, hardy horse of about eight hundred fifty pounds, his requirements were less than those of larger, more impressive animals, but he was known for his good appetite and as usual appreciated his regular meals.

The four divisions of the Second Corps began arriving on December 1. Jim Lewis and the rest of Jackson's staff were among the first to show up, providing Jackson with at least one more mount. Although Little Sorrel is the only horse mentioned during the days leading up to the battle in Fredericksburg, Jackson still owned Big Sorrel and may have owned or could have borrowed others. His next best-known horse—the handsome bay stallion named Superior—didn't arrive until the following February.

Jackson was presented with still another good-looking bay a month after his arrival in Fredericksburg. But all evidence suggests that he had two horses to choose from during these important days of preparation for battle and the horse he usually chose was Little Sorrel.

Work for a corps commander's horse during the first ten days of December consisted mostly of brief trips. The four divisions of Jackson's Second Corps had been assigned to form the right wing of the Army of Northern Virginia during the coming battle. The front was only two miles long, so Little Sorrel traveled mostly short distances as Jackson arranged his divisions and checked in on their commanders.

The left wing, under First Corps commander James Longstreet, defended the river crossing from a strong position on heights directly to the west of Fredericksburg. Because of the excellence of the position, Longstreet's corps stretched out over five miles north to south. Jackson's corps waited in a more exposed position and he was forced to concentrate two of its divisions into a much shorter two-mile front, easier on a horse during preparations but making it more likely that the Union attack would focus on them.

During the first week in December, Jackson, Little Sorrel, and some members of the staff took a longer twenty-mile trip southeast, paralleling the Rappahannock as it headed toward its mouth. Their destination was Port Royal, where one of the Second Corps divisions was still stationed, protecting the strategically located town and, more important, the river. The possibility existed that Burnside might order a crossing there rather than Fredericksburg. The Port Royal troops were also to protect against any Federal gunboats that might try to sneak up the river toward Fredericksburg.

"The river with its southern hills made a strong line of defense," James Power Smith observed in his memoirs. He also noted that the Port Royal area "afforded no facility for an aggressive movement." Jackson decided that while Port Royal still needed to be defended, it was an unlikely spot for the main Federal thrust. But he did assess how long it would take his Port Royal division to reach Fredericksburg.

Topographer Jedediah Hotchkiss, charged with drawing a map of Caroline County, made the same trip to Port Royal and noticed how the horses of that division suffered badly from "greasy heel," sometimes called mud rash or mud fever. The disease was less debilitating than some equine illnesses common during war, but it was uncomfortable for the horses. The bacterial skin condition was hard to treat during the pre-antibiotic era, and it was equally difficult to prevent in the circumstances faced by Civil War armies. The solution would have been to stable the horses in dry conditions, an impossibility for the artillery and staff horses that were suffering near Port Royal. Little Sorrel, receiving the close attention of the affectionate Jim Lewis, had his feet dried and groomed daily, even if he didn't enjoy the protection of a stable.

On December 11 the waiting ended. In the early hours of the morning, the Mississippi pickets on the west side of the river heard the unmistakable sounds of Federal efforts to lay bridges on portable pontoons, signaling that Union soldiers were about to cross the river. Couriers hurried with the information to Lee and both corps commanders.

Mississippi sharpshooters made sure that the Union engineers would not have an easy time building their bridge. After a few hours of back-and-forth sniper fire and the shelling of Fredericksburg, Union troops completed their first bridge and began moving slowly across the Rappahannock. The crossing continued through the day and over night.

Jackson ordered Little Sorrel saddled and ready to go well before dawn on December 12. The Confederate command thought and hoped that Burnside would not have his troops across and ready to attack that day, so Jackson, whose troops were spread over a twenty-mile front, had time to call them in. After dispatching couriers, Jackson mounted and rode north to confer with Lee and check various sites within Fredericksburg. He rode Little Sorrel back to his own lines to position troops, and then the pair traveled ahead of the Confederate lines, along with Lee and Stuart, to get a good view of the Federal troops, who were now completing two pontoon bridges in front of Jackson's Second Corps.

All agreed that the Federal forces were likely to hit hardest here. Jackson liked his position, with nearly a mile and a half of open fields between the river and his troops. But Longstreet's First Corps, on a high ridge behind Fredericksburg, was even better off. After further work on positioning, Jackson rode south with topographer Hotchkiss to check on where the newly arriving divisions would be placed, then returned to a new campsite nearer to the expected center of action. Both Jackson and Little Sorrel had every right to be exhausted, but there was no sign of fatigue in either one of them.

Hotchkiss observed Jackson whistling as they went along. After a day of sporadic artillery shelling, the foggy night was eerily quiet, and both general and horse apparently got a good night's sleep.

Well before dawn on Saturday, December 13, Jackson, his staff, and their horses were awake. Soldiers struck their tents, loaded the wagons, and everything unnecessary for battle went to the rear. The big sorrel went to the rear with Jim Lewis, and Jackson again mounted Little Sorrel. As usual, the horse showed no sign of having been heavily used for days. One thing was not usual, though: Jackson prepared for battle by dressing in the magnificent new gray general's coat given to him the previous October by J. E. B. Stuart. He added a new gold-trimmed cap in place of the tattered blue hat from his Virginia Military Institute days.

"Altogether he looked so spick and span that the boys could scarcely believe their eyes, so unlike was he to the battered, sunburnt Old Jack of the valley," said aide James Power Smith in a memoir. "But the sorrel horse he rode and the same following of staff and couriers reassured the troops."

Former aide Henry Kyd Douglas, back with his original unit, was impressed with the sartorial splendor of the general, even though some the soldiers in his new command shook their heads at the change. Still, Douglas thought, the effect was altogether extraordinary.

According to Douglas, even Little Sorrel looked better than usual, apparently also impressed with his rider's appearance. That was high praise from a man who tended to be snobbish about horses.

The warm days and cold nights ensured heavy fog every morning, and December 13 was no exception. Federal cannons began sporadic booming as Jackson rode north shortly after sunrise to confer with Lee, Longstreet, and Stuart, whose cavalry stood ready to protect the far right of the Confederate line. Stuart, always excited by the prospect of battle, was pleased to see Jackson in his handsome new coat. If he was less pleased to see Little Sorrel, he wisely said nothing about it. Artilleryman William Page Carter later claimed that he got his first-ever look at Jackson mounted on a "superb bay horse," but other observers who knew Jackson better were convinced it was Little Sorrel that carried their commander.

The fog began to lift slowly, and all four generals knew that their predictions were about to be confirmed. The initial attack would come against Jackson's corps. Jackson remounted Little Sorrel and returned to his own troops shortly after 9:00 AM. An hour later, the fog had lifted entirely and Jackson, who had a magnificent view from an elevated position behind his troops, could see the spectacle of seventy thousand soldiers in blue ready to move ahead.

A signal set the Union front lines in motion, and on they came. Fire from a two-gun battery of Stuart's horse artillery, stationed at an angle to the passing Union troops, caused some damage and a great deal of confusion. The artillery action prompted an hour of heavy Federal artillery bombardment. Jackson remained on horseback in his exposed position, where he could see everything that was going on with the Federal attack.

Jackson was "calm and deliberate," according to one observer. Little Sorrel, to the same soldier's amazement, "had the appearance of dozing under the music of the guns." Jackson may have been pretending to be more calm than he actually felt to reassure any troops and officers who could see him. But Little Sorrel was behaving exactly as he felt. An artillery barrage, no matter how heavy, wasn't enough to excite him.

Federal pontoon bridges cross the Rappahannock as Jackson waits on Prospect Hill.
ALEXANDER GARDNER PHOTOGRAPH, LIBRARY OF CONGRESS

The Union infantry renewed its forward advance, nearly breaking through a poorly defended Confederate sector, but Jackson's repositioning of the Confederate troops forced the Federals to fall back. The attack on the southern front was over by early afternoon. The battle moved north to Longstreet's line, where repeated Union attacks with fresh troops also failed. The two-pronged Union offensive in Fredericksburg proved to be a double disaster.

As the second act of the Battle of Fredericksburg passed to the north, Jackson and Little Sorrel moved about their half of the field checking on human and equine casualties. Many artillery horses were lost, but the number of human casualties was far greater. Casualties in Jackson's corps were nearly the same as those on the Union side, but Jackson's came out of a total force less than half the size of the Union's. In spite of the proportionally greater losses, Jackson was thinking about immediate counterattack.

By late afternoon he knew it would have to be a night attack, something almost never done during the Civil War. He changed his mind after a renewal of Union artillery fire on his scattered command. If he had gone ahead with an attack, Little Sorrel would have gone along without resistance or complaint.

During the day, Alexander Boteler, Jackson's good friend and a member of the Confederate Congress, had arrived from Richmond eager to experience the Confederate success firsthand. After nightfall, Jackson and Boteler rode among the troops forming the right of the line, the area Jackson thought was most vulnerable to a possible renewed Federal attack in the morning. Boteler was a great admirer of the "patient, easy-going, and reliable" Little Sorrel. Although they probably didn't talk about the horse that night, it was obvious to both men that Little Sorrel had fully lived up to his reputation.

Jackson sent Boteler to his own tent with instructions for Jim Lewis to fix him supper and find him a place to sleep. The general himself returned after midnight, leaving his horse to Lewis for feeding and grooming. At 2:00 AM Jackson was awake again, and he was still awake when an aide to Maxcy Gregg arrived. Gregg, a brigadier general from South Carolina, had been critically wounded during the afternoon's fighting and wanted to see Jackson once more before his expected death. Jackson asked Lewis to saddle Little Sorrel.

A few minutes later when Jackson left his tent to mount his horse, he was annoyed to discover Big Sorrel waiting for him. According to an article Boteler wrote for a Pennsylvania newspaper twenty years later, Jackson demanded to know why Lewis had ignored his order. "Old Sorrel was dead tired 'cause you'd been riding him all day," Lewis said, according to Boteler. "I sort of promised him some rest." Lewis assured Jackson that he would come to the front himself with Little Sorrel as soon as he heard the first gun go off. With no further complaint, Jackson mounted the big sorrel and rode off to a deathbed visit with Maxcy Gregg.

Jim Lewis, among many others, believed there would be no attack from the Union army in the morning, but Jackson, after visiting the dying Gregg, spent December 14 strengthening his right while his troops waited. Throughout the day, there was sporadic artillery fire from the Union side, answered even more sporadically by the Confederates, who were protecting their limited ammunition stores. It's unclear if this prompted the return to action of Little Sorrel. If not, the big sorrel must have performed adequately.

During the early morning of December 16, the chance of attack or counterattack passed when the Union army slipped away under the cover of the nightly fog. Rumor of a Federal crossing and attack twenty miles southeast in Port Royal had Jackson, again on Little Sorrel, leading his entire corps toward the east. When word came back that the rumor was false, it was dark and cold. The wagons carrying tents and food for both soldiers and horses were well out of reach.

When told by his staff that they were near the well-known Moss Neck Plantation, Jackson refused to impose on the owners, the Corbin family. He instead found a clearing that made an acceptable bivouac for the night near the south bank of the Rappahannock, about halfway between Port Royal and Fredericksburg. The rest of his corps found similarly cold spots within a few miles.

"One young man there was disappointed and mad," wrote James Power Smith years later, referring to himself, as he prepared for a cold, hungry night. An officer brought cold biscuits and ham, but apparently no hay, from the Moss Neck house. Jackson soon relented and allowed his staff to seek shelter for all of them in the house.

Jackson, his staff, and their horses were warmly welcomed the night of December 16 by the Corbin family, consisting at the moment of five adult women, a fifteen-year-old boy, and three small children. Only a few older slaves remained of what had been a large contingent. The man of the house, Richard Corbin, was away with the army, but his wife, Roberta, and sister Kate managed to keep the house functioning. It was warm and there was ample food.

The enthusiasm of the Corbins probably meant that Little Sorrel received at least some hay and grain that night and possibly a dry stall in the extensive Moss Neck stables and barns, almost empty of horses at this point in the war. A few days earlier, Roberta and Kate Corbin had been able to find only two riding horses, the remnants of a large herd, to ride out to get a distant glimpse of the action in Fredericksburg.

The following morning, December 17, Roberta and Kate prepared an elaborate breakfast for Jackson and his staff. The women offered a wing of the big house to Jackson for use as a headquarters, but his wagons, carrying their tents and other equipment, managed to find their way to Moss Neck by noon and the general declined the offer. He told the Corbin ladies that he thought a general should share the living conditions of his men, much to the disappointment of his staff. They immediately set up their tents on the Moss Neck grounds.

Although none of the journal keepers mention it, Little Sorrel and the other staff horses may have been allowed to remain in the nearly empty stables, protected from what turned out to be an exceptionally cold and snowy winter. But the horses enjoyed little rest during the next several weeks.

For nearly a month, Jackson and the rest of Lee's army were unsure if the Army of the Potomac planned to renew hostilities. Ambrose Burnside was sure he wanted to and where he wanted to do it, but he was entirely unsure just how to carry it off. The Confederates received several reports that the Union army had not yet gone into winter quarters, signaling the end of fighting until spring. The Second Corps was ready to act if necessary.

As it turned out, Burnside did eventually move, heading northwest along the northern bank of the Rappahannock, intending to cross the river and attack the rear of the Army of Northern Virginia. But he waited too long to move and most of his army got bogged down in the mud, so he finally had to give up his plans for attack. The Federal forces went into winter quarters, and the Army of Northern Virginia did the same. The soldiers and officers of the Second Corps were especially happy, turning the extensive woods around Moss Neck into lumber for winter huts. Water from the river was clean, and the railroad depot at Guiney Station was only ten miles away, allowing for delivery of the limited food and supplies available to the army.

Food for Jackson and his staff was not a problem. The days on either side of Christmas brought a deluge of gifts from Virginia citizens to Jackson's tent. He had received the lion's share of attention and public gratitude from the victory at Fredericksburg, a reality that must have annoyed James Longstreet, whose success had been equal and whose performance hadn't included inadvertently leaving a gap between divisions that had been exploited by the Federals, if only briefly.

Shortly before Christmas, three plump turkeys arrived at headquarters, followed by a ham, cakes, wine, biscuits, and pickles. Jackson's staff, as well as officers from Lee's and Stuart's staffs, enjoyed a Christmas dinner more like a prewar celebration than what they had been expecting.

A particularly fine gift arrived at Moss Neck at the end of the month. On December 31 an excellent bay mare arrived, the gift of several important political gentlemen from Staunton in Augusta County, complete with saddle, bridle, and other necessary equipment. Jackson immediately wrote a note of thanks, which the gentlemen made sure was published in the local newspaper a week later. What prompted the gift is unknown. Quartermaster John Harman, the man who chose the big and little sorrels from the rail car in Harpers Ferry, was from Staunton, and Jackson's mapmaking friend Jedediah Hotchkiss was from a place just outside the town.

Both Harman and Hotchkiss had been home for Christmas, and both had spent time in town catching up with friends and acquaintances. Harman is more likely to have been the source of the idea that Jackson needed a better—or just an additional—horse, but Hotchkiss was closer to the general. Little Sorrel was due to turn thirteen early in 1863, and Hotchkiss and Harman may have realized that he shouldn't be used quite so heavily.

One of the two of them may actually have brought the gift mare to Jackson, since they arrived from Staunton at about the same time she did. But Hotchkiss, who was delayed a little and arrived just after the first of the year, doesn't talk about the gift mare in his otherwise extensive diary entries for those days.

There is no evidence that Jackson used the mare much during the next few months, but he did retain ownership of her and was grateful for the gift. Jim Lewis was also grateful, even though he now had more work to do. He often got to ride the extra horses, and the bay mare must have been better looking than the angular Big Sorrel.

Little Sorrel's reaction to the young interloper is unknown, but he probably accepted the new arrival with the same nonchalance with which he greeted every unexpected event. Most horses like to be around other horses, and the more the better. Some can become jealous of other horses, but it's almost certain that the easy-going Little Sorrel was not one of the resentful ones.

After a few days in his tent, Jackson became ill with a cold and earache. He acquiesced to his surgeon's advice to accept the hospitality of the Corbins and move inside. He accepted the offer of the plantation's office building and established his personal winter quarters there.

The regiments of the Second Corps were scattered over a nearly twenty-mile area, and for Little Sorrel winter quarters didn't mean an absence of work. Jackson spent hours in the saddle inspecting the fortifications at their positions. In January, before the worst of the winter weather set in, the division and regimental commanders drilled their troops and Jackson often rode out to watch them.

Moss Neck Plantation, where Little Sorrel spent the winter months of 1863.
CONFEDERATE VETERAN MAGAZINE, JANUARY 1912

He made frequent twenty-five-mile round trips to Lee's headquarters, and he probably rode the sure-footed Little Sorrel when the weather was particularly bad. One day he and aide James Power Smith made the ride in the middle of a snowstorm.

"A worse ride than that one," Smith said later, "I have never had." After meeting Lee, who was shocked that Jackson made the trip during such a storm, they turned around and rode back to Moss Neck. Little Sorrel, certainly Jackson's mount that day, made the trip without incident.

On February 6, Jackson received another welcome gift, which he described as an "excellent horse" sent to him by Colonel Michael Harman and William J. Bell of Staunton. This was most likely the bay horse he named Superior, an animal that was to play an important role in the last few months of Jackson's life. James Power Smith wrote many years later that Harman and Bell had presented Superior to Jackson the previous autumn in Winchester, but Jackson himself wrote a letter to his wife Anna on February 7, 1863, saying that the "excellent horse" had arrived the day before, so Smith apparently remembered the date incorrectly.

Harman was the brother of Jackson's quartermaster John Harman and had himself been a quartermaster with the Confederate army before becoming colonel of the Fifty-Third Virginia Infantry, part of Jackson's Second Corps. Whether the mare that arrived five weeks earlier had failed to work out or he thought that Jackson needed a fourth horse, Michael Harman made sure he got a good one.

Jackson was proud of Superior and rode him when he wanted to make a good impression. Shortly after receiving the horse, Jackson rode Superior to visit Lee's headquarters, again accompanied by James Power Smith, who was not as impressed with Superior as Jackson was. After the meeting with Lee, Smith led Jackson to a shortcut that ran along the Rappahannock.

"Before long we came to a wide ditch," Smith wrote, "difficult at any time, but especially so with its banks covered with snow." Smith crossed easily, then looked back to see Jackson trying to coax Superior across the ditch. "What do you think of your bay now?" he claimed to have asked Jackson. The general, he said, laughed heartily.

Whether or not Smith really spoke so impertinently to the general, the story illustrates a fact that everyone in Jackson's command knew. The beautiful stallion was fine for show, but the plain little gelding was what Jackson needed when the stakes were high. Still, Jackson enjoyed showing to the world that he had and could handle a magnificent horse.

At about the time Superior arrived, Jackson loaned or, more probably gave, Big Sorrel to Beverly Tucker Lacy, recently appointed by Jackson to be chaplain of the Second Corps. The two had met in Lexington before the war, but it was during the quiet time at Moss Neck that Jackson realized that Lacy's religious beliefs mirrored his own.

Jim Lewis had often been permitted to ride the big sorrel and he soon discovered that the arrangement was to continue with Superior. The care of a stallion meant harder work, but Lewis, like Jackson, enjoyed being admired astride a good-looking mount.

The winter months of 1863 proved to be exceptionally snowy with no grazing at all available to the horses of the Second Corps around Moss Neck. During some winters, the lack of snow cover meant that the dry survivors of the summer's blades of green grass helped to fill equine bellies with volume if not nutrition. This particular winter there was almost nothing, and it was a terrible season for all the horses of the Army of Northern Virginia.

As the favorite mount of a commanding general, Little Sorrel fared better than thousands of the army's surviving horses. Most received far too little feed to rebuild their strength after the long, exhausting, but mostly successful campaign of 1862. The concentration of the army in response to the Union's Fredericksburg offensive had devastated the supply of both feed and horses in central Virginia. The railroads ran erratically, often unable to carry hay from the agricultural regions within reach—the Shenandoah Valley and North Carolina. The quartermasters made an effort to carry hay by wagon, but the only horses big enough to haul heavily loaded wagons were the very ones that had been badly weakened by lack of feed.

Robert E. Lee hoped there would be no new Federal offensive during the winter. Joseph Hooker replaced Ambrose Burnside as the commander of the Army of the Potomac and word came across the Rappahannock that he was busy reorganizing his army. Lee was so concerned about the condition of his horses that he took a great risk and decided to scatter elements of the army. Part of the cavalry was sent off to the Shenandoah Valley where they could find hay and grain and perhaps a little midwinter grazing.

Artillery horses were sent east and west where some feed and forage was available. These were bigger animals, though less active than cavalry horses, and they needed a great deal of feed to have the strength to pull cannons. Some horses had to stay and suffer. Transportation horses, needed to haul horse feed and human food as well as military and medical supplies, remained and worked. Horses used by couriers for communication and officers' mounts remained and also had to be fed.

There was insufficient food for the soldiers too, so Lee took the most drastic step of all and sent half of James Longstreet's First Corps, along with Longstreet himself, to southeastern Virginia with a double purpose. Longstreet was to find food for humans and forage for horses. His absence would also lessen the demand on the stores of edibles remaining in central Virginia. Nearly twenty thousand men and perhaps a thousand horses, Lee hoped, could live off the land by confiscating what they needed.

The horses owned by Jackson, his other generals, and their staffs almost certainly received less feed than they wanted but more than the other horses of the corps enjoyed. All horses lose weight when they don't get enough to eat, except, apparently, Little Sorrel. Henry Kyd Douglas was again impressed with the fact that Little Sorrel retained condition even with short rations. His endurance, Douglas reported, was wonderful. It was not the first time in the war that Little Sorrel had been hungry and amazed his human family with his ability to carry on regardless.

Jim Lewis had already become famous among Jackson's staff for finding and cooking food for them, no matter how short the supply appeared to be. Most likely, he managed to obtain forage for Little Sorrel and his other equine charges as well during this long winter.

By mid-March, with a spring campaign in sight, the time required to travel between Moss Neck and Lee's headquarters south of Fredericksburg became burdensome. Jackson decided to move his own headquarters closer. He chose land owned by the prominent Yerby family just southwest of Lee's headquarters tents. Thomas Yerby's mansion, known as Belvoir, stood just a mile and a half from Lee's headquarters. Jackson, now that the weather was better, chose to pitch his tents even closer and settled less than a mile from Lee.

Belvoir had already served as a field hospital during the battle of Fredericksburg, and Jackson had visited the house himself on December 14 to see the dying Maxcy Gregg. Two weeks after Jackson moved to the Yerby property, Lee became ill with the first signs of the heart disease that he would live with for the rest of his life and spent several days in the Yerby mansion.

Jackson moved into Belvoir himself for nine days in late April. His wife Anna and infant daughter, Julia, arrived for a visit on April 20, and the three, plus a nursemaid, stayed at Belvoir. Presumably, Jim Lewis was given lodging nearby as well. Each day Jackson rode the short distance to his headquarters to work, usually on Little Sorrel.

One morning he rode back to Belvoir from his headquarters, leaving Little Sorrel and returning on Superior with the intention of impressing his wife. She was indeed impressed.

"After bringing him up to the steps of the house and showing him off," she wrote later, "he remounted him and galloped away at such a John Gilpin speed that his cap was soon borne off by the velocity." John Gilpin was a popular comic figure in a ballad about a man carried at breakneck speed through the English countryside by a runaway horse. In the end, however, Anna Jackson, like everyone else, was more impressed by the intelligence and good nature of Little Sorrel than the beauty and speed of Superior.

The nine-day visit would have presented Anna with the opportunity to ride Little Sorrel, but she never mentions doing it. It was now obvious to Anna that her husband would never give up Little Sorrel until the war was over, and possibly not even then. She must have thought that Jackson may never have intended to give her Little Sorrel but somehow didn't want to admit that an ordinary-looking little horse appealed to him so much.

The idyll for both soldiers and horses ended on April 29. Well before dawn, Jackson was awakened at Belvoir by Major Samuel Hale of General Jubal Early's staff. Early's division was stationed along the Rappahannock River in Fredericksburg and Hale told him that Union forces had begun crossing the river.

CHAPTER 11

Triumph and Tragedy

Stonewall Jackson had enjoyed the approval that came to him whenever he rode the magnificent Superior in public during the quiet winter months. Although two years of war had accustomed him to receiving respect for his talent for war, admiration of his appearance was something new and welcome. But the renewal of war had now moved from prospect to reality, and the horse he called for on the morning of April 29 was Little Sorrel.

Even so, Jackson dressed in his handsome new gray coat, the gift he received seven months earlier from the always well-dressed J. E. B. Stuart. Little Sorrel also benefited from the equipment given to Jackson over the winter season, dashing off to the opening of the 1863 campaign in a new bridle with a yellow noseband that nearly matched the gold armbands on Stuart's gift coat.

Horse and rider traveled first to Jackson's headquarters near the railroad depot at Hamilton's Crossing, a trip of less than five minutes from Belvoir. Most likely Jackson urged Little Sorrel into his impressively fast pace, not significantly slower than a gallop yet much safer to horse and rider in the foggy predawn light. At his headquarters Jackson issued orders to his staff, who had been awakened earlier by Samuel Hale.

Jackson dispatched his aide-de-camp James Power Smith to inform General Lee of the Federal crossing, and he alerted couriers to the possible need to inform his division commanders that Union troops were coming. Jackson, still astride Little Sorrel, moved forward to see for himself what had happened.

He and Lee had expected an attempted river crossing from Union forces, though they had no idea where along the thirty-mile front it would occur. The Rappahannock River itself had formed a useful defensive line for months, but the Confederate troops were thinly stretched over that distance and their commanders knew the line was vulnerable. At a dozen or more points the river could be forded on foot or crossed with pontoon bridges, awkward but highly portable with the seemingly endless supply of new horses that the Union quartermasters enjoyed.

At first light that misty morning, Jubal Early deployed his troops to face the advancing Union forces, but he commanded only four brigades. The question he, Jackson, and Lee would have to answer was whether this was Joseph Hooker's main assault or a feint, a mere ruse to disguise the primary crossing of the Rappahannock miles to the north and west. If it was the principal assault, the bulk of the Army of Northern Virginia would have to be moved in. If not, deploying too many soldiers here could lead to disaster upriver.

When Jackson arrived at the front, the soldiers of the Georgia and Louisiana brigades arrayed there immediately noticed two things, one unexpected and one familiar. The unexpected was the commander's appearance, at least in dress.

"He was clad in a new uniform," marveled Captain William J. Seymour of General Harry Hays's Louisiana brigade, presenting, Seymour said, "an unusually spruce appearance." But Seymour's more important observation was that Jackson and his horse stood for many minutes inspecting the Federal deployment. "As musket balls whizzed about him," Seymour said, "Stonewall calmly studied the position of the enemy through his binoculars." Beneath him, Little Sorrel stood just as calmly, ignoring as usual the clamor of returned fire and the smell of gunpowder.

A thorough examination told Jackson that the Federal troops were firing and returning fire, but they were not advancing much beyond their river crossing. Jackson turned his horse. Urging Little Sorrel into his fastest gait, Jackson quickly traveled the short distance to Lee's headquarters. If it had been his choice, the always-aggressive Jackson might have decided to meet the advance with attack. But the decision belonged to Lee.

Lee agreed with Jackson's idea to consolidate the rest of his corps in front of the Federal crossing but still thought the real attack would likely come elsewhere. A few days earlier, Stuart had reported that some Union troops were headed north and west, but not across the Rappahannock. The cavalry chief thought they might be moving to the Shenandoah Valley. Perhaps crossing south of Fredericksburg was a diversion to keep Lee from pursuing those troops.

Jackson spent the rest of the day supervising the recall of his corps from as far as eighteen miles away. He did make a brief and rainy visit to the front to confirm that the Union troops remained stationary, but most of his work was done at his tent headquarters.

Little Sorrel had an easy day, nibbling on what new grass was left around Second Corps headquarters, where horses had been kept since December. He had already put on weight during the previous nine days at Belvoir, where the cool, wet spring had led to flourishing pastures. At no time during the next few weeks was Little Sorrel referred to as "raw-boned." It was inaccurate during the thinnest of times and entirely untrue now.

As Jackson watched and planned, Lee finally received several pieces of information that gave him a better idea of what lay ahead for the

Army of Northern Virginia. Separate reports from Stuart and Richard Anderson, commander of the troops on his far left wing, told him that Union forces had indeed crossed the Rappahannock and its tributary the Rapidan at several points. He now knew that Hooker intended to get around the left flank of the Confederate troops. The goal may have been to cut communications and supply routes from Richmond, or it may have been more sinister. Preparations became more urgent.

After two years of war, Little Sorrel was quite familiar with what happened during the hours or days after battle became inevitable: prepare and then wait. Jim Lewis had Little Sorrel and Jackson's other horses as ready as they could be. Lewis would have checked their feet and made sure that their shoes were well set. A horse's hooves couldn't survive a battle without the protection of well-fitting and well-secured horseshoes. A lost shoe could lead to lameness at a critical time.

The red horse's tough Narragansett Pacer feet stayed sound through-out the war, but just like every other horse, he often wore out or lost shoes. Most divisions included professional farriers, both to fit premade wrought iron shoes and fashion custom ones. But the farriers' portable forges were often in use to repair iron on wagons and artillery pieces, so many cavalry troopers and officers carried enough equipment themselves to reset loose shoes and do minor repairs. Jackson, as a corps commander, wouldn't have been expected to do this. Jim Lewis was, and did.

Lewis would have checked other equipment because a broken girth or stirrup leather could also have deadly consequences. Lewis would have struggled to keep hooves and leather as dry as possible, difficult work in the rainy conditions of the night of April 29. The rain continued through the night, finally stopping by the morning of April 30. But the new day was foggy and damp.

It was to be a day of decision, and Jackson and Little Sorrel left early for Lee's headquarters. After a few minutes inside Lee's tent, the two generals emerged and mounted their horses—Jackson on Little Sorrel and Lee perhaps not on his famous gray Traveller. After the war, Lee remembered that he had been on Traveller on the final day of the battle, suggesting that he may have used different horses on other days.

Little Sorrel's companion that day may have been the small chestnut mare Lucy Long—like Jackson's coat, a gift of J. E. B. Stuart. She was in Lee's retinue during that period, and the commander enjoyed her quiet nature and common sense. Traveller was a magnificent horse in battle but possessed a rough trot and an inability to stand still during quiet periods. "He fretted a good deal," remembered Robert E. Lee Jr. after the war. If the other horse was indeed Lucy Long, Little Sorrel would have been pleased. Traveller was known to be hard on other horses, sometimes kicking and nipping if they got too close. Traveller's famous good looks would not have impressed Little Sorrel as they did his human observers.

From the high ridge overlooking the Rappahannock near the Fredericksburg crossing, Lee and Jackson studied the Union regiments on each side of the river. They both realized that the Union forces here weren't as strong as they first thought, weaker in fact than Jackson's corps. Jackson urged attack, but Lee was more convinced than ever that the main attack would come above Fredericksburg.

Then, Jackson said, an assault here might force Hooker to send help. At the very least, it would upset the Union commander's plans for his upriver attack. Lee agreed that Jackson might attack if he believed it would work. In the end, after he and Little Sorrel rode the front line again for further examination, Jackson decided it was not a good idea to attack in Fredericksburg. He and Lee spent the rest of the daylight hours in Lee's headquarters tent.

"Smiling and elated," according to chaplain Beverly Tucker Lacy, Jackson returned to his own headquarters in the evening. The prospect of battle always made him feel that way. Little Sorrel, sensitive to his owner as all good horses are, undoubtedly felt some of the euphoria. Staff members called to the headquarters tent also noticed the "high spirits" and "good humor," as Henry Kyd Douglas described Jackson's mood.

Lee's orders were for Jackson to move the bulk of his troops west, leaving at daybreak the next day, May 1, to reinforce the weak left wing near the place where Hooker appeared to be converging his forces. It was an otherwise insignificant crossroads known as Chancellorsville, which Jackson now knew, was where his next major battle would be fought.

Oddly, Jackson chose to ride another mile to Belvoir that night to visit the Yerby family, where he had spent nine days with Anna and his baby. It was late, though. Anna had already left for Richmond, and the family was no longer awake. Jackson returned to headquarters. Little Sorrel was now finished for the day, left to the care of Jim Lewis for unsaddling and grooming, while Jackson worked through the night. He sent couriers to his four division commanders. Jubal Early was told to remain at the site of the Federal crossing, making his division look bigger than it was, while the other three were told that they would begin their march to battle at three o'clock in the morning, several hours earlier than the daybreak departure that Lee had ordered.

Hooker, Jackson thought, might strike early, and he wanted to make sure that he was at the front line of the Confederate left wing in time to attack rather than defend. Always attack; defend only if you must.

Another white fog lay over the road to Chancellorsville as the first units of the column marched. That, and the silence demanded by Jackson, masked the massive movement of troops that should have been visible under a nearly full moon. Union forces lay just a few miles away, so Jackson marched the column to the south at first, as a diversion in case spies were watching, then turned them west toward Chancellorsville.

At nine o'clock in the morning, General Hooker received a report that a large column of Confederate infantry was moving upriver, but the report was vague and, he thought, indicated only that Lee was reinforcing existing positions. Hooker had no idea of the grave threat he faced.

Jackson and Little Sorrel traveled at the head of the column, so far ahead that they reached the front well in advance of the marching divisions. No memoir or other eyewitness account of the Chancellorsville campaign mentions Jackson aboard any horse other than Little Sorrel during the four days of preparation and battle. It would have made no sense for him to choose the handsome Superior, a horse that was untried in battle and had already shown himself to be afraid to cross water. Jackson may still have owned Big Sorrel at this point, but that horse was less comfortable to ride during a march and less trustworthy under fire. Little Sorrel was never aggressive, but in almost every other way he perfectly mirrored his rider. The choice was obvious.

Superior, Big Sorrel, and the bay mare wouldn't have been immediately available if something happened to Little Sorrel. By normal practice on a day of potential battle, Jim Lewis would have traveled toward the back of the column with the extra horses, probably riding Superior. Jackson could have taken the horse of a subordinate or sent a courier to fetch Superior if necessary.

During the five-and-a-half-hour march, Jackson followed his usual habit and rode up and down the column. Jackson urged the troops to remain close to each other to maximize the impact once contact was made with the Union forces. Jackson made himself visible for an additional reason. At this point in the war, he knew that the sight of him was enough to motivate his soldiers.

Never mind the dusty uniform, the worn-out cap, and the odd little pacing horse, he was still Stonewall Jackson and an object of inspiration wherever he appeared. The magnificent new uniform he wore that day may have puzzled a few of them, but the little horse was the same, and they thought all must certainly be well with the army.

Jackson arrived at the front line at about 8:30 AM, three hours after sunrise, taking field command of the two divisions of soldiers already there. In an instant, those divisions changed their role. They were no longer to form a defensive roadblock to Union troops heading east toward Fredericksburg. They were now to be, as Jackson told their commanders, the vanguard of an attacking Confederate force, the bulk of which was still several hours east. The order to advance came a couple of hours later, when the first regiments of Jackson's own divisions were close.

The first shots of the Battle of Chancellorsville were fired shortly before eleven o'clock on the morning of May 1, when skirmishers of the two armies met up about three miles east of the crossroads. Fighting began in earnest half an hour later.

The oblivious General Joseph Hooker had ordered a slow advance of Federal troops on the turnpike that headed east from Chancellorsville to Fredericksburg, expecting resistance, but not too much. He was still under the delusion that most of Jackson's corps remained along the Rappahannock south of Fredericksburg. Hooker himself was comfortably settled in a strong defensive position around the Chancellorsville crossroads, ready to repulse any Confederates that got through. He was also in position to follow in support of Union troops headed to Fredericksburg.

His lead regiments got the resistance they expected, but they were confused by it. Hooker's carefully thought-out and, so far, well-executed plan depended on the relatively weak Confederate left wing falling back to Fredericksburg under the Union onslaught and making their defensive stand in the city, where they would be overwhelmed by a Federal force twice their size.

But these Confederate troops seemed for all the world like they were advancing, not falling back. In the decades since Chancellorsville, Hooker has been both attacked and defended for his actions in the first week of May 1863, but neither supporters nor detractors can understand why he would base his entire plan on the twin assumptions that Stonewall Jackson could not get his corps up quickly and that, once there, he and Robert E. Lee would choose to fight a defensive battle.

Jackson, still riding his brave Little Sorrel, was so determined to know the strength and intentions of the Federal forces that he rode for a time in front of his advancing troops, a position far too reckless for a man so important to his army. What he saw was a Union force not eager to advance but ready to fight through the resistance that the Confederates presented. The Union troops surprised him when they began withdrawing. It was an orderly withdrawal, to be sure, but they were making no effort to continue forward. The Union soldiers fired, pulled back, fired again, and pulled back again.

These actions mystified Jackson, who knew that Hooker was aggressive by nature. The Union artillery had found itself an effective position on high ground south of the crossroads, so the Confederate advance was slow and difficult in spite of the Federal infantry withdrawal.

Late in the afternoon, Jackson and Little Sorrel, accompanied by one aide, hurried to a spot farther south where he could examine the Federal defensive position. Joined by Stuart and a handful of the cavalry chief's aides, he dismounted, leaving the perfectly behaved Little Sorrel in the company of the other horses, and climbed up a small knoll. It was a terribly exposed position, with artillery shells exploding all around the group.

"General Jackson, we must move from here," Stuart announced. Jackson agreed.

They walked down the knoll and remounted, but not before two things happened. First, a shell fragment struck Stuart's adjutant Channing Price, who had been standing just a few feet from Jackson. The wound, although it appeared not to be serious, severed an artery and ultimately killed the young aide. Second, Jackson got a good view of the dense, tangled stand of trees and brush that stood between him and the Union position near the Chancellorsville crossroads. The vegetation was thick and tall enough to mask a marching column of soldiers, should a general want to send one south and west. Jackson rode Little Sorrel back to the front.

Shortly before sunset, Lee and Jackson met less than a mile from the Chancellorsville crossroads. The Union troops appeared to have retreated into their strong defenses. Dismounting and leaving Little Sorrel and Lee's mount to be held by aides, the two generals sat on fallen logs and talked about the surprising Union retreat. Jackson thought it might mean Hooker was ready to pull out of his strong defensive position in Chancellorsville. Lee disagreed.

They did agree to send out a pair of trusted aides to scout the Federal positions. The scouts found the front extremely well defended. A direct assault on the crossroads would be difficult and bloody. But the Union right flank beyond the crossroads was weak and poorly laid out.

Lee's question: could Jackson's troops somehow get around seventy-two thousand Union soldiers and hundreds of pieces of artillery to smash into the vulnerable Union right flank? It was a rhetorical question since Lee had already decided the flank attack was the only option. Most of those seventy-two thousand would be in the center and could not be struck head on. How to do it was something for Jackson to sleep on. Little Sorrel was long since dozing when his owner lay down himself.

A couple of hours later Jackson was wide awake, sitting on a discarded Union hardtack crate, examining maps, and thinking about that dense growth he had seen from his risky hill climb the previous afternoon. Scouts and local guides told him there were routes well south, out of sight of even the sharpest-eyed Federal observers, and that he could lead his troops south and then north to hit the only part of the Union line where a column of twenty-eight thousand men could have an impact on a line of seventy-two thousand.

The march got under way at 7:00 AM, later than Jackson's predawn preference. But he was confident that he could keep his soldiers mostly hidden, and Lee knew everything that Hooker had done the day before spoke to the Union commander's determination to fight a defensive battle.

Jackson joined the march after one of his fifteen regiments of infantry got under way. For the fourth straight day, he rode Little Sorrel. He might have liked to rest the little horse, but he knew today would be pivotal, for himself, for the army, for the entire Confederacy. Lee had ordered and planned a long and risky march to attack a wing of an enormous Union army. Failure would have meant disaster, and Jackson chose again to ride his most trusted horse.

There was an added advantage. The march would be at least a dozen miles, and he and his horse would add a few more than that, riding up and down the column to see and be seen. The comfortable pacing gait, the first thing Jackson had noticed about the little horse two years earlier, would be a blessing.

Lee waited near the previous night's meeting place to have a few final words with Jackson, a moment noted by biographers and painted by artists. The conversation was brief and nobody knows what was said. Lee never wrote about it afterward, and if he told anyone else, they kept his confidence. The two generals parted, and Jackson returned to his audacious march around Hooker's army. Lee returned to his duty: commanding the two divisions left to him, no more than fourteen thousand men, trying to persuade Hooker that forty thousand soldiers remained in front of him.

Not long after the march began the column passed through a small clearing, suddenly becoming visible to Federal observers posted a mile and a quarter away in tall pine trees. A few hours later shells began crashing into the clearing, most of them falling short, as the last of the infantry marched through. The shelling did little damage, and the remaining soldiers were hurried through the clearing. The trailing supply wagons were directed on a longer, more southerly route, well out of sight and range of Union weapons.

News of the Confederate movement had clearly gotten to General Hooker from the tree-top observers, as did a handful of other reports

Robert E. Lee and Stonewall Jackson meet for the last time on May 1, 1863.
RANDOLPH, *THE LIFE OF GEN. THOMAS J. JACKSON*, 1876

from scouts, but he managed to convince himself that the troop move-ment meant that Lee was retreating. It was what he expected, what he wanted, and therefore it must have been what was happening.

A Georgia regiment trailing and protecting the column was attacked and badly damaged in late morning, but the attack was eventually fought off by reserves. Otherwise, the march moved forward through the hot, dry, and narrow footpaths that wound through the tangled desolation known as the Wilderness. The tireless Little Sorrel was in constant motion, carrying Jackson forward and backward around marching sol-diers, urging them to keep up with the men in front of them.

Just after two o'clock in the afternoon, General Fitzhugh Lee of Stu-art's cavalry division intercepted Jackson. Lee and his cavalry had been acting as a screening force for the march and located the far right wing of Hooker's army.

"Bring only one courier," Fitzhugh Lee told Jackson, "as you will be in view." Jackson, his courier, Lee, and possibly cavalry Colonel Thomas

Munford rode to the top of a wooded hill. Jackson and Little Sorrel stood for several minutes, in plain view and within sharpshooter range of the Eleventh Corps of Hooker's army. The soldiers had stacked arms and were completely at ease, cooking, smoking, and otherwise enjoying a warm, sunny afternoon. If they had looked up from their pleasures, everybody's day might have ended differently.

Jackson told the courier to hurry to the front of the marching column and tell the commanding general to wait for him. The courier dashed away.

"One more look upon the Federal lines," Fitzhugh Lee wrote later of Jackson, "and then he rode rapidly down the hill, his arms flapping to the motion of his horse, over whose head it seemed, good rider as he was, he would certainly go."

When he reached his column, Jackson changed his plans and orders. He told the officers to continue farther north than originally intended, so that the attack would come, not just on the flank of the right wing of Hooker's army, but at the back, a far greater challenge to an army that had already been caught napping.

It took nearly two hours for enough of the trailing division to reach Jackson's chosen point of assault and be directed to their positions, mostly in the dense thickets of the Wilderness. Although racing sundown, Jackson was composed, almost serene, as he waited with line officers to pass on the word to attack. Little Sorrel, whose efforts during the march would have tested any horse, matched his owner in unruffled serenity.

"Upon his stout-built, long-paced little sorrel," said his aide James Power Smith, "General Jackson sat, with visor low over his eyes and lips compressed, and with his watch in his hand."

Lt. Octavius Wiggins of the Twenty-Seventh North Carolina Infantry also watched Jackson prepare to order the assault. He was more poetic in his description of Jackson and his horse. "There sat General Jackson on the little sorrel," Wiggins wrote later, "as calm as if sitting upon the seashore a thousand miles away from a battlefield." Stonewall Jackson undoubtedly had worries and doubts during this day of his most difficult and daring march, but the choice of a horse to carry him was not among them.

With the words "You can go forward" from Jackson, twenty-one thousand men burst out of the thickets with the unearthly Rebel yell and muskets crashing onto the unsuspecting Eleventh Corps of Joseph Hooker's Army of the Potomac. It was a rout.

Some Union soldiers tried to stand their ground and fight; some arranged themselves into an organized retreat, returning fire when possible; and some simply ran, a few as far as the Rappahannock River. By the time the sun went down the Confederates had advanced nearly a mile and a half, to within sight of the Chancellorsville crossroads. Artillery support from the Union Twelfth Corps, plus disorganization within the front ranks of Jackson's corps, had brought the attack to a standstill.

But the attack had been an improbable and breathtaking success and Jackson, in whom elation and aggression fused during battle, was determined to regroup and carry on. Night assaults were rare and dangerous, but the moon was nearly full. A campaign that began under the shroud of white fog would not be stopped by a curtain of darkness.

At just after 9:00 PM, Jackson decided to see for himself what was happening in front. Aboard Little Sorrel, as he had been for fourteen hours, he gathered around him his staff, a few couriers, and a young local man from Stuart's cavalry division to act as a guide. There were ten men in all.

It was now two hours past sunset with no trace of daylight remaining, but the full moon offered some visibility. Jackson's party could see the soldiers forming the front line but generally could not see precisely who these soldiers were. If it had been possible to ask Little Sorrel and the other horses, they could have told their riders who was there. The night vision of horses is much superior to that of humans.

Shortly after starting the ride to the front, Jackson's group met up with General A. P. Hill, commander of the division that held the front line. Jackson told Hill about his planned scout and Hill felt obligated

At 9:00 PM on May 2 Jackson and Little Sorrel head out from this spot to scout the Union line.
LIBRARY OF CONGRESS

to join the ride forward. Eight other men were with Hill. An additional man was added when Jackson gave Hill the use of his own engineer, Captain James Keith Boswell, as a guide. Jackson's group moved forward first.

They heard noise from Federal soldiers in the dark ahead as well as random firing from skirmishers on both sides. The nineteen riders found themselves between the front lines of the Confederate and Union forces, and Jackson, who did not consider himself reckless, realized the danger was too great. He ordered his men to turn around.

Peril came from all directions. The Union troops appeared to be forming for the expected Confederate advance just ahead, so turning back made sense. But Confederates were also firing at a Pennsylvania regiment just to the south, the crash of musketry clearly audible to both Hill and Jackson and the North Carolina troops in front of them.

Hill, who had been following, was now leading the two groups and, just sixty yards from the safety of the Confederate line, he heard the shout, "Yankee cavalry!" followed by a volley of musket fire. A horse might have known that the nineteen silhouetted riders wore Confederate uniforms, but the soldiers of the Eighteenth North Carolina infantry did not.

The volley struck the A. P. Hill party first and hardest. Jackson and his followers had veered off into heavy woods and were screened somewhat by trees and distance, but the gunfire devastated both groups. In Hill's group, the general and his mount were the only pair in which one or both were not killed, wounded, or captured. Jackson's engineer, James Keith Boswell, riding next to Hill, died instantly from two bullets to the heart.

In terms of numbers, Jackson's party suffered less from the catastrophic friendly fire. One courier and two horses died immediately. Several horses were wounded, possibly including Little Sorrel, and two men were struck as well. But fewer casualties did not mean less consequence.

Stonewall Jackson was struck three times, once by a smoothbore ball that broke two bones in his right hand. The other wounds were more serious. Two bullets tore through his left arm, one through outside of the forearm and a second smashing through bone a few inches below the shoulder. The first of these bullets, which left an exit wound on the inside of Jackson's left wrist, may have struck Little Sorrel, who was described by one of the party as suffering from a neck wound.

Whether it was pain, fear, or a response to the distress of his trusted rider, Little Sorrel wheeled and dashed away from the gunfire, crashing through thick woods toward the Union line, causing Jackson's face to be gashed by low tree limbs. Jackson's bridle hand, the left, was useless, but

A nineteenth-century woodcut shows Jackson's wounding and a startled Little Sorrel moving in something like a pacing gait.
CASLER, *FOUR YEARS IN THE STONEWALL BRIGADE*, 1906

he managed to control his horse with his less-injured right hand and direct him back to the Confederate line.

Two aides who had escaped injury dashed up to horse and rider, stopped Little Sorrel, and eased Jackson from the saddle to begin care of his wounds. It would be the last time Stonewall Jackson and Little Sorrel saw each other.

CHAPTER 12

Afterward

The catastrophe of Stonewall Jackson's wounding drew dozens of men desperate to help, in spite of the danger from enemy and friendly fire. Little Sorrel, not as important to the army, was almost ignored. He stood quietly in place as Jackson was helped from the saddle, remaining stationary as work began to stop the general's bleeding. This was the behavior so familiar to the men who knew Little Sorrel.

Captain William F. Randolph, chief of the couriers riding with the group, had been behind Jackson when the bullets struck. He was uninjured, although his horse suffered several minor wounds. After regaining control of his terrified horse, Randolph moved him ahead to where Jackson had been placed.

"I saw the general's horse, which I recognized at once," Randolph wrote years later. Little Sorrel, he said, "was standing close to the edge of the road with his head bent low and a stream of blood running from a wound in his neck."

The wound to Little Sorrel is left out of other accounts. Understandably, most witnesses paid almost all their attention to Jackson, not his horse. Moreover, the rest of Randolph's account is highly suspect. He describes dismounting, rushing to the supine Jackson's side, and lifting the general's head and shoulders up.

"Not a living soul was in sight then," continued Randolph, "but in few moments A. P. Hill rode up, and then Lieutenant Smith, one of his aides." All that was true, but it was Jackson's chief signal officer Richard Wilbourn, one of the men who helped Jackson down from Little Sorrel, who had given the first assistance, not Randolph.

So Randolph's account has been mostly ignored, even though some of the descriptions of the events are compelling and believable. The account of Little Sorrel's wound may well be one aspect of the narrative that was true.

The brave little horse had showed utter calm under fire all day. Bullets had zoomed by his head and shells had crashed at his feet. The headlong dash toward enemy lines was atypical for Little Sorrel and most likely would not have happened unless pain was added to the noise and confusion.

To be fair, a good horse is always sensitive to his rider and Little Sorrel would have felt Jackson's shock and been aware of his pain. But bolting was not in this horse's repertoire. A wound, perhaps not as severe as Randolph described, may well have been the cause. The two bullets that struck Jackson's left arm were never found, and later trajectory analysis suggests that the horse's neck might have been in line with the lower of the wounds, especially given Jackson's crouching posture on horseback.

Randolph said he was sent off, first in search of a horse-drawn ambulance and then to inform General Stuart, second only to Jackson and A. P. Hill in terms of rank. The man who took charge of Little Sorrel after the incident was Private John Webb of Moorman's Battery of J. E. B. Stuart's Horse Artillery.

The battery would normally have been with Stuart, several miles away at this point. But Jackson had ordered a gun from Moorman's Battery and two others to participate in the late afternoon assault. Three pieces were still in place at the time of the barrage of bullets, just a few yards from the point where Jackson was removed from Little Sorrel. The commander of one of the pieces, Major Marcellus N. Moorman, had been a student of Jackson's at the Virginia Military Institute.

Webb held on to Little Sorrel in spite of the confusion and the sporadic firing, also catching the horses of two other wounded officers. Members of Moorman's Battery said later that they were unsure of the identity of Little Sorrel and that he and the other riderless horses were used for a few days after the wounding. Eventually Little Sorrel was recognized and turned over to Moorman. Moorman was both fond of horses and ambitious, and he was careful with Stonewall Jackson's horse. Little Sorrel joined the other horses of the battery.

One account from 1866 written by Jackson's brother-in-law General D. H. Hill, who wasn't present, claimed that Little Sorrel disappeared after the wounding and then improbably wandered into J. E. B Stuart's camp thirty miles away a week later. But the early biographers of Jackson acknowledged Moorman's version, although they all left out Moorman's name. During the 1880s and 1890s Moorman became active in speaking and writing about his experiences at Chancellorsville, particularly his role at the time of Stonewall Jackson's wounding. Critics were quick to jump on inconsistencies and exaggerations in other aspects of his narrative, so he failed to become part of the ongoing historical record.

At the same time that Moorman began speaking out about his experiences after the wounding, a few newspaper reporters began making the existing story more interesting by claiming that Union soldiers had captured Little Sorrel. Perhaps the symmetry of a horse repatriating himself appealed to them. But the truth of what happened to Little Sorrel was lost.

Eventually the idea that Little Sorrel had completed his bolt toward the Union lines and had been captured by Federal forces reached writers of Jackson biographies. Since it was well known what happened to the horse later in his life, the biographers assumed that the Federals must have either given him back or lost him in a subsequent recapture. Even the finest of the Jackson biographies, with a very few exceptions, include some version of this story.

The time frame for his period in Federal hands ranged from a few hours to a few months, depending on the writer. The final issue of *Confederate Veteran* magazine, published in December 1932, had a compromise story, with Little Sorrel disappearing briefly, then being recovered by Stuart's troops early the next morning.

A few former Union soldiers helped the Union capture story along. Among the best known was Charles H. Lewis of the Twenty-Second New York Cavalry. He claimed to have captured Stonewall Jackson's sorrel horse during fighting in the Wilderness. "It was the greatest horse I ever rode," Lewis told family members, who passed the story on to reporters. Lewis, of Cherry Valley in Otsego County, described how the horse was taken away from him a few days later when he was captured himself by the Confederates and sent off to the Andersonville prison in Georgia.

Lewis, like so many others, got his action confused. The Twenty-Second New York Cavalry was not engaged at Chancellorsville but was involved in the Battle of the Wilderness over the same ground a year later. He spent the summer and fall of 1864, not 1863, at Andersonville. Lewis may well have taken a fine sorrel horse from the Confederate army, but it was not Little Sorrel. Jackson's little red horse was almost certainly never out of the control of the Army of Northern Virginia.

Meanwhile, the battle continued on the morning of May 3 with the most intense fighting of the campaign. With masterful management and the help of Stuart substituting for the wounded Stonewall Jackson,

Robert E. Lee managed to reunite the two parts of his army while fighting off an attack from the rear by the Federal corps that had finally left Fredericksburg. Hooker's army was driven back to the fords of the Rappahannock they had been so proud to cross the week before. The Army of the Potomac escaped across the river on May 6.

Jackson and Little Sorrel were sent in different directions, Jackson south and east to Guiney Station, deeper in Confederate territory for better protection as he recuperated, and Little Sorrel north and west with Stuart's cavalry. The horse artillery saw little action during the final days of the battle, but it was kept in constant motion. Little Sorrel traveled with Moorman's men until they reached Raccoon Ford on the Rapidan River on May 7. Men and horses were exhausted, probably including Little Sorrel, but the spring grass gave the horses plenty to eat. Little Sorrel was lovingly cared for by John Webb, who had found him, and another artillery private, Thomas R. Yeatman.

On May 9, Stuart's division arrived at Orange Court House in Orange County, setting up camp at a site just south of the village. It was an area known as Scott's Hill. "Our headquarters were established on one of the hills forming a semicircle round one side of the beautiful little valley in which the pleasant village of Orange Court-house is situated," wrote Heros von Borcke in his *Memoirs of the Confederate War.* "We overlooked the town, as well as a great part of the rich country around it."

Von Borcke, the volunteer aide to Stuart, had always found Jackson and his little horse amusing. It's not known if he realized that Jackson's horse was part of Stuart's contingent on Scott's Hill.

On May 10, eight days after the wounding, Moorman sent a letter to Jackson, assuming that the general had continued the recovery that he and the rest of the army had heard about. He told Jackson that he had possession of his little sorrel horse and asked what the general wanted done with him. Jackson died at 3:15 that afternoon of pneumonia, which had set in a few days earlier.

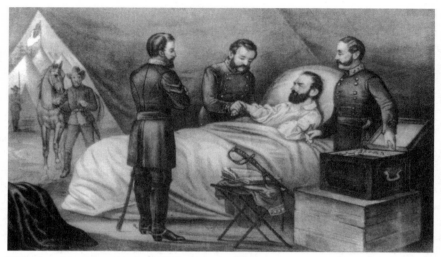

Little Sorrel is shown in an 1872 lithograph, but he was not actually present on May 10, 1963, when Stonewall Jackson died.
CURRIER AND IVES, LIBRARY OF CONGRESS

The letter most likely did not arrive before Jackson's death. If it did, Jackson was in no condition to understand its contents. Although it would be good to think that he knew before his death that his beloved little horse was safe, that was unlikely. Jim Lewis probably did know, and the news was most likely a small comfort to him.

News of Stonewall Jackson's death raced through the Army of Northern Virginia. Moorman may have known by the night of May 10. He certainly was aware by the next day and immediately asked Stuart what should be done with Little Sorrel. Stuart made the arrangements to send the horse to Richmond. According to Moorman, John Webb kept the yellow noseband as a souvenir.

Little Sorrel was taken to the stables at the Governor's Mansion, where Governor John Letcher took charge of the favorite horse of his neighbor and friend. The horse did not march in Stonewall Jackson's funeral procession. Many people then and since have assumed that he was indeed the riderless horse that followed the hearse as the funeral procession traveled the half mile between the Governor's Mansion to the state capitol building on May 12.

There are no surviving photographs, so modern historians may be forgiven for assuming the place of honor went to Little Sorrel. Contemporary observers should have noticed that Little Sorrel had become dark bay and must have grown five or six inches. The horse in the procession was Superior.

Jackson's newer horse may have been chosen for the honor because he was considered more handsome, or maybe Little Sorrel's neck wound was thought to be unsightly. Most likely, the horse hadn't reached Richmond in time for the procession and he simply wasn't available. When he did arrive, he stayed in the Letcher stables for two weeks, possibly to recover fully from his wound, and then was put on a train to North Carolina, to Anna Jackson's family home near Charlotte.

In June, Jackson's estate was probated. He left no will, but Anna was sole heir and the valuation and distribution were completed without controversy. The family home in Lexington, Virginia, was valued at $8,548 and converted to rental property. Four slaves were valued at a total of $5,700 and soon emancipated. Assorted stocks and investments were sold to pay debts. Anna kept the two horses owned by Stonewall Jackson at the time of his death.

"A sorrel horse, not present" and a "bay mare" were listed in the appraisal of Jackson's estate and valued at $400 to $450 each. The sorrel horse was obvious. That was Little Sorrel, already sent to Anna Jackson in North Carolina. The bay mare is more difficult to figure out. The mare was presumably the horse given by citizens of Staunton on December 30, 1862. There is no record of Jackson using her, but she may still have been in his possession.

He certainly owned the bay stallion Superior at the time of his death. Superior did eventually end up in Anna Jackson's possession, but he was emphatically not a mare. There is no record of when Superior was shipped to North Carolina, but he was there by early 1865. So Jackson's second horse was either the mare given by the gentlemen from Staunton in December or a misidentified Superior. The mare, later named Molly Jackson, was never sent to North Carolina and was owned after the war by Fielding Templeton of Staunton and later by Templeton's nephew McDowell Adair.

Little Sorrel lived in peace for nearly two years at Cottage Home, the Morrison plantation in Lincoln County, North Carolina. The plantation house was hardly a cottage. Anna's father, Robert Hall Morrison, had transferred the name from the family's smaller original home when they inherited a much larger property from his wife's parents.

Robert Morrison was a Presbyterian minister and a former college president in nearby Charlotte, but his marriage had placed him securely within the plantation aristocracy of North Carolina. So Little Sorrel now enjoyed the most luxurious circumstances he had ever known, not that

Cottage Home, North Carolina, where Little Sorrel was sent after Jackson's death.
ARNOLD, *EARLY LIFE AND LETTERS OF GEN. THOMAS J. JACKSON, "STONEWALL" JACKSON*

a horse in the habit of lying down in an army bivouac for a quick nap would have much cared.

The plantation house itself was a three-story, twelve-room country mansion, but to the horses, the important structures were huge barns. Even more important were the extensive pastures. There was plenty of room at Cottage Home for two extra horses. The farm was now mostly in food production. By mid-1863 the Union navy's blockade made it difficult to ship cotton overseas, and the Northern markets for cotton were gone. Food, on the other hand, found a ready market for the Confederate army and the civilian population in Virginia, whose farms had suffered terribly from foraging armies of both sides.

Little Sorrel, called Fancy around the farm, became a favorite for transporting family and workers around the eight-hundred-acre Cottage Home plantation. He was also a favorite mount of Anna's young nephew Paul Barringer, son of her late sister Eugenia. Paul's father, Rufus Barringer, served in Stuart's cavalry division, eventually rising to brigadier general.

Paul Barringer, born in 1857, spent much of the war at Cottage Home. It's through his memoirs, written in the 1880s but not published until 1949, that the story of Little Sorrel in North Carolina survives. Because of his youth, some historians doubt that Barringer's memories are entirely accurate, but what he writes in his memoir corresponds with other sources. The most important of his recollections involves the day war came calling again on Little Sorrel.

By the last week in March 1865, the Confederacy was held together by a quickly diminishing thread. The country's government knew it would have to evacuate the capital of Richmond within days—it happened on April 2—and Lee was unable to feed his shrinking army. After a week of trying desperately to find a way south to unite his army with that of Joseph Johnston's in North Carolina, Lee surrendered on April 9 at Appomattox Court House. The end had been in sight for months.

Even though Lieutenant General Ulysses S. Grant knew better than anyone else that the Confederacy could not long survive, the Union commander-in-chief was determined to end the war once and for all. His method was to be a final attack on the war-making ability of the South. He would take care of the Confederate army. Cavalry general George Stoneman would take care of the capacity to feed that army.

George Stoneman.
LIBRARY OF CONGRESS

Stoneman would operate in eastern Tennessee and North Carolina, which had been so far mostly untouched by war. Stoneman, who had been a roommate of Stonewall Jackson's at West Point in the 1840s, would make war on the economic lives of the people.

Stoneman's Raid—the word has been capitalized ever since—got under way on March 23 in Knoxville, Tennessee. The cavalry division plundered its way out of Tennessee and across North Carolina, reaching Virginia on April 2. The raid continued in southern Virginia as Lee and Grant played their endgame to the north and on April 9, the day of the surrender, they moved back into North Carolina. Even though Johnston's army was still in the field, it seemed to the people whose property was taken or destroyed that it was all overkill. Whom, they asked, could their farm support at this point except for their own children?

Stoneman's raiding party was made up of three brigades of three regiments each, and the people of Lincolnton, North Carolina, were fortunate that it was Stoneman's First Brigade that rode into town on April 17. The First was under the command of Col. William J. Palmer, a Quaker abolitionist from Delaware.

As a Quaker, Palmer opposed war, but as an abolitionist, he fought for the end of slavery. He managed to remain honorable through four years of war. The looting and physical violence against civilians suffered by other towns in North Carolina were minimal in those raided by Palmer's brigade. But he was assiduous in one of the primary goals of the raid. Stoneman had ordered his troopers to take any useable horse or mule they could find, both for service of the Union army and to deny them to the Confederates.

On the morning of April 18, Palmer divided two regiments of his brigade, the Tenth Michigan and the Twelfth Ohio, into raiding parties and sent them out in search of horses. Young Paul Barringer had spent the day of April 18 with his aunt Anna and the rest of the family at Cottage Home. "That evening a full regiment of Yankee cavalry passed by,"

Barringer wrote later, "stopping long enough to take all the horses and mules on the place, including Fancy and General Jackson's other horse, a stallion named Superior."

Anna Jackson, aware that her husband and Stoneman had known each other at West Point, wrote a note to the general, asking him to return the two horses. Young Paul and "old Abram"—presumably a slave—took the note to the raiders' camp, a mile away near the millpond of Dr. C. L. Hunter, a friend and colleague of Robert Hall Morrison. This was the camp of the Twelfth Ohio Cavalry and, upon arrival, Paul was sent to the commanding colonel. Paul, only eight at the time, was unable to recall the colonel's name years later, but he was almost certainly Robert H. Bentley, the acting commander of the Twelfth Ohio. More than thirty men of that regiment, including the adjutant William Heddleston, were from Hillsboro, Ohio, the town Little Sorrel may have left to go to war four years earlier.

Colonel Bentley took Paul and Abram to the corral where the day's horse haul was being held. Paul spotted Little Sorrel immediately and, with a Union bridle provided by the colonel, brought him out of the corral. Abram claimed a large white mule named Old Kit, and, with the amused permission of Col. Bentley, chose a few more that may or may not have been the Cottage Home mules. The colonel sent a note of apology to Anna with Paul, who rode Little Sorrel home, followed by Abram and the mules. Bentley assigned three troopers to protect Cottage Home, and, the next day, returned Superior to Anna with further apologies.

This was not the only instance of the First Brigade returning the property of prominent civilians. In Lincolnton, Col. Palmer returned a trunk filled with valuables to Harriet Vance, wife of the governor of North Carolina. But the widow of Confederate general Leonidas Polk, killed the previous summer in the defense of Atlanta, was unfortunate enough to be caught up in a raid by Stoneman's Second Brigade. A major from the Eleventh Kentucky Cavalry took the dead general's dress sword and refused to return it to the widow.

Anna Jackson's nephew Paul Barringer, who helped rescue Little Sorrel.
TYLER, *MEN OF MARK IN VIRGINIA*, 1906

The Morrison plantation survived the weeks of Stoneman's Raid better than many other North Carolina farms, but the end of the raid and the end of the war ushered in a period of great hardship. Finances became increasingly strained in the years after the war, as they were at most plantations in the former Confederate states. The Morrison family found it impossible to farm the acreage themselves, so they offered much of it in sharecropping arrangements with former slaves, including at least one of their own, a man named Jake Morrison.

"We must try to live on what we get," wrote the elderly Dr. Morrison to his sister Sarah three years after the war. The family, once enjoying the services of as many as sixty-six enslaved workers, was down to two paid servants, a woman and her young son.

In the summer of 1867, Anna moved to sell off some of the items she had inherited to raise much-needed cash. One of the things she decided she could part with was the bay stallion Superior. Little Sorrel's sale was never considered, for both emotional and practical reasons.

"A charming little horse," one visitor called him. Not only was he Jackson's favorite, he was a favorite around the farm for his usefulness and personality. His habit of undoing the latches of his own and other horses' stall doors provided entertainment, as did his ability to topple the top rail of a fence to make the barrier low enough to jump. The freed horses could always be found in the nearest well-grown pasture, so the humans were able to laugh at Little Sorrel's antics.

Anna originally planned to send Superior to Jackson supporters in Baltimore. The city's postwar economy was thriving and she was told that they would get a good price for him there. In June, a Jackson admirer in Macon, Georgia, made a generous offer and Little Sorrel's partner of four and a half years was gone. But the mules and possibly a pony or two remained and his human companions were always ready to pay him attention.

He became a regular mount for Anna's brother Robert H. Morrison Jr., a physician who needed comfortable and trustworthy transportation for trips to see patients. On the rare occasions that the elder Robert Morrison left the property, Little Sorrel transported him, either under saddle or harness. He became a familiar and well-loved figure in Lincoln County.

A story made the rounds that the Morrisons had once sent a servant on an errand to the Brevard railroad station aboard Little Sorrel. The trouble began when the chore was completed. "The old horse started

An elderly Little Sorrel enjoyed a place of honor in Anna Jackson's biography of her husband.
ARNOLD, *EARLY LIFE AND LETTERS OF GEN. THOMAS J. JACKSON, "STONEWALL" JACKSON*

home at a leisurely pace," one newspaper article reported. Then, according to the article, the servant "began beating him unmercifully." This was not going to happen to the dearly loved horse of a revered Confederate general. A posse of citizens pursued the offender. "If they had succeeded in overtaking him," the article continued, "his life would probably have paid the forfeit." The story is suspect, since Brevard is at least one hundred miles from Cottage Home, a long way to send a servant on an elderly horse, but the sentiment was true. Little Sorrel was a hero of the Confederacy and he was going to be treated as such.

The Morrisons tried to raise money for the upkeep of the farm by selling souvenir photographs of Little Sorrel, but Anna was unable to afford to keep him. In 1883 she made a difficult decision. Little Sorrel was now thirty-three-years-old, a very advanced age for a horse in the late nineteenth century. He was still healthy and alert, but he had trouble keeping on weight and was stiff in the joints. He was no longer capable of carrying Dr. Morrison on long trips, and Anna felt she couldn't

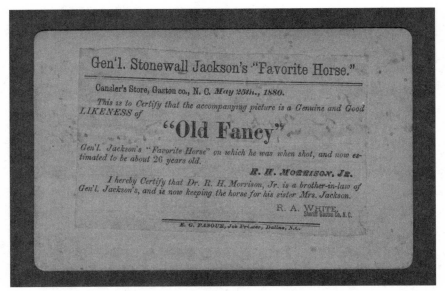

Anna Jackson's family tried several times to raise money by selling pictures of the famous old horse.
"OLD FANCY" CIVIL WAR COLLECTION, STUART A. ROSE MANUSCRIPT, ARCHIVES, AND RARE BOOK LIBRARY, EMORY UNIVERSITY

afford to keep a horse if he had no other use. She decided to offer him to the Virginia Military Institute in Lexington, Virginia, which had the stabling, grazing, and human help required to assure him comfort in his final few years.

On August 21 the little red horse was taken to Charlotte, where John E. Brown, a veteran of the Fiftieth North Carolina infantry, prepared him for shipment. Col. Brown, who operated a large stable in Charlotte, had been on the field with Jackson at Malvern Hill.

The next day Little Sorrel was led aboard a special car of the Richmond and Danville Railroad. He traveled as far as Lynchburg by train, then was transported to Lexington, where a hero's welcome awaited him. Only about two thousand eight hundred people lived in Lexington the year of Little Sorrel's arrival, but it was a place of pilgrimage. Not only

In 1884 Little Sorrel was back in Virginia for the first time in nineteen years to take up residence at Virginia Military Institute.
1884 POSTCARD

was Jackson buried there, so were Robert E. Lee and his famous gray horse Traveller. Visitors from North and South alike came to see the graves and were soon surprised and pleased to discover that a living relic of the war also resided in Lexington.

Little Sorrel had been losing hairs from his mane and tail since he became famous in 1862, but the pillaging escalated during his time at VMI. Although cadets were detailed to protect him, distinguished visitors managed to purloin sizeable sections of hair. A few weeks after Little Sorrel's arrival at VMI, Charles Thurman, son of a prominent Lynchburg family, arrived from Nashville with an appointment in hand as inspector-general of Tennessee and a state commission as a brigadier general.

General Thurman returned to Nashville with "a large band of hair cut from the mane of the old sorrel horse which General Stonewall Jackson rode during the war," according to a Nashville newspaper. He presented the mane hair to the Tennessee Historical Society, undoubtedly pleased to know that most Little Sorrel hair exhibits included a much smaller supply of rusty red tail hairs.

In late October, just three months after his arrival, Little Sorrel was taken to the Shenandoah Valley Agricultural Fair in Winchester, where he had seen so much action during the war. A proud corps of cadets accompanied him. The horse lost more hair during this expedition, in spite of strenuous efforts to protect him. But fairgoers were pleased to see him look so well. "Although thin," the *Winchester News* reported, "he is looking quite well." Another newspaper described him as "a handsome sorrel of good form."

Little Sorrel found that there was pleasure to be had in a life full of new people, new activities, and—above all—new sounds. He was put out to graze on the parade ground and soon discovered that its appeal lay in more than its fine grass.

"When the cadets, in practice, began firing rifle or cannon," post surgeon R. B. James told *Confederate Veteran* magazine, "Old Sorrel would come running onto the parade ground, sniffing the air and snorting loudly, with head and tail up."

His health was so good that fourteen months after his arrival at VMI he was strong enough to take a trip by railroad into Maryland, following nearly the same route that he had twenty-two years earlier when the Army of Northern Virginia had invaded the North for the first time. In 1862 Little Sorrel trailed somewhere behind the marching column. In 1884 he enjoyed a special railroad car and a greeting befitting a returning hero.

He was the guest of honor at one of the most important agricultural events in the country, the Great Hagerstown Fair. He traveled at the request of Hagerstown resident Henry Kyd Douglas, who had retained the great fondness for the horse that he had developed when he served as an aide to Stonewall Jackson.

The fair was enormously popular in Maryland, southern Pennsylvania, West Virginia, and Virginia, and four different rail lines brought thousands of visitors for the two-week event. Horses were particularly popular—rivaled only by the thousands of poultry shown—and the fair featured in-hand showings of draft horses, riding horses, and breeding stock. The harness races were especially well attended, and after the final race of the day on October 20, Little Sorrel's appearance was announced.

The huge crowd roared as the old horse, led by ten-year-old Johnny Beckenbaugh on a Shetland pony, paced his way past the grandstand. By this point in his life he was well used to crowds of admirers, but he seemed particularly alert this day. The trotting races may have awakened some distant memory, a recollection even older than combat. But when the band struck up "Dixie," there was no doubt what he was remembering. "The old sorrel threw his venerable head in the air," the *Hagerstown News* reported, "and pranced over the track with much of his old time fire." The reporter was unaware that there was little fire, even in the old times. What the fairgoers saw that day was an animal that enjoyed his life but still remembered his past.

Life became a little more difficult over the next few months. The visit to Hagerstown was so successful that the Institute's leadership decided to ship the horse to New Orleans to have him appear in a paid exhibit at the 1885 New Orleans World's Fair, officially named the World's Industrial and Cotton Centennial Exposition.

What followed was an unseemly squabble between VMI and Anna Jackson over who would have the honor of exhibiting the old horse and who would profit from the tickets. In the end, Mrs. Jackson won, and her choice for traveling companion was Major Andrew R. Venable, who had seen action as an artillery officer in several of Jackson's battles but was better known as an aide to J. E. B. Stuart.

Venable and Little Sorrel were in place in New Orleans by late February 1885 after a tour that stopped at several Southern cities. Although the tour was criticized as being too stressful for a thirty-five-year-old horse, he arrived in New Orleans without incident. "He is in good condition," the *New Orleans Daily Picayune* reported on February 25. "He has eyes as bright as a 3-year-old's although he doesn't appear to have ever been a stylish animal."

He looked so well and alert that Major Venable was forced to tell the newspaper a few weeks later that this was truly Stonewall Jackson's horse and he really was thirty-five years old. Doubters had appeared, questioning that a horse of that age could have survived a trip of hundreds of miles and the attentions of thousands of spectators.

He was a popular exhibit, especially after the beginning of April when he began to shed. Many visitors were treated to a lock of his hair to keep as a souvenir, some of which survive in public and private collections. While he was in New Orleans, possession of the famous old horse changed. According to Anna's wishes, the profits from the twenty-five-cent fee to look at him were to go to a new rest home for poor and disabled Confederate veterans that was recently opened in Richmond.

Little Sorrel left New Orleans on May 1 and began another tour of Southern cities on his way to his new home. He was hauled through the South in a special four-compartment car, with two sections for two human companions, one for hay, feed, and water, and one special padded compartment for the old horse himself.

"Old men fell upon its neck and wept like children," reported the *Cincinnati Enquirer* of his stop in Knoxville, Tennessee. Other cities saw similar displays as Little Sorrel took part in what amounted to a railroad procession to his new destination. Once there, he was welcomed by men who had seen him at war and others who had only heard about him.

The twenty years after the war had been difficult for most residents of the old Confederacy, but they were particularly hard on the older and disabled veterans of the war. By the early 1880s, destitute soldiers numbered many thousands around the South and probably a thousand or more in Virginia, whose economy had finally begun to improve.

In 1884 better-off former Confederates raised $14,000 to buy a thirty-six-acre tract of lightly wooded land and an old house in the western part of Richmond. More money poured in to build cottages for Confederate veterans with no way to support themselves, as well as a chapel, a hospital, and other outbuildings. The Robert E. Lee Camp of the Confederate Soldiers' Home was occupied over its more than half-century life by hundreds of elderly and disabled veterans and, for seven months, by one old horse.

The home opened its doors to its first veterans in January 1885, and Little Sorrel—usually called Old Sorrel at this point—arrived from New Orleans in August. At thirty-five he was, in terms of relative age, by far the oldest resident. The life expectancy of a full-sized horse today is twenty-five to thirty years, several years more than it was in the nineteenth century, when twenty was a good long life. Even today, a thirty-five-year-old horse is the equivalent of a nearly hundred-year-old human. In 1885 Little Sorrel was a centenarian by anybody's standards. Hardly anybody at the soldiers' home had seen or even heard talk of a horse so old.

There were plenty of eager hands to groom him, feed him, caress him, and talk to him about the war that had ended more than twenty years earlier. Some of the veterans had actually seen him in wartime, not in his youth exactly because he was no longer young when John Harman took him off the livestock car in Harpers Ferry. They happily told the others about their memories of Little Sorrel and his master.

The trip to New Orleans may have been harder on the old horse than anyone thought, or perhaps the years were finally too many. Little Sorrel began his final decline a few months after his arrival at the soldiers' home.

When word spread around the country that he was nearing his end, a young woman from Hillsboro, North Carolina, sent him a gift for the holidays. "This apple is for Old Sorrel," Anna Cameron wrote on a card attached to an enormous apple that arrived by express shipment in late December. Others used stronger language.

"Take off your hats, boys. Bow your heads. Old Sorrel is dying," said the *Times-Picayne* (New Orleans). "He is only a brute, true, but he is a marked figure in a grand historical pageant. The Great Commander is fast closing up the column, and ere long even the rear guard will have passed over the river to rest under the shade of the trees." The writer used the reputed last words of Stonewall Jackson, who died never dreaming that his little red horse would outlive him by a full twenty-three years.

By the first weeks of 1886, just after the old soldiers helped him celebrate his thirty-sixth birthday, Little Sorrel reached the point where he could no longer get up on his own. He could lie down, as most horses like to do for an hour or two a day, but his front legs were too weak for him to rise independently.

The soldiers fashioned a block-and-tackle system with bands around his belly to help hoist him up, but the contraption broke, severely injuring the old horse. During the second week in March, Virginia governor Fitzhugh Lee, who had played a role in the success of the flank march at Chancellorsville, paid a visit to the dying horse. Lee caressed his mane and tail, acquiring a few hairs as so many others had done. On March 16, 1886, at six o'clock in the morning, Little Sorrel died at the Confederate Soldiers' Home. The flag outside the home was immediately lowered to half-staff.

Plans had been made even before the old horse left North Carolina in 1883 for his hide to be mounted and displayed to maintain the thread that connected Americans—Southerners mostly but Northerners too—to one of the Civil War's greatest heroes. There was no delay in making arrangements for his body.

The famous taxidermist Frederic Webster had been notified as soon as Little Sorrel was injured, and immediately had the horse's remains transported to his studio in Washington, D.C. Upon completion, the mount, with head up as if he were focusing on the sight of troops marching and the sound of cannons, was returned to the soldiers' home, where it remained for more than fifty years.

When the last resident died in 1941, the property was taken over by the State of Virginia and Little Sorrel took a final trip, back to VMI. He remains on display today in the museum in Jackson Hall, named, appropriately, for the man he carried to glory, a glory that was shared by both of them.

Two and a half years earlier, Dr. R. B. James had marveled at how much life remained in Little Sorrel so many years after the vast majority of horses that participated in the war were gone. "Game to the end," said Dr. James of the little red horse. His other description of Little Sorrel was most accurate. "A glorious warrior," Dr. James said.

CHAPTER 13

The Legend

Little Sorrel began to find his place in history within minutes of his death, as Stonewall Jackson himself had done nearly a quarter century before. But Jackson died early, at only thirty-nine, so he was to remain forever young in memory. Little Sorrel lived to an extraordinary age, and all but one of the known photographs of him were taken when he was elderly. That, combined with the inevitably aged-looking mount created by Frederic Webster, ensured that stories of a homely little warhorse would be given credence forever.

Little Sorrel's reputed appearance was further solidified in people's imaginations when Stonewall Jackson became a cornerstone of the Lost Cause concept that began within weeks of the war's end. The Lost Cause got its name from a book published in 1866 by Southern historian Edward A. Pollard, *The Lost Cause: A New Southern History of the War of the Confederates.*

The Pollard theme was that the Confederacy, although composed of fine soldiers, citizens of high moral and social standing, and a righteous cause, was doomed to defeat by the overwhelming size and technological superiority of the North. So it was not the fault of the Confederate army that it was defeated. The Lost Cause idea was first voiced, at least in part, by none other than Robert E. Lee, who in April 1865 tried to soothe the pain of the loss after the surrender at Appomattox. "[T]he Army of Northern Virginia has been compelled to yield to overwhelming numbers and resources," Lee wrote in his farewell to the army. Over the next few months, Lee quietly compiled figures of comparative strength of manpower and weaponry between his own army and that of Ulysses S. Grant during the time Grant commanded the Army of the Potomac.

The Lost Cause movement soon developed another basic concept, one that had less of a basis in reality. The war, according to Lost Cause historians, was not about slavery but about states' rights. Besides, they argued, slavery wasn't so bad anyway and enslaved people were mostly happy about it. Modern historians from any region never make the argument that slavery was a good thing, and few pretend that threats to slavery and its expansion weren't the most immediate cause of war, pointing out that even the Confederate constitution itself was careful to prevent member states from doing anything to limit slavery.

But many people in the North and South do still believe in another keystone of the Lost Cause movement: that Robert E. Lee and Thomas "Stonewall" Jackson were essentially perfect examples of the kind of military figure that the prewar South could produce. They were, the argument went, tactically brilliant, brave beyond the normal, and morally upright leaders of men. An additional Lost Cause object of admiration was the ordinary Confederate foot soldier, a hungry, homespun-clad, dirty hero who carried on magnificently despite overwhelming odds. It suited the story that a noble figure—Stonewall Jackson—would be mounted on the equine version of the shabby Confederate foot soldier.

The first two major biographers of Stonewall Jackson each played important but contradictory roles in the development of the Lost

Cause model of Jackson and Little Sorrel. Robert Lewis Dabney, the Presbyterian minister who worked briefly and with limited success as chief of staff for Jackson, certainly knew the general's horse. He fails to mention Little Sorrel by name in his authorized biography, first published in 1866, but he presents a fully realized heroic portrait of Jackson as an ideal Christian soldier.

Dabney published an earlier contribution to the Lost Cause concept in his 1863 *Defense of Virginia*, which was primarily a pro-slavery manifesto. Dabney didn't pretend that Jackson was in the field for any reason other than the desire to defend the institution "in the name of God and the Right." Dabney's Jackson was the ultimate Christian soldier and a martyr to his beliefs. His book, written at least partially from personal experience, became the definitive biography for generations. But no Little Sorrel was to be found, perhaps because he didn't suit Dabney's image of Jackson.

That omission was corrected by the second of the early biographers. John Esten Cooke was a successful poet and novelist when he joined J. E. B. Stuart's staff early in the war. Cooke, more on the lookout for a good story than Dabney was, presented a heroic but eccentric Jackson in a quickly written biography published in 1863 and expanded in 1866. Cooke's Stonewall went to battle sucking lemons and raising his hand to heaven. Cooke had some personal experience of Jackson, and he realized that Jackson's odd little horse was part of a colorful—and saleable—story. His description has lasted for 150 years. "His horse was not a fiery steed but an old raw-boned sorrel," Cooke wrote, "gaunt and grim but a horse of astonishing equanimity." Cooke must have formed his impression of Little Sorrel during winter or early spring, because the horse was neither raw-boned nor gaunt the rest of the time.

In her own biography of her husband, Anna Jackson takes pains to point out that Little Sorrel was plump and round by nature, and she spent many more years with the horse than anyone else, including her husband.

As the years went by, biographers drew from Dabney, Cooke, and Anna Jackson. As staff members and others who saw Jackson and Little Sorrel in person added their own memories to the historical record, a generally accepted portrait emerged of a brilliant and pious Christian soldier with peculiarities and a strange-looking little horse. Modern biographers tend to downplay Jackson's peculiarities and pay more attention to the incidents of less-than-perfect leadership in battle. But most continue the story of a poor rider riding an even worse horse.

Fortunately for his reputation, artistic depictions of Little Sorrel didn't always parallel the written version as the decades passed. The traditions of equestrian art required a noble horse as well as a noble rider, and Little Sorrel was the victim or beneficiary, depending on your point of view. With only a few exceptions, the sculpted and painted Little Sorrel was a much more magnificent animal, in appearance at least, than the living one.

During the war and for several years after it ended, most graphic art was produced in the North. Even before the war came, the Confederate states had limited facilities for printing art and those that existed were seriously compromised by the war. But the Northern printmakers were willing to fill the gap and produce items intended to be sold in the former Confederate states. Stonewall Jackson and Robert E. Lee were also favorite subjects in the North, and many prints and paintings of the two famous Confederates included horses. Both Traveller and Little Sorrel were known in the North, thanks to wartime newspaper reporting, and many of the artists made an effort to represent the horses they heard about with some degree of accuracy. In the case of Traveller, they succeeded. In the case of Little Sorrel, they mostly failed.

One of the popular scenes to show a mounted Jackson represented the last meeting of Jackson and Lee. The most famous was an oil painting by E. B. D. Julio, *The Last Meeting of Lee and Jackson*. Completed in 1869, the painting was soon engraved and reproduced by the thousands. Julio apparently realized that Jackson's horse was a sorrel, but he gave him a wide white blaze instead of an unmarked face. The various engravers and lithographers who repeated the scene showed a similar horse, a sorrel with a blaze.

The famous and widely distributed Currier and Ives lithograph *The Death of Stonewall Jackson* showed a believable Little Sorrel, a small alert horse being held by an aide outside the tent where Jackson lay dying of his wounds at Chancellorsville. Other than the horse's appearance, mostly everything else about the scene was fantasy. Jackson died in a building, not a tent, at Guiney's Station, not Chancellorsville, and Little Sorrel was miles away at the time of his death. Most of his staff, probably even Jackson himself, believed that Little Sorrel had disappeared during the chaos of the shooting incident. But it was touching to think that Jackson's favorite horse, who had been with him through so much danger, was still with him as he lay on his deathbed, and the printmakers were determined to include the horse.

Artist and printmaker David Bendann, who had been a photographer in prewar Richmond, made an effort to create a realistic Stonewall Jackson and Little Sorrel. Bendann's equestrian oil of Jackson, done in Baltimore late in the nineteenth century possibly with the help of a hired artist, was widely reproduced in the early twentieth century. Although it shows a more elegant horse, the color and relative size were correct. The Bendann portrait remains one of the most important works issued under the Bendann name and is certainly one of the best-known images of Jackson and Little Sorrel.

Other engravings and lithographs, sold in both the North and the South, made more egregious mistakes about the horse. Some lost the blaze but changed Little Sorrel to bay. Some added white ankles or legs. But most did have one thing in common. The artists converted the small, round horse into a specimen of equine perfection. They also gave Jackson what they considered to be a better and more graceful seat in the saddle.

David Bendann produced a painting and a successful print edition of a handsome Stonewall Jackson and Little Sorrel.
DAVID BENDANN, C. 1913

In 1911 the celebrated illustrator N. C. Wyeth produced an oil painting of Stonewall Jackson on foot overlooking the Shenandoah Valley and holding an unusually small horse. Wyeth created it as the frontispiece for *The Long Roll*, a novel by Mary Johnston. The horse appears to be bay rather than sorrel or chestnut and Wyeth may have been producing a generic horse rather than Little Sorrel, in spite of the animal's size. The portrait of the horse is good, but that of Jackson was somewhat abstract and highly controversial. It was "more the likeness of some brutal prize-fighter of physical figure and countenance," complained Anna Jackson, the general's widow, who was still alive in 1910. Wyeth was taken aback by the vigor of her complaints and eventually gave the original canvas to Mary Johnston rather than exhibiting or selling it.

This N.C. Wyeth painting of Jackson and Little Sorrel in the Shenandoah Valley was controversial.

JOHNSTON, *THE LONG ROLL*, C. 1911

An early twentieth-century painting shows the most accurate Little Sorrel among any done while there were people still living who had seen the horse in life. This one was in an entirely different medium, a large mural on the wall of a wing of what is now the Virginia Historical Society. It was the work of French artist Charles Hoffbauer, a lover of American scenes, historical events, heroic scale, and generous commissions.

The Confederate Memorial Association chose Hoffbauer to create four large wall panels for its headquarters showing the progression of the war from the point of view of the Confederate army. Stonewall Jackson was to be the centerpiece of one of the panels. The grouping was eventually named *The Four Seasons of the Confederacy* and the Jackson panel represented spring, more specifically the spring of 1862, and the still-famous Shenandoah Valley campaign.

Accuracy was important to Hoffbauer. He amassed a collection of thousands of Civil War photographs, built clay models, and hired dozens of people to pose for the unknown figures in the murals. Perhaps most important to the accuracy of the mounted portrait of Jackson and Little Sorrel, he visited the Confederate Soldiers' Home next door, where Little Sorrel had spent his last year. The mount was still there when Hoffbauer created his murals.

Hoffbauer was able to look at something very close to the real thing as he sketched the horse. The artist spoke to residents of the home, some of whom had actually seen horse and rider in life. The result was an equestrian portrait that was as accurate as possible for a scene that was never photographed and was reimagined from a distance of more than fifty years. Little Sorrel is small and attractive, not an inspiring war charger, but precisely suited to his rider. Hoffbauer realized that the Little Sorrel of his painting should be a twelve-year-old in the spring rather than a thirty-six-year-old with a winter coat. He's standing still, so there is no way to know if Hoffbauer was aware that Little Sorrel was a pacing horse.

There was no sculptor equivalent of Charles Hoffbauer. The most important equestrian statues of Stonewall Jackson were erected during a period of just over twenty years, between 1919 and 1940. The dedication ceremony of the earliest monument included a number of Confederate veterans, several of whom had seen Jackson and Little Sorrel in life. The next, two years later, included fewer survivors, but there were still a few who had firsthand knowledge. By 1940, when the last of the three major individual statues was unveiled, there was only one veteran still alive who claimed to have seen Jackson and Little Sorrel in person, and he wasn't at the ceremony. But the fact that observers had no knowledge of what the real thing looked like didn't keep them from criticizing the statues. In each case, most of the complaints centered on the depiction of the horse rather than the interpretation of Stonewall Jackson.

The first of the three statues was the most conservative and the least criticized, although the veterans and others who had known Little Sorrel were disappointed to see that, while the rider looked like Stonewall Jackson, the horse looked nothing like his favorite mount. It was no mistake, claimed the sculptor. The horse was Superior, not Little Sorrel at all, even though Jackson probably never rode Superior in battle. This was the mounted Stonewall Jackson on Monument Avenue in Richmond.

F. William Sievers, the sculptor commissioned to create the seventeen-foot bronze statue, was an Indiana-born resident of Richmond. Sievers was classically trained and preferred to mount Jackson on the Thoroughbred-like Superior rather than the chunky Little Sorrel. His sense of proportion and balance also made him give Jackson a more acceptable seat. In the Monument Avenue statue, Stonewall Jackson sits back in the saddle with stirrups only a tiny bit shorter than normal.

Shortly after the Richmond statue was unveiled, another Stonewall Jackson equestrian statue was on its way. This one was intended to show Jackson specifically aboard Little Sorrel and an effort was made to do it accurately. It has one major mistake, but many people believe it to be among the best equestrian statues ever sculpted in America, inaccurate or not.

Early in 1919, eight months before the Monument Avenue statue of Jackson and Superior was dedicated, a Charlottesville financier and philanthropist gave the city a parcel in the center of town in order to develop a park around a statue of Stonewall Jackson and Little Sorrel. The donor, Paul Goodloe McIntire, was a lover of horses and history and had dreamed for years of such a statue. He commissioned prominent sculptor Charles Keck of New York City to create the monument.

Like Sievers in Richmond, Keck was classically trained, but he was more of a modernist in his style. So the bronze he created for Charlottesville, although very realistic, was a highly unusual equestrian statue in which movement predominates. Jackson's familiar cap is gone, lost in the wind. The general rides with his shorter-than-normal stirrups, leaning far forward, as he did in real life. Little Sorrel's mane and tail are blown back as he races to the front.

An accurate depiction of the horse was important to Keck and his sponsor. The sculptor traveled to central Virginia to study local horses and horsemanship and used McIntyre's own favorite riding horse among other live models for Little Sorrel. Some observers complained that the horse was too small for the tall Jackson, but they were quickly quieted with the explanation that the real Little Sorrel did indeed look too small for his rider. But Charlottesville-area horsemen had other complaints. They wanted Little Sorrel to look like "the best kind of Virginia horse," which of course he never was.

"The rump is weak and should be filled out a little," one horse expert said after seeing the model for the proposed bronze. "The rump is fallen," noted another. "Looks like a damn skabe," stated a third. Of course, the real Little Sorrel had a low-set tail, a sloping croup, and hindquarters smaller than his shoulders. He was a pacer and that's exactly how he should have looked. Keck possibly didn't know about his gait, but he probably had seen photographs of Little Sorrel and accurately depicted the horse's obvious pacing conformation.

Keck took his work on the horse as seriously as he did his sculpting of Stonewall Jackson himself. The result was a remarkable depiction of a horse—one so real that he appeared to be trotting briskly across Jackson Park in the center of Charlottesville, and that is precisely the problem with the sculpture.

"Little Sorrel is shown proceeding at an animated trot with his proper left front leg and proper right hind leg elevated," reads the description in Charlottesville's application for the statue to be placed on the National Register of Historic Places. The relative height is correct, the conformation is correct, the attitude is correct, but the gait is not. The pacer Little Sorrel trots in the best statue that was ever sculpted of him.

The quality of the Charlottesville sculpture was recognized as soon as it was unveiled on October 19, 1921, as part of a Confederate veterans' reunion. Five thousand people, including school children arrayed to represent the Confederate flag, marched to Jackson Park to get the first look at the statue.

A copy of the Keck statue stands on Courthouse Square in Clarksburg, West Virginia, Jackson's birthplace. The site is appropriate for both Jackson and his horse since it was in what is now West Virginia that the future Stonewall Jackson first laid eyes on the future Little Sorrel when John Harman chose him from a load of Yankee horses to show his commander as a potential warhorse.

A less appropriate location is the site of the final and most familiar of the three individual equestrian statues, the massive sculpture at the Manassas National Battlefield Park. This statue shows a huge, heavily muscled, arch-necked horse that has nothing in common with Little Sorrel except his species.

Plans for the Manassas statue got under way in the late 1930s when the government announced the establishment of the national park at the

The best sculpted likeness of Little Sorrel is that of the Charles Keck statues in Charlottesville, Virginia, and Clarksburg, West Virginia, even though he trots rather than paces.

site of two important Civil War battles, the First and Second Battles of Manassas. The Sons of Confederate Veterans agreed to donate land they owned on Henry Hill, the place where Jackson received the name "Stonewall," provided a statue of Jackson was commissioned and erected there.

In 1938 the Virginia legislature appropriated $25,000 for the memorial and gave the Virginia Art Commission the responsibility for acquiring a suitable statue. The requirements were minimal: that Thomas J. "Stonewall" Jackson and his horse "Little Sorrel" be portrayed in bronze and that the "nature, quality, and significance of Stonewall Jackson be expressed and considered in the design of the monument."

The commission decided to conduct a contest to find a sculptor, and their choice among eighty entries was Italian-born New Yorker Joseph Pollia, whose previous work had included well-received Civil War statues. Both the model and the final sculpture drew an outpouring of complaints so loud and relentless that some people called the controversy the "Third Battle of Manassas."

There were complaints that Jackson's face looked too old. After all, he was less than forty when he died. There were complaints that the figure was dressed in a cape, a uniform item that he rarely, if ever, wore. Besides, the Manassas battles were in July and August, hardly cape season. There were further complaints that Pollia had given Jackson muscles that he didn't possess in life.

But most of the criticism centered on the horse. The sculpted animal looked nothing at all like Little Sorrel, but the sculptor hadn't even made him more handsome, which might have been forgivable. He was a big, clumsy-looking animal, much heavier in front than a riding horse should be. But he was a dramatic creature, as was the figure riding him.

"Little Sorrel was a Thoroughbred and not a farm horse," complained Mrs. G. T. Kern of the Richmond chapter of the United Daughters of the Confederacy. She was wrong about that, but she was right that Pollia's horse was not an accurate representation of Jackson's favorite mount.

Sculptor Joseph Pollia created a fantasy Stonewall Jackson and Little Sorrel in his statue on the Manassas battlefield.

A few people objected to the specific location of the statue, on the opposite side of Henry Hill from the spot where Stonewall received his name at the First Battle of Manassas. But apparently nobody objected to the fact that perhaps Little Sorrel shouldn't have been memorialized on Henry Hill at all. Jackson wasn't aboard him at the first battle. Little Sorrel was used at Second Manassas, but Henry Hill was James Longstreet's sector, not Jackson's.

The twenty-first century is unlikely to see any new military equestrian statues, particularly of Confederate generals, so the question of Little Sorrel's accurate depiction in bronze or stone won't likely come up again. But Civil War art is alive, well, and highly realistic. Stonewall Jackson and Little Sorrel are favorite subjects of modern painters. Portraits of Jackson alone appear, but scenes, often mounted, are more popular.

The scenes are usually of specific, identifiable events, sometimes battles, but often much simpler scenes. The best artists employ nearly photographic realism and almost all portray a convincing Jackson. They also show a believable horse, although the horse sometimes doesn't look much like Little Sorrel.

One artist who has made a determined effort to portray an accurate Little Sorrel is Bradley Schmehl, who has included Jackson and Little Sorrel in seven of his Civil War works. Accuracy is vital in a genre that appeals to people used to the reality of photography, and one that knows what it's looking for.

"Painting for an audience of historical enthusiasts, many of whom are quite knowledgeable, required me to do my due diligence," Schmehl says. He chose a retired racing Arabian for Little Sorrel's model, a horse that was small enough to be convincing as Stonewall Jackson's undersized mount. The horse did require that his white blaze be painted out before he posed for the paintings.

Artist John Paul Strain finds accuracy so important that he gave Jackson the correct blue uniform in his "Jackson Meets Little Sorrel." The painting represents the first contact between a man and a horse destined to be famous. On May 10, 1861, Jackson hadn't yet traded his blue Virginia Military Institute uniform for Confederate gray.

Strain also wanted to capture the feelings of both in what became one of his most best-known paintings. "My depiction shows the immediate connection that Jackson had with him at Harpers Ferry," Strain says.

More than one hundred fifty years after the end of the Civil War Stonewall Jackson remains an icon, second only to Robert E. Lee as a mythic symbol of the war. The appetite for Jackson biographies and images may be greater in the South than the North, but not by much. The myth everywhere usually imagines Stonewall Jackson on horseback, and he's on an animal known alternately as Fancy, Old Sorrel, and today, Little Sorrel. The horse still appears in books and art, but not always as he really looked. But no matter how he's portrayed and what name is used, the little Yankee horse is an important part of the image and an even greater part of the legend.

Endnotes

INTRODUCTION: LAID TO REST AT LAST

The decision to inter the bones of Little Sorrel and the subsequent ceremony were well covered by newspapers, particularly in Virginia, during the spring and summer of 1997. Most of the coverage was straightforward, but a few writers couldn't resist a little mockery. Examples of the first kind are in the bibliography, as is Tony Horwitz's "Stonewall's Steed Was Ugly, But His Hide Was Tough," from the *Wall Street Journal*. Horwitz quotes a local newspaper editor as saying, "You turn a corner in the VMI museum and come face to face with the mighty Stonewall's mighty war-horse—and it looks like it couldn't pull Donald Duck in a wagon."

The events surrounding the original taxidermy work, the separation of the hide and the bones, and the travels of each part of Little Sorrel were also well covered in newspapers of their respective times and there are examples of each in the bibliography. For an examination of Frederic Webster's technique, see Oliver Davie, *Methods in the Art of Taxidermy*.

CHAPTER 1: WARRIORS UNDER SADDLE

An overview of the conflicting attitudes of Virginians as war approached can be found in James McPherson's *Battle Cry of Freedom*, the best single-volume history of the Civil War. Jackson's own prewar ambivalence is well described in S. C. Gwynne's *Rebel Yell*.

The story of how Jackson came to own Little Sorrel has been repeated by almost everyone who has written extensively about Jackson, although not by the two men most closely involved. Jackson had no opportunity to write his memoirs and John A. Harman, his quartermaster, never did. There are contemporary newspaper accounts of the train seizure and the capture of horses, but none mention Jackson or any specific horse. An example that includes a report that the consignor of the confiscated horses was paid is in the *Staunton Spectator*, May 21, 1861.

The most detailed account of Jackson at Harpers Ferry in 1861 is John Imboden's. The eventual cavalry brigadier general wrote his memories of Jackson in *Century Illustrated Magazine* in 1885, later reprinted in the voluminous *Battles and Leaders of the Civil War*. Imboden fails to mention Little Sorrel's acquisition, but Jackson aide Henry Kyd Douglas, whose *I Rode with Stonewall* is the greatest single source of information about the horse, does. Douglas completed his memoirs in the 1890s, but they weren't published until 1940. Jackson's widow, Mary Anna, also writing in the 1890s, tells much the same story of the seizure that Douglas does.

Other details of the early days at Harpers Ferry are in *Stonewall Jackson's Way: A Sketch of the Life and Services of Major John A. Harman* by Alexander Garber, a relative of Harman's, and *Legends of Loudon* by Harrison Williams, who details the split loyalties of the region where Jackson and Harman went hunting for horses.

One especially good source of information on the domestication of the horse appears in *The Horse: The Epic History of our Noble Companion* by Wendy Williams, but you'll find others in the bibliography. Williams thinks the Botai of Kazakhstan may not have been the first to domesticate the horse.

Louis DiMarco's *War Horse: A History of the Military Horse and Rider* is a good overview of the history of horses at war. For a disturbing look at the equine catastrophes of the Crimean War and, particularly the Charge of the Light Brigade, see Terry Brighton's *Hell Riders: The True Story of the Charge of the Light Brigade.*

CHAPTER 2: HORSEMAN

The best source for family background of Stonewall Jackson is Roy Bird Cook's *The Family and Early Life of Stonewall Jackson*, originally published in the 1920s. Stephen Wayne Brown's *Voice of the New West: John G. Jackson, His Life and Times* has details of Jackson's father, Jonathan, and his gambling problems. More recent discoveries in the area of family and early history, as with almost every other topic related to Stonewall Jackson, are in James Robertson's *Stonewall Jackson: The Man, the Soldier, the Legend.* The bibliography includes several other books with more in-depth information on the Scots-Irish immigration and convict transportation to America. The story of David Ross, the convict merchant, is in James Johnston's *From Slave Ship to Harvard: Yarrow Mamout and the History of an African American Family.*

Although the book concentrates on Quarter Horses, Alexander Mackay-Smith's *The Colonial Quarter Race Horse* offers a thorough look at all horse racing in Virginia and Maryland in the seventeenth and eighteenth centuries. The story of the Reverend Hindman's racing career is in Charles Kemper's "The Settlement of the Valley," *Virginia Magazine of History and Biography*, published by the Virginia Historical Society in 1922.

Information about the Spanish riding style Jackson would have used in Mexico City appears in Kathleen Sands's *Charrería Mexicana: An Equestrian Folk Tradition*, although Sands focuses on changes to that style that occurred in Mexican ranching. Deb Bennett, in her *Conquerors: The Roots of New World Horsemanship*, also describes Spanish and Mexican equitation.

Jackson described his Mexican horse purchase in a letter to his sister Laura reprinted in *Early Life and Letters of General Thomas J. Jackson*, compiled by his nephew Thomas Jackson Arnold. Information about the first Fancy, the horse Jackson owned at Fort Hamilton, appears in Anna Jackson's *Life and Letters of General Thomas J. Jackson (Stonewall Jackson).*

CHAPTER 3: MYSTERY HORSE

A modern biography of George Washington, *Washington: A Life* by Ron Chernow gives, like almost all full biographies of Washington, details about the general's choice of warhorses. Napoleon's white horse has merited a biography of his own, *Marengo: The Myth of Napoleon's Horse* by Jill Hamilton.

Detailed (but understandable) information about the genetics of coat color—gray, dun, and chestnut—can be found in *Horse Genetics* by Ernest Bailey and Samantha A. Brooks. A much earlier discussion of color genetics and the names in common use a century ago is found in Walter Anderson's *The Inheritance of Coat Colors in Horses*, published in 1914.

Almost every veterinary textbook of the nineteenth century contains information on the why and how of equine castration. Dr. Leonard Conkey's 1890 text *Veterinary Medicine, Animal Castration, Surgery and Obstetrics Simplified* summarizes most of what was known in the nineteenth century. Gene Armistead's *Horses and Mules in the Civil War* is a good source for the sex as well as color, fate, and other details of animals known by name who participated in the conflict.

What was known about dental aging of horses in the mid- to late nineteenth century is included in *Soundness and Age of Horses: A Veterinary and Legal Guide to the Examination of Horses for Soundness* by Matthew Horace Hays. In this 1887 book, Hayes claims that age can be determined with considerable accuracy using teeth.

Go the Distance: The Complete Resource for Endurance Horses by Nancy Loving has good information on the value of small horses as well as conformation characteristics that are needed in a heavily used riding horse, most of which apply to Little Sorrel. Information about the pacing gait is found in most books about the gaited breeds; several are listed in the bibliography. *The American Trotter* by John Hervey is a classic. In spite of the title, the pacing horse, including the Narragansett Pacer, is part of the discussion. Edward Channing's *The Narragansett Planters: A Study of Causes* describes the circumstances in Rhode Island that created and destroyed the breed. The accounts of the last few Narragansett Pacers in Connecticut appear in the *American Stallion Register* by Joseph Battell from 1911.

The story that makes Little Sorrel a native of Somers, Connecticut, is contained in an undated typescript, apparently written by Erwin Avery sometime before 1920, in the archives of the Congregational Church of Somers. A copy is in the Somers Public Library. Details of the relationship of Fuller to Noah Collins, supposed breeder of Little Sorrel, can be found in *Genealogy of Some Descendants of Edward Fuller of the Mayflower* by William H. Fuller. William Montague's *Biographical Record of the Alumni of Amherst College* contains a good biography of William O. Collins. A biography of William H. Trimble appears in Paul Teetor's *A Matter of Hours: Treason at Harper's Ferry*, while information about the relationship of Trimble and Collins appears in publications of St. Mary's Episcopal Church in Hillsboro, Ohio, as well as articles about the Highland County Fair throughout the 1850s.

The only report of Little Sorrel's capture in Stoneman's Raid comes from Anna Jackson's nephew Paul Barringer, who was just seven years old at the time. Barringer's memoir, *The Natural Bent*, wasn't published until 1949, but it appears from the context that it was written in the late 1880s, while his aunt was still living. While he may have confused details, it's likely that the story itself was true. Accounts of the raid, including Chris Hartley's recent *Stoneman's Raid, 1865*, coincide with Barringer's memoirs in terms of dates and events.

CHAPTER 4: LITTLE SORREL GOES TO WAR

The best—or at least the most colorful—stories of the first few months of Stonewall Jackson's Civil War history were written by John Newton Lyle, who completed a manuscript of his war memoirs in 1903. This document, entitled "Sketches Found in a Confederate Veteran's Desk," was given to Washington and Lee University upon his death. The accessible version is *A Reminiscence of Lieutenant John Newton Lyle of the Liberty Hall Volunteers*, edited by Charles Turner and published in 1986. Other information on the early months comes from the work of Susan Pendleton Lee, daughter of artillerist William Pendleton. Her *Memoirs of William Nelson Pendleton* reprints letters between her parents that touch on this period.

James Thomson's loan of a horse to Jackson for the First Battle of Bull Run is found in John Esten Cooke's second biography of Jackson, *Stonewall Jackson: A Military Biography*. Cooke's first attempt, *The Life of Stonewall Jackson*, published in 1863, doesn't mention it. But other sources describe Jackson aboard a horse that obviously wasn't Little Sorrel that day.

Richard Williams's *Stonewall Jackson: The Black Man's Friend* has what's known of Jim Lewis and Stonewall Jackson's other slave property and makes the argument that, on balance, Jackson was a reluctant and benevolent slave owner. *Battle-fields of the South: From Bull Run to Fredericksburgh*, written by Thomas Caffey under the pseudonym An English Combatant, has contemporary descriptions of black camp servants and their duties. Historian and teacher Kevin Levin (whose website is www.cwmemory.com) writes frequently on camp and body servants during the Civil War.

CHAPTER 5: WAR IN WINTER

The Romney expedition is covered by all Jackson biographers. Because of the misery involved, memoirists and letter writers also wrote extensively about it. William Pogue and Henry Kyd Douglas, whose later descriptions of Little Sorrel became so important, first took notice of the unusual little horse during the campaign.

One full-length work on the campaign is *Stonewall Jackson's Romney Campaign, January 1–February 20, 1862*, by Thomas Rankin, which follows Jackson's—and by association, Little Sorrel's—daily activities. Anna Jackson's *Life and Letters of General Thomas J. Jackson (Stonewall Jackson)* includes relatively little about Romney, even though she was present in Winchester before and after the campaign. But her husband told her enough about the expedition for her to realize that it was during these weeks that he became inseparable from Little Sorrel.

Susan McBane's *The Horse in Winter: How to Care for Your Horse during the Most Challenging Season of the Year* describes some of the difficulties that even modern, well-stabled horses face in winter. The renowned horseman Oscar Gleason, whose 1892 *Gleason's Horse Book* was a bible to veterinarians and horse owners, offers information on the challenges of winter conditions during the nineteenth century.

CHAPTER 6: INTO THE VALLEY

As befits one of the most famous military campaigns in world history, Stonewall Jackson's Shenandoah Valley campaign is the subject of dozens of books, both of the campaign as a whole and of specific battles. Peter Cozzens's *Shenandoah 1862: Stonewall Jackson's Valley Campaign* is a good overview. References to Little Sorrel abound in soldiers' memoirs, several of which are mentioned in the text.

Jedediah Hotchkiss came into Stonewall Jackson's life during the Shenandoah Valley campaign and his papers are a vital source for the everyday activities of man and horse during this period. The papers, including his diaries, are at the Library of Congress, but Hatchkiss and Archie McDonald's well-edited *Make Me a Map of the Valley: The Civil War Journal of Stonewall Jackson's Topographer* is a more accessible substitute. Robert K. Krick's *Conquering the Valley: Stonewall Jackson at Port Republic* is especially useful on the story of Jackson and Little Sorrel's near miss at Port Republic.

Richard Ewell's description of Jackson as "crazy as a March hare" and "an enthusiastic fanatic" can be found in almost every biography of Ewell, but a good interpretation of the opinion is in Wallace Hettle's *Inventing Stonewall Jackson: A Civil War Hero in History and Memory*. Ewell's subordinate Richard Taylor's *Destruction and Reconstruction* features vivid accounts of the valley campaign and a colorful description of Little Sorrel during this period.

CHAPTER 7: RIVER OF DEATH

The Seven Days have merited almost as many studies as the Shenandoah Valley campaign, but in this case the interest has been more in mistakes made than in goals accomplished. Stonewall Jackson's performance has been widely criticized and closely analyzed, with little agreement on why the hero of the valley should function so poorly so soon after his greatest achievement.

Douglas Southall Freeman devotes a chapter to the mystery in his classic work *Lee's Lieutenants: A Study in Command, Vol. 1—Manassas to Malvern Hill*. For a book that follows Jackson's movement during the battles around Richmond, see Brian K. Burton's *The Peninsula and Seven Days: A Battlefield Guide*. Details about Little Sorrel's activities are more often found in the memoirs and narratives of participants such as John William Jones, John Hinsdale, William Blackford, and others noted in the bibliography.

A nearly contemporary description of Chickahominy Fever is found in William Aitken's medical text *The Science and Practice of Medicine, Volume 1*, on page 495. Much information on that and other illnesses and the other physical miseries of the Seven Days is in Ted Tunnell's *Edge of the Sword: The Ordeal of Carpetbagger Marshall H. Twitchell in the Civil War and Reconstruction*.

CHAPTER 8: RISK AND REDEMPTION

Stonewall Jackson and Robert E. Lee both regarded the Battle of Cedar Mountain as a significant victory, but others were less certain. Robert K. Krick in *Stonewall Jackson at Cedar Mountain* offers a complete review from a primarily Confederate perspective. As to what Little Sorrel went through that day, the memoirists are again the most useful.

In addition to Henry Kyd Douglas and Jedediah Hotchkiss, two new men, both recently assigned to Jackson, provide invaluable references to Little Sorrel during this battle. Letters and comments of Charles M. Blackford and his wife, Susan, were first published in a small edition for family and friends in 1894 but republished as *Letters from Lee's Army* in 1947. As Blackford did, cavalry captain John Blue published his stories in the 1890s—in Blue's case, in the *Hampshire Review* of Romney, West Virginia. These accounts have been republished as *Hanging Rock Rebel: Lieutenant John Blue's War in West Virginia and the Shenandoah Valley*. Both Blackford and Blue, probably because they were cavalrymen, paid special attention to Jackson's horse.

They and other observers also noted the considerable risk Jackson took with himself and his horse. He had been doing this for months, at least since the second battle of the Shenandoah Valley campaign, but as Blue in particular noted, the risk-taking approached a new high at Cedar Mountain.

Jackson continued his risk-taking at the Second Battle of Manassas. John Hennessy's *Return to Bull Run: The Campaign and Battle of Second Manassas* provides the overview. Again, memoirists and letter-writers were most likely to pay attention to a horse and again provided much of what we know about Little Sorrel during the last weeks of August 1862.

Dueling memoirs are especially important in terms of the biggest mystery of Little Sorrel during the Civil War—what happened to him between the final day of Second Manassas and a few days into the invasion of Maryland. Full references can be found in the bibliography. Two unpublished works offer some insight into the use of Little Sorrel and the possible reason for his being sent to the rear. They are John Hennessy's "Historical Report on the Troop Movements for the Second Battle of Manassas, August 28 through August 30, 1862," a work done for the National Park Service that describes Union general Abner Doubleday's sight of Jackson on Little Sorrel within small arms range at the Battle of Groveton. The June 2015 newsletter of the Texas Division of the Sons of Confederate Veterans contains an extensive article on the Black Horse Cavalry by Andrew Harris that tells the story of the Black Horse cavalryman who suffered a fatal injury while holding Jackson's horse.

CHAPTER 9: INVASION

The story of the Harwoods and Three Springs Farm comes from the *History of Frederick County, Maryland* by Thomas J. C. Williams, first published in 1910. The Black Horse Cavalry version of the events in Boonsboro comes from "Black Horse Troop" in the *Southern Historical Society Papers* of 1902, pages 142–46.

The Battle of Antietam, known as America's bloodiest day, is second only to Gettysburg in the volume of books and articles devoted to it. There is a selection in the bibliography. Ethan S. Rafuse's *Antietam, South Mountain, and Harpers Ferry: A Battlefield Guide* makes it easy to follow Jackson's movements.

The near miss for Jackson and Lafayette McLaws was reported by Henry Lord Page King, aide-de-camp of McLaws and repeated by Dennis Frye in *Antietam Revealed*.

CHAPTER 10: DEFENDING THE RAPPAHANNOCK

The best source for the trip to Fredericksburg, the days surrounding the battle of Fredericksburg, and winter quarters is James Power Smith, who was Jackson's aide-de-camp and favored courier during the time. Smith never produced a complete memoir, but he was an assiduous writer on his career with Jackson. His "With Stonewall Jackson in the Army of Northern Virginia" was published in the *Southern Historical Society Papers* in 1920. More information about Thomas Chandler's Fairfield Plantation is found in Marshall Wingfield's *A History of Caroline County, Virginia: From Its Formation in 1727 to 1924.*

Most overviews of Fredericksburg focus on the Union side, since their disaster was so great. But *The Fredericksburg Campaign: Decision on the Rappahannock* edited by Gary Gallagher includes both sides.

The Civil War journals of Jedediah Hotchkiss (*Make Me a Map of the Valley* is the easiest reprint to follow) have considerable detail about the day-to-day events of the time frame. Anna Jackson repeats the story of William Page Carter, the artilleryman who claimed to see Jackson riding a "superb bay horse" in her *Life and Letters of General Thomas J. Jackson (Stonewall Jackson).* For details of the incident between Jackson and Jim Lewis over the use of Little Sorrel, see "Night with Jackson: Reminiscences of the Confederate Leader after the Bloody Battle of Fredericksburg" by Alexander Boteler in the *Philadelphia Times,* July 31, 1881. The story of the gift horse from Staunton is in the *Staunton Spectator,* January 6, 1863.

James Power Smith and Jedediah Hotchkiss each write extensively of winter quarters at Moss Neck. Roberta Cary Corbin in "Stonewall Jackson in Winter Quarters" in *Confederate Veteran,* January 1912, offers more detail.

Jackson's second residence of winter quarters is described in "Belvoir: The Thomas Yerby Place, Spotsylvania County" by John Hennessy. Anna Jackson, who writes in *Life and Letters* of Jackson's acquisition of Superior, also describes her visit to Belvoir in April and her husband's pride in owning the handsome horse. The difficulties faced by the Army of Northern Virginia and its horses during this time is explained by Charles W. Ramsdell in "General Robert E. Lee's Horse Supply, 1862–1865" in *American Historical Review,* July 1, 1930.

CHAPTER 11: TRIUMPH AND TRAGEDY

The best-known modern overview is Stephen Sears's *Chancellorsville,* but that book focuses on Joseph Hooker and his Union army. For a focus on the Confederate side, see Douglas Southall Freeman's *Lee's Lieutenants: A Study in Command, Vol. 2—Cedar Mountain to Chancellorsville.*

William J. Seymour's description of Stonewall Jackson on April 29 is in *The Civil War Memoirs of Captain William J. Seymour: Reminiscences of a Louisiana Tiger.* Lucy Long appears in *Recollections and Letters of General Robert E. Lee,* compiled after the war by Robert E. Lee Jr.

Three outstanding works on the final days of Stonewall Jackson's military life are Chris Mackowski and Kristopher D. White's *The Last Days of Stonewall Jackson,* Robert K. Krick's *The Mortal Wounding of Stonewall Jackson,* and Mathew Lively's *Calamity at Chancellorsville: The Wounding and Death of Confederate General Stonewall Jackson.* Lively, almost alone among modern writers on Chancellorsville, correctly has Little Sorrel remaining in the hands of the Confederates after Jackson's wounding.

Chapter 12: Afterward

The two narratives that relate to Little Sorrel in the minutes following the wounding are William F. Randolph's "Chancellorsville: The Flank Movement That Routed the Yankees," in *Southern Historical Society Papers*, 1901. Randolph is the man who reported seeing a bloody wound on Little Sorrel's neck. Marcellus Moorman's "Narrative of Events and Observations Connected with the Wounding of General T. J. (Stonewall) Jackson" in the *Southern Historical Society Papers*, 1902, describes what he did with Little Sorrel after Jackson's injury.

The postshooting story that has Little Sorrel finding his own way back to J. E. B. Stuart's camp some days later comes from *The Land We Love* magazine, May to October 1866. Among the newspaper reports of Charles Lewis's story was one in the *Amsterdam (NY) Daily Democrat and Recorder*, on January 23, 1928. The Virginia Historical Society owns the letter sent on May 10 by Marcellus Moorman to Jackson.

The valuation of Jackson's estate appears in Roy Bird Cook's *The Family and Early Life of Stonewall Jackson*. Details of the later lives of Jackson's other horses can be found in Louise Dooley's "A Warhorse for Stonewall" in *Army* magazine on April 1, 1975.

Much of the information on Cottage Home and the Morrison family comes from Sarah Marie Eye's unpublished master's thesis from Virginia Tech, "Religion, Slavery and Secession: Reflections on the Life and Letters of Robert Hall Morrison." The sources for George Stoneman's raid at Cottage Home and Little Sorrel's capture by Union cavalrymen appear in the notes for chapter 4 above.

Superior's sale to Macon, Georgia, is in the *Anderson (SC) Intelligencer*, July 24, 1867. The story of the servant punishing Little Sorrel comes from the *Landmark* newspaper of Statesville, North Carolina, August 19, 1886.

The transfer of Little Sorrel to the Virginia Military Institute was widely covered in newspapers around the country in the summer of 1883. "Something about Stonewall Jackson's Old War Horse" from the *Charlotte Observer*, August 22, 1883, is an example. The horse's life at VMI is discussed by R. B. James in "Last Days of Famous Old Horses," *Confederate Veteran*, 1930.

Trips to the Hagerstown Fair and the New Orleans exposition were also widely reported in newspapers. Examples are in the bibliography. Also of interest is the *Practical Common Sense Guidebook through the World's Industrial and Cotton Centennial Exposition at New Orleans*, published in 1885.

February through April 1886 saw hundreds of newspaper stories published about the decline and death of Little Sorrel. A moving example is in the *Western Sentinel* of Winston-Salem, North Carolina, on March 26, 1886. The hair acquired by Fitzhugh Lee a few days before the horse's death is now at the Dolph Briscoe Center for American History at the University of Texas.

Chapter 13: The Legend

Two excellent books cover the growing and changing legend of Stonewall Jackson. His horse figures in both. The first is Wallace Hettle's *Inventing Stonewall Jackson: A Civil War Hero in History and Memory*, a book that follows and comments on the postwar development of the legend. Mark Neely and Harold Holzer's *The Confederate Image: Prints of the Lost Cause* covers the lithographs, engravings, and—to a lesser extent—the paintings that depict Jackson and Little Sorrel. The Virginia Historical Society website at www .vahistorical.org is the best source for information on the Hoffbauer mural.

The Sievers statue in Richmond is discussed in "The South's Tribute to Stonewall Jackson" in *Confederate Veteran*, 1920. The best description of the Charles Keck statue in Charlottesville is in the application papers for its place on the National Register of Historic Places. The controversy surrounding the Manassas statue is covered in Joan Zenzen's *Battling for Manassas: The Fifty-Year Preservation Struggle at Manassas National Battlefield Park* and in Shae Adams's "Cultural Distortion: The Dedication of the Thomas 'Stonewall' Jackson Monument at Manassas National Battlefield Park" in the *Gettysburg College Journal of the Civil War Era*, Spring 2011.

Bibliography

Adams, Shae. "Cultural Distortion: The Dedication of the Thomas 'Stonewall' Jackson Monument at Manassas National Battlefield Park." *Gettysburg College Journal of the Civil War Era*, Spring 2011, 9–26.

Aitken, William. *The Science and Practice of Medicine, Volume 1*. Philadelphia: Lyndsay and Blakiston, 1868.

Alamance Gleaner (Graham, NC). "News Items," January 21, 1886.

Alfriend, Edward M. "Recollections of Stonewall Jackson." *Lippincott's Monthly Magazine*, January–June 1902, 582–88.

Allan, William. "History of the Campaign of General T. J. (Stonewall) Jackson in the Army of Northern Virginia from November 4, 1862, to June 17, 1862." *Southern Historical Society Papers*, September 1, 1920, 111–295.

Amsterdam (NY) Daily Democrat and Recorder. "Rode Stonewall's Horse," January 23, 1928.

Anderson (SC) Intelligencer. "Stonewall Jackson's War Horse Superior," July 24, 1867.

Anderson, Walter S. *The Inheritance of Coat Colors in Horses*. Lexington, KY: State University Press, 1914.

Andersson, Lisa S., Martin Larhammar, Fatima Memic, Hanna Wootz, et al. "Mutations in DMRT3 Affect Locomotion in Horses and Spinal Circuit Function in Mice." *Nature*, August 30, 2012, 642–46.

Andrews, William Hill. *Diary of W. H. Andrews 1st. Sergt. Co. M, 1st Georgia Regulars from February 1861, to May 2, 1865*. East Atlanta, GA: publisher not identified, 1891.

Anson (NC) Times. "Old Sorrel Is Dying," March 19, 1886.

Armistead, Gene C. *Horses and Mules in the Civil War: A Complete History with a Roster of More Than 700 War Horses*. Jefferson, NC: McFarland, 2013.

Arnold, Thomas Jackson. *Early Life and Letters of General Thomas J. Jackson, "Stonewall" Jackson*. New York: Fleming H. Revell, 1916.

Atlanta Constitution. "Riderless War Steed: General Stonewall Jackson's Old Sorrel in Rome Caressed by Soldiers," February 14, 1885.

Avery, Erwin D. "History of Prink Street." Typescript. Archives of Congregational Church of Somers, Connecticut.

Bailey, Ernest, and Samantha A. Brooks. *Horse Genetics*. 2nd ed. Boston: CABI, 2013.

Barber, John Warner. *Connecticut Historical Collections Containing a General Collection of Interesting Facts, Traditions, Biographical Sketches, Anecdotes, &c., Relating to the*

History and Antiquities of Every Town in Connecticut, with Geographical Descriptions. New Haven, CT: J. W. Barber, 1836.

Barringer, Paul B. *The Natural Bent: The Memoirs of Dr. Paul B. Barringer.* Chapel Hill: University of North Carolina Press, 1949.

Battell, Joseph. *American Stallion Register, Volume 2.* Middlebury, VT: American Publishing Company, 1911.

Baylor, George. *Bull Run to Bull Run; or, Four Years in the Army of Northern Virginia. Containing a Detailed Account of the Career and Adventures of the Baylor Light Horse, Company B., Twelfth Virginia Cavalry, C.S.A., with Leaves from My Scrapbook.* Richmond, VA: B.F. Johnson Publishing Company, 1900.

Bennett, Deb. *Conquerors: The Roots of New World Horsemanship.* Solvang, CA: Amigo Publications, 1998.

Biographical Cyclopedia and Portrait Gallery with Historical Sketches of the State of Ohio, Volume 4. Cincinnati, OH: Western Biographical Publishing Company, 1887.

Blackford, Susan Leigh, and Charles Minor Blackford. *Letters from Lee's Army; or, Memoirs of Life in and out of the Army in Virginia during the War Between the States.* New York: Scribner, 1947.

Blackford, W. W. *War Years with Jeb Stuart.* New York: Scribner, 1945.

Blue, John, and Daniel P. Oates. *Hanging Rock Rebel: Lt. John Blue's War in West Virginia and the Shenandoah Valley.* Shippensburg, PA: Burd Street Press, 1994.

Bobskill, Laurie. "Historian Mounts Drive to Link Famous Steed to Somers." *Springfield (MA) Daily News,* December 28, 1978.

Boteler, A. R. "Night with Jackson: Reminiscences of the Confederate Leader after the Bloody Battle of Fredericksburg." *Philadelphia Times,* July 31, 1881.

Brighton, Terry. *Hell Riders: The True Story of the Charge of the Light Brigade.* New York: Henry Holt, 2004.

Brown, Stephen Wayne. *Voice of the New West: John G. Jackson, His Life and Times.* Macon, GA: Mercer, 1985.

Bruce, Philip Alexander. *Social Life of Virginia in the Seventeenth Century.* Williamstown, MA: Corner House Publishers, 1968.

Burton, Brian K. *The Peninsula and Seven Days: A Battlefield Guide.* Lincoln: University of Nebraska Press, 2007.

Caffey, Thomas E. (An English Combatant). *Battle-fields of the South: From Bull Run to Fredericksburgh: With Sketches of Confederate Commanders, and Gossip of the Camps.* New York: John Bradburn, 1864.

Cannan, John. *The Antietam Campaign August–September 1862.* Conshohocken, PA: Combined Books, 1994.

Carrington-Farmer, Charlotte. "Slave Horse/War Horse: The Narragansett Pacer in Colonial and Revolutionary Rhode Island." Paper delivered at SOAS University of London, May, 2014.

Carrollton (GA) Free Press. "Stonewall Jackson Relic," September 5, 1884.

Casler, John O. *Four Years in the Stonewall Brigade.* Girard, KS: Appeal Publishing Company, 1906.

Channing, Edward. *The Narragansett Planters: A Study of Causes*. Baltimore: Johns Hopkins University Press, 1886.

Charlotte (NC) Observer. "Something about Stonewall Jackson's Old War Horse," August 22, 1883.

Chase, William C. *Story of Stonewall Jackson: A Narrative of the Career of Thomas Jonathan (Stonewall) Jackson, from Written and Verbal Accounts of His Life*. Atlanta: D.E. Luther, 1901.

Chernow, Ron. *Washington: A Life*. New York: Penguin, 2010.

Conkey, Leonard L. *Veterinary Medicine, Animal Castration, Surgery and Obstetrics Simplified*. Grand Rapids, MI: Valley City Printing, 1890.

Cook, Roy Bird. *The Family and Early Life of Stonewall Jackson*. 3rd ed. Charleston, WV: Charleston Print., 1948.

Cooke, John Esten. *The Life of Stonewall Jackson. From Official Papers, Contemporary Narratives, and Personal Acquaintance. By a Virginian*. New York: Charles B. Richardson, 1963.

———. *Stonewall Jackson: A Military Biography, with a Portrait and Maps*. New York: Appleton & Company, 1866.

Corbin, Roberta Cary. "Stonewall Jackson in Winter Quarters." *Confederate Veteran*, January 1912, 24–26.

Cozzens, Peter. *Shenandoah 1862: Stonewall Jackson's Valley Campaign*. Chapel Hill: University of North Carolina Press, 2008.

Cullen, Joseph P. *The Peninsula Campaign, 1862: McClellan and Lee Struggle for Richmond*. Harrisburg, PA: Stackpole Books, 1973.

Dabney, Robert Lewis. *Life and Campaigns of Lieut.-Gen. Thomas J. Jackson, (Stonewall Jackson)*. New York: Blelock & Co., 1866.

Davie, Oliver. *Methods in the Art of Taxidermy*. Columbus, OH: Hahn & Adair, 1894.

Davis, William C. *Battle at Bull Run: A History of the First Major Campaign of the Civil War*. Garden City, NY: Doubleday, 1977.

DiMarco, Louis A. *War Horse: A History of the Military Horse and Rider*. Yardley, PA: Westholme Publishing, 2008.

Dinkins, James. "Famous War Horses." *Confederate Veteran*, December 1932, 423–27.

Dooley, Louise K. "A Warhorse for Stonewall." *Army*, April 1, 1975, 34–39.

Douglas, Henry Kyd. "Stonewall Jackson in Maryland." *Century Magazine*, October 1, 1886, 285–95.

———. *I Rode with Stonewall, Being Chiefly the War Experiences of the Youngest Member of Jackson's Staff from the John Brown Raid to the Hanging of Mrs. Surratt*. Chapel Hill: University of North Carolina Press, 1940.

Earle, Alice Morse. *Customs and Fashions in Old New England*. New York: Scribner, 1893.

Ehrenborg, Gwendoline. *From Dawn to Eclipse*. Lulu.com, 2013.

Evans, Clement A. *Confederate Military History: A Library of Confederate States History, Volume 3*. Atlanta, GA: Confederate Publishing, 1899.

Eye, Sarah Marie. "Religion, Slavery and Secession: Reflections on the Life and Letters of Robert Hall Morrison." Unpublished master's thesis, Virginia Tech, 2003.

Farwell, Byron. *Stonewall: A Biography of General Thomas J. Jackson.* New York: W.W. Norton, 1992.

Frederick (MD) News. "T.N. Harwood's Will," February 25, 1902.

Freeman, Douglas Southall. *Lee's Lieutenants: A Study in Command, Vol. 1—Manassas to Malvern Hill.* New York: Scribner, 1942.

———. *Lee's Lieutenants: A Study in Command, Vol. 2—Cedar Mountain to Chancellorsville.* New York: Scribner, 1943.

Frye, Dennis E. *Antietam Revealed: The Battle of Antietam and the Maryland Campaign as You Have Never Seen It Before.* Collingswood, NJ: Civil War Historicals, 2004.

Fuller, William Hyslop. *Genealogy of Some Descendants of Edward Fuller of the Mayflower.* Palmer, MA: C.B. Fiske & Co., 1908.

Gallagher, Gary W. *The Fredericksburg Campaign: Decision on the Rappahannock.* Chapel Hill: University of North Carolina Press, 1995.

———. *The Myth of the Lost Cause and Civil War History.* Bloomington: Indiana University Press, 2000.

———. *The Shenandoah Valley Campaign of 1862.* Chapel Hill: University of North Carolina Press, 2003.

Garber, Alexander M. *Stonewall Jackson's Way: A Sketch of the Life and Services of Major John A. Harman, Chief Quartermaster of Second Corps, Army Northern Virginia, and of the Army of the Valley District, on the Staffs of Generals Stonewall Jackson, Ewell and Early.* Staunton, VA: "Spectator" Job Print, 1876.

Gilbert, David T. *A Walker's Guide to Harpers Ferry, West Virginia: Exploring a Place Where History Still Lives.* 5th ed. Harpers Ferry, WV: Harpers Ferry Historical Association, 1995.

Gimbel, Gary. "The End of Innocence: The Battle of Falling Waters." *Blue and Gray Magazine,* Fall 2005, 10–12.

Gittings, John G. *Personal Recollections of Stonewall Jackson, Also Sketches and Stories.* Cincinnati, OH: Editor Publishing, 1899.

Gleason, Oscar R. *Gleason's Horse Book: The Only Authorized Work by America's King of Horse Tamers.* New York: Allison and Webster, 1892.

Gocher, W. H. "Narragansett's Famous Pacers in Early Days." *Brooklyn Eagle,* April 2, 1933.

Goodhart, Briscoe. *History of the Independent Loudoun Virginia Rangers U.S. Vol. Cav. (Scouts) 1862–65.* Washington, DC: Press of McGill & Wallace, 1896.

Green, Ben K. *Horse Conformation as to Soundness and Performance.* Rev. ed. Flagstaff, AZ: Northland Press, 1975.

Griffin, Patrick. *The People with No Name: Ireland's Ulster Scots, America's Scots Irish, and the Creation of a British Atlantic World, 1689–1764.* Princeton, NJ: Princeton University Press, 2001.

Gwynne, S. C. *Rebel Yell: The Violence, Passion, and Redemption of Stonewall Jackson.* New York: Scribner, 2014.

Hagerstown (MD) Herald and Torch Light. "The Big Fair," October 29, 1885.

Hamilton, Jill. *Marengo: The Myth of Napoleon's Horse.* London: Fourth Estate, 2000.

Harris, Andrew. "The Bravest of the Brave." *Sons of Confederate Veterans, Texas Camp, John H. Regan Camp News*, June 2015.

Harrison, James C., and Ralph N. Baldwin. *Care and Training of the Trotter and Pacer.* Columbus, OH: United States Trotting Association, 1968.

Harrisonburg (VA) Daily News-Record. "Old Sorrel Goes to the Cleaners," November 18, 1940.

Hartley, Chris J. *Stoneman's Raid, 1865.* Winston-Salem, NC: John F. Blair, 2010.

Hayes, Matthew Horace. *Soundness and Age of Horses: A Veterinary and Legal Guide to the Examination of Horses for Soundness.* London: W. Thacker, 1887.

Hazard, Thomas R., and Rowland Gibson Hazard. *The Jonny-cake Papers of "Shepherd Tom," Together with Reminiscences of Narragansett Schools of Former Day.* Boston: Printed for the Subscribers, 1915.

Helm, Henry T. *American Roadsters and Trotting Horses: Being a Sketch of the Trotting Stallions of the United States, and a Treatise on the Breeding of the Same.* Chicago: Rand, McNally & Co., 1878.

Henderson, G. F. R. *Stonewall Jackson and the American Civil War.* Two volumes. New Improved Edition. London: Longmans, Green, 1904.

Hennessy, John. "Historical Report on the Troop Movements for the Second Battle of Manassas, August 28 through August 30 1862." Unpublished report for the United States Department of the Interior, National Park Service, Denver Service Center, Northeast Team, 1985.

———. *Return to Bull Run: The Campaign and Battle of Second Manassas.* New York: Simon & Schuster, 1993.

———. "Belvoir: The Thomas Yerby Place, Spotsylvania County." National Park Service document.

Hershberger, H. R. *The Horseman: A Work on Horsemanship; Containing Plain Practical Rules for Riding, and Hints to the Reader on the Selection of Horses. To Which Is Annexed a Sabre Exercise for Mounted and Dismounted Service.* New York: H. G. Langley, 1844.

Hervey, John. *The American Trotter.* New York: Coward-McCann, 1947.

Hettle, Wallace. *Inventing Stonewall Jackson: A Civil War Hero in History and Memory.* Baton Rouge: Louisiana State University Press, 2011.

Heubsch, John. "The Ross House in Bladensburg, Maryland." A thesis as an initiation requirement for Tau Beta Pi, April 8, 1932.

Hinsdale Family Papers. William R. Perkins Library. Duke University, Durham, NC.

Hoefling, Larry J. *Chasing the Frontier: Scotch-Irish in Early America.* Lincoln, NE: IUniverse, 2005.

Hopewell, H. Lynn. "Cavaliers and Lawyers: The Black Horse Cavalry." *News and Notes from the Fauquier (VA) Historical Society*, Winter 1983, 1–5.

———. *A Biographical Register of the Members of Fauquier County Virginia's "Black Horse Cavalry," 1859–1865.* Warrenton, VA: Black Horse Press, 2003.

Horwitz, Tony. "Stonewall's Steed Was Ugly, But His Hide Was Tough." *Wall Street Journal*, July 25, 1997.

———. *Confederates in the Attic: Dispatches from the Unfinished Civil War*. New York: Vintage, 1999.

Hotchkiss, Jedediah, and William Allan. *The Battle-fields of Virginia Chancellorsville; Embracing the Operations of the Army of Northern Virginia, from the First Battle of Fredericksburg to the Death of Lieutenant-General Jackson*. New York: D. Van Nostrand, 1867.

Hotchkiss, Jedediah, and Archie P. McDonald. *Make Me a Map of the Valley: The Civil War Journal of Stonewall Jackson's Topographer*. Dallas: Southern Methodist University Press, 1973.

Howard, McHenry. *Recollections of a Maryland Confederate Soldier and Staff Officer under Johnston, Jackson and Lee*. Baltimore: Williams and Wilkins, 1914.

Howard, Robert West. *The Horse in America*. Chicago: Follett, 1965.

Hull, Lewis Byrum. *Diary of Lewis Byrum Hull 1861–1862*. www.ancestry.com.

Hyland, Ann. *The Horse in the Ancient World*. Westport, CT: Praeger, 2003.

Imboden, John. "Stonewall Jackson in the Shenandoah." *Century Illustrated Monthly Magazine*, May–October 1885, 279–93.

Isaac, Rhys. *The Transformation of Virginia, 1740–1790*. Chapel Hill: University of North Carolina Press, 1990.

Jackson, Mary Anna. *Life and Letters of General Thomas J. Jackson (Stonewall Jackson)*. New York: Harper & Brothers, 1892.

James, R. B. "Last Days of Famous Old Horses." *Confederate Veteran*, 1930, 5.

Johnson, Clint. *In the Footsteps of Stonewall Jackson*. Winston-Salem, NC: John F. Blair, 2002.

Johnson, James Ralph, and Alfred Hoyt Bill. *Horsemen, Blue and Gray: A Pictorial History*. New York: Oxford University Press, 1960.

Johnson, Robert Underwood, and Clarence Clough Buel. *Battles and Leaders of the Civil War: Being for the Most Part Contributions by Union and Confederate Officers, Volumes 1 and 2*. New York: Century Company, 1887.

Johnston, James H. *From Slave Ship to Harvard: Yarrow Mamout and the History of an African American Family*. New York: Fordham University Press, 2012.

Johnston, Mary. *The Long Roll*. Boston: Houghton Mifflin, 1911.

Jones, J. William. "Down in the Valley under 'Stonewall's Quartermaster.'" In *Southern Historical Society Papers*. Vol. 9, 185–89. Richmond, VA: Southern Historical Society, 1881.

———. "Seven Days around Richmond." In *Southern Historical Society Papers*. Vol. 9, 557–70. Richmond, VA: Southern Historical Society, 1881.

Jordan, Rudolf. *The Gait of the American Trotter and Pacer*. New York: W.R. Jenkins, 1910.

Kemper, Charles E. "The Settlement of the Valley." *Virginia Magazine of History and Biography*. Richmond: Virginia Historical Society, 1922, 178–79.

Kincheloe, Kathleen. *State Council of Higher Education for Virginia Update*, 2008, 3–4.

Krick, Robert K. *Stonewall Jackson at Cedar Mountain*. Chapel Hill: University of North Carolina Press, 1990

———. *Conquering the Valley: Stonewall Jackson at Port Republic*. New York: Morrow, 1996.

————. *The Mortal Wounding of Stonewall Jackson*. A UNC Press Civil War Short, excerpted from *Chancellorsville: The Battle and Its Aftermath*, edited by Gary W. Gallagher. Chapel Hill: University of North Carolina Press, 2011.

Lazelle, Henry Martyn, and Leslie J. Perry. *The War of the Rebellion: A Compilation of the Official Records of the Union and Confederate Armies*. Series I, vol. 30. Washington, DC: Government Printing Office, 1887.

Lee, Robert E., and Robert E. Lee Jr. *Recollections and Letters of General Robert E. Lee*. New York: Doubleday, Page & Company, 1904.

Lee, Susan P. *Memoirs of William Nelson Pendleton, D.D., Rector of Latimer Parish, Lexington, Virginia; Brigadier-general C.S.A.; Chief of Artillery, Army of Northern Virginia*. Philadelphia: Lippincott, 1893.

Littauer, Vladimir Stanislavovich. *Horseman's Progress: The Development of Modern Riding*. Princeton, NJ: D. Van Nostrand, 1962.

Lively, Mathew W. *Calamity at Chancellorsville: The Wounding and Death of Confederate General Stonewall Jackson*. El Dorado Hills, CA: Savas Beatie, 2013.

Longacre, Edward G. *Lee's Cavalrymen: A History of the Mounted Forces of the Army of Northern Virginia, 1861–1865*. Mechanicsburg, PA: Stackpole Books, 2002.

Longrigg, Roger. *The History of Horse Racing*. New York: Stein and Day, 1972.

Louisiana Democrat (Alexandria). "Stonewall Jackson's Old Battle Horse," February 22, 1885.

Louisville (KY) Courier-Journal. "Stonewall Jackson's Sorrel Horse," August 12, 1885.

Loving, Nancy S. *Go the Distance: The Complete Resource for Endurance Horses*. North Pomfret, VT: Trafalgar Square, 1997.

Luvaas, Jay, and Harold W. Nelson. *A Guide to the Battles of Chancellorsville & Fredericksburg*. Lawrence: University Press of Kansas, 1994.

Mackay-Smith, Alexander. *The Colonial Quarter Race Horse: America's First Breed of Horses, America's Native Breed of Running Horses, the World's Oldest Breed of Race Horses, Prime Source of Short Speed*. Middleburg, VA: H. K. Groves, 1983.

Mackowski, Chris, and Kristopher D. White. *The Last Days of Stonewall Jackson*. El Dorado Hills, CA: Savas Beatie, 2013.

Maury, Dabney Herndon. *Recollections of a Virginian in the Mexican, Indian, and Civil Wars*. New York: Scribner, 1894.

McBane, Susan. *The Horse in Winter: How to Care for Your Horse during the Most Challenging Season of the Year*. Guilford, CT: Lyons Press, 2003.

McCarr, Ken. *The Kentucky Harness Horse*. Lexington: University Press of Kentucky, 1978.

McClendon, W. A. *Recollections of War Times by an Old Veteran While under Stonewall Jackson and Lieutenant General James Longstreet: How I Got In, and How I Got Out*. Montgomery, AL: Paragon Press, 1909.

McClure, Alexander K. *The Annals of the War Written by Leading Participants North and South*. Philadelphia: Times Company, 1879.

McKim, Randolph H. *A Soldier's Recollections, Leaves from the Diary of a Young Confederate, with an Oration on the Motives and Aims of the Soldiers of the South*. New York: Longmans, Green and Company, 1910.

McPherson, James M. *Battle Cry of Freedom: The Civil War Era*. New York: Oxford University Press, 1988.

———. *Crossroads of Freedom: Antietam*. New York: Oxford University Press, 2002.

Mellin, Jeanne. *The Complete Morgan Horse*. Lexington, MA: S. Greene, 1986.

Michaelis, David, and N. C. Wyeth. *N. C. Wyeth: A Biography*. New York: Knopf, 1998.

Miller, Francis Trevelyan, and Robert S. Lanier. *The Photographic History of the Civil War*. New York: Review of Reviews, 1911.

Miller, William J. *Mapping for Stonewall: The Civil War Service of Jed Hotchkiss*. Washington, DC: Elliott & Clark, 1993.

Montague, William Lewis. *Biographical Record of the Alumni of Amherst College 1821– 1896*. Amherst, MA: 1896.

Moore, Edward Alexander, and Robert E. Lee. *The Story of a Cannoneer under Stonewall Jackson: In Which Is Told the Part Taken by the Rockbridge Artillery in the Army of Northern Virginia*. Lynchburg, VA: J.P. Bell, 1910.

Moorman, Marcellus N. *Letter. Capt. Marcellus N. Moorman to Lt. Gen. T. J. Jackson, Orange Court House, VA, 10 May 1863*. Archives of the Dabney-Jackson Collection, Library of Virginia, Richmond, VA.

———. "Narrative of Events and Observations Connected with the Wounding of General T. J. (Stonewall) Jackson." In *Southern Historical Society Papers*. Vol. 30, 110–17. Richmond: Southern Historical Society, 1902.

Morrison, James L. *"The Best School in the World": West Point, the Pre-Civil War Years, 1833–1866*. Kent, OH: Kent State University Press, 1986.

Neely, Mark E., and Harold Holzer. *The Confederate Image: Prints of the Lost Cause*. Chapel Hill: University of North Carolina Press, 1987.

Neese, George Michael. *Three Years in the Confederate Horse Artillery*. New York: Neale, 1911.

New York Times. "Reverse at Harper's Ferry," September 18, 1862.

———. "Statues of Lee, Jackson, and Clark are given to town," May 8, 1921.

Oates, William C. *The War between the Union and the Confederacy and Its Lost Opportunities, with a History of the 15th Alabama Regiment and the Forty-eight Battles in Which It Was Engaged*. Dayton, OH: Morningside Bookshop, 1974.

Philadelphia Times. "R. E. Lee Camp Soldiers' Home," October 17, 1897.

Phillips, Deane. *Horse Raising in Colonial New England*. Ithaca, NY: Cornell University Agricultural Experiment Station, 1922.

Phillips, V. N. *Between the States: Bristol, Tennessee/Virginia during the Civil War*. Johnson City, TN: Overmountain Press, 1997.

Pittsburgh Post-Gazette. "Move Relic of Sorrel Says Donor," July 29, 1939.

Poague, William Thomas. *Gunner with Stonewall: Reminiscences of William Thomas Poague, a Memoir, Written for His Children in 1903*. Jackson, TN: McCowat-Mercer Press, 1957.

Pollard, Edward Alfred. *The Lost Cause: A New Southern History of the War of the Confederates: Comprising a Full and Authentic Account of the Rise and Progress of the Late Southern Confederacy*. New York: E.B. Treat, 1866.

Practical Common Sense Guidebook through the World's Industrial and Cotton Centennial Exposition at New Orleans. Harrisburg, PA: Lane S. Hart, 1885.

R.S.P. "Black Horse Troop: Some Reminiscences of This Famous Command." In *Southern Historical Society Papers.* Vol. 30, 142–46. Richmond: Southern Historical Society, 1902.

Rafuse, Ethan S. *Antietam, South Mountain, and Harpers Ferry: A Battlefield Guide.* Lincoln: University of Nebraska Press, 2008.

Ramsdell, Charles W. "General Robert E. Lee's Horse Supply, 1862–1865." *American Historical Review,* July 1, 1930, 758–77.

Randolph, Sarah Nicholas. *The Life of Gen. Thomas J. Jackson.* Philadelphia: Lippincott, 1876.

Randolph, William F. "Chancellorsville: The Flank Movement That Routed the Yankees." In *Southern Historical Society Papers.* Vol. 29, 329–37. Richmond, VA: Southern Historical Society, 1901.

Rankin, Thomas M. *Stonewall Jackson's Romney Campaign, January 1–February 20, 1862.* Lynchburg, VA: H. E. Howard, 1994.

Reed, Peter Fishe. *Incidents of the War, or, The Romance and Realities of Soldier Life.* Indianapolis, IN: Asher & Co., c. 1862.

Richmond (VA) Dispatch. "Old Sorrel Gone: Death at Soldiers' Home of Stonewall Jackson's War-horse," March 16, 1886.

Robertson, James I. *Stonewall Jackson: The Man, the Soldier, the Legend.* New York: Macmillan, 1997.

Rodenbough, Theodore. *Photographic History of the Civil War, The Cavalry* (Volume 4). New York: Review of Reviews Company, 1911.

Sands, Kathleen M. *Charrería Mexicana: An Equestrian Folk Tradition.* Tucson: University of Arizona Press, 1993.

Santa Cruz (CA) Sentinel. "New Orleans Letter," February 26, 1885.

Scott, W. W. *A History of Orange County, Virginia: From Its Formation in 1734 (o.s.) to the End of Reconstruction in 1870, Compiled Mainly from Original Records.* Richmond, VA: Everett Waddey Company, 1907.

Sears, Stephen W. *Landscape Turned Red: The Battle of Antietam.* New York: Ticknor & Fields, 1983.

———. *To the Gates of Richmond: The Peninsula Campaign.* New York: Ticknor & Fields, 1992.

———. *Chancellorsville.* Boston: Houghton-Mifflin, 1996.

Seymour, William J., and Terry L. Jones. *The Civil War Memoirs of Captain William J. Seymour: Reminiscences of a Louisiana Tiger.* Baton Rouge: Louisiana State University Press, 1991.

Sidnell, Philip. *Warhorse: Cavalry in Ancient Warfare.* London: Hambledon Continuum, 2006.

"Sketches of Gen. Jackson," *Land We Love, A Monthly Magazine Devoted to Literature, Military History, and Agriculture,* Vol. 1, 312.

Smith, James Power. "Stonewall's Last Battle." *Century Magazine,* October 1, 1886, 921–26.

———. "With Stonewall Jackson in the Army of Northern Virginia." In *Southern Historical Society Papers, Jackson Number*. Vol. 43, 1–110. Richmond, VA: Southern Historical Society, September 1, 1920.

"Soldiers' Home Richmond, Virginia." In *Southern Historical Society Papers*. Vol. 20, 315–24. Richmond, VA: Southern Historical Society, 1892.

"The South's Tribute to Stonewall Jackson," *Confederate Veteran*, February 1920, 47–48.

Sponenberg, D. Phillip, and Bonnie V. G. Beaver. *Horse Color*. College Station: Texas A&M University Press, 1983.

Stackpole, Edward J. *From Cedar Mountain to Antietam*. 2nd ed. Harrisburg, PA: Stackpole Books, 1993.

Statesville (NC) Landmark. "Lincoln County News," August 19, 1886.

———. "On the Wing," August 22, 1886.

Staunton (VA) Spectator. "Several Carloads of Cattle and Some Horses Were Captured at Harpers Ferry," May 21, 1861.

———. "Letter to Lieut. Gen. Thomas J. Jackson," January 6, 1863.

———. "Stonewall Jackson's War Horse," November 4, 1884.

———. "Fancy or Old Sorrel," February 25, 1885.

Steinmetz, Martin. "The Fair's Written History: A Historical Sketch of The Union Agricultural Society." Prepared for the Four Town Fair, Somers, Connecticut, April 1980. http://www.fourtownfair.com/history.

Stiles, Robert. *Four Years under Marse Robert*. New York: Neale, 1903.

Tanner, Robert G. *Stonewall in the Valley: Thomas J. "Stonewall" Jackson's Shenandoah Valley Campaign, Spring 1862*. Garden City, NY: Doubleday, 1976.

Taylor, Louis. *The Horse America Made: The Story of the American Saddle Horse*. New York: Harper & Row, 1961.

Taylor, Richard. *Destruction and Reconstruction: Personal Experiences of the Late War*. New York: D. Appleton & Company, 1879.

Teetor, Paul R. *A Matter of Hours: Treason at Harper's Ferry*. Rutherford, NJ: Fairleigh Dickinson University Press, 1982.

Thomas, Emory M. *Bold Dragoon: The Life of J. E. B. Stuart*. New York: Harper & Row, 1986.

Thomas J. Jackson Estate Document (1863 June 5). Jackson Papers, Virginia Military Institute.

Times-Picayune (New Orleans), March 15, 1886.

Toney, Marcus Breckenridge. *The Privations of a Private: The Campaign under Gen. R.E. Lee; the Campaign under Gen. Stonewall Jackson; Bragg's Invasion of Kentucky; the Chickamauga Campaign; the Wilderness Campaign; Prison Life in the North*. Nashville, TN: Printed for the Author, 1905.

Transactions of the Connecticut State Agricultural Society for the Year 1855. Hartford, CT: Press, Case, and Company, 1855.

Trout, Robert J. *Galloping Thunder: The Story of the Stuart Horse Artillery Battalion*. Mechanicsburg, PA: Stackpole Books, 2002.

Tunnell, Ted. *Edge of the Sword: The Ordeal of Carpetbagger Marshall H. Twitchell in the Civil War and Reconstruction*. Baton Rouge: Louisiana State University Press, 2001.

Turner, Charles W., ed. *A Reminiscence of Lieutenant John Newton Lyle of the Liberty Hall Volunteers*. Roanoke, VA: Virginia Lithography and Graphics Company, 1986.

Tyler, Lyon Gardiner. *Men of Mark in Virginia, Ideals of American Life: A Collection of Biographies of the Leading Men in the State*. Washington, DC: Men of Mark Publishing Company, 1906.

Updike, Wilkins. *History of the Episcopal Church in Narragansett, Rhode-Island; including a History of Other Episcopal Churches in the State; with an Appendix Containing a Reprint of a Work . . . Entitled: America Dissected, by Rev. J. Macsparran, D.D.* New York: Henry N. Onderdonk, 1847.

Vaver, Anthony. *Bound with an Iron Chain: The Untold Story of How the British Transported 50,000 Convicts to Colonial America*. Westborough, MA: Pickpocket Publishing, 2011.

von Borcke, Heros. *Memoirs of the Confederate War for Independence by Heros von Borcke, Lately Chief of Staff to Gen. J.E.B. Stuart*. London: William Blackwood and Sons, 1866.

Watkins, Samuel R. *1861 vs. 1862 "Co. Aytch," Maury Grays, First Tennessee Regiment; or, A Side Show of the Big Show*. Nashville, TN: Cumberland Presbyterian Publishing House, 1882.

Waugh, John C. *The Class of 1846: From West Point to Appomattox: Stonewall Jackson, George McClellan, and Their Brothers*. New York: Warner Books, 1994.

Welcome to St. Mary's Church: A Self-Guided Tour. Hillsboro, OH: St. Mary's Church.

Western Sentinel (Winston-Salem, NC). "Gen. Jackson's Horse: Soldiers Lift Your Hats; Old Sorrel Is Dying," March 26, 1886.

White, William Spottswood. *Sketches of the Life of Captain Hugh A. White of the Stonewall Brigade*. Columbia: South Carolinian Steam Press, 1864.

Wilbourn, Richard E. *Letter to C. J. Faulkner. May 1863. Eyewitness account of Stonewall Jackson's wounding*. Virginia Historical Society. http:// vahistorical.org.

Williams, Harrison. *Legends of Loudon*. Richmond, VA: Garrett & Massie, 1938.

Williams, Richard G. *Stonewall Jackson: The Black Man's Friend*. Nashville, TN: Cumberland House, 2006.

Williams, Thomas J. C., and Folger McKinsey. *History of Frederick County, Maryland*, Vol. 1. Baltimore: Regional Publishing Company, 1967.

Williams, Wendy. *The Horse: The Epic History of Our Noble Companion*. New York: Scientific American/Farrar, Straus and Giroux, 2015.

Wilmington (NC) Sun. "Stonewall Jackson's Horse Photographed," January 31, 1879.

Wingfield, Marshall, and Edward Maria Wingfield. *A History of Caroline County, Virginia: From Its Formation in 1727 to 1924*. Richmond, VA: Trevvet Christian, 1924.

Worsham, John Henry. *One of Jackson's Foot Cavalry: His Experience and What He Saw during the War, 1861–1865. Including a History of "F Company," Richmond, Va., 21st Regiment Virginia Infantry, Etc.* New York: Neale, 1912.

Zenzen, Joan M. *Battling for Manassas: The Fifty-Year Preservation Struggle at Manassas National Battlefield Park*. University Park: Pennsylvania State University Press, 1998.

Index